Golf Architecture

Golf Architecture

A WORLDWIDE PERSPECTIVE

VOLUME ONE

COMPILED AND EDITED BY **PAUL DALEY**

Pelican Publishing Company
Gretna 2003

Published by arrangement in North America by
Pelican Publishing Company, Inc., 2003

*Jacket, text design, typesetting, and layout by Andrew
  Cunningham—Studio Pazzo*
Sketches by Barry King, Melbourne

*Photo on page ii: Eleventh hole, Pacific Dunes, Oregon, USA.
  (Photo by Wood Sabold © Bandon Dunes Resort.)*

Throughout the book, all references to hole and course lengths
will be consistent with the system of measurement of that country.
American courses use the imperial system, while European and
Commonwealth courses use the metric system.
An anomaly occurs in Japan where the metric system is used
throughout the country except in the context of golf where the
convention is to retain imperial terminology.

Printed in China

Published by Pelican Publishing Company, Inc.
1000 Burmaster Street, Gretna, Louisiana 70053

Contents

Foreword

Geoffrey S. Cornish

In a worldwide outpouring of creativity, the most beautiful landscapes ever created by our species are arising from the drawing boards of contemporary golf course architects.

Golf has been played for half a millennium or more in Scotland, on a handful of hallowed and natural links amidst breathtaking scenery. As the game spread far from its homeland, playing fields were still established on links, but with many more arising on pastures, prairies, ranges, and other areas of short grass. Many were informal and primitive with routings that constantly changed, and many were abandoned following a few seasons of play. Then, around the end of the nineteenth century and the beginning of the twentieth, the superb heathland courses emerged near London. They rivalled the ancient Scottish and other links in England and Ireland.

Unlike pasture courses and links, those on the heathlands required the clearing of trees, the moving of earth, and the cultivation of grass to produce interesting golf holes. The profession and art form of golf course architecture was born.

Almost at the same time, the landmark courses were emerging in the United States and Canada, and work was soon underway on the National Golf Links of America by Charles Blair Macdonald. Completed in 1909, this Long Island course officially opened in 1911. Its excellence set a standard for course architecture worldwide, and caused both the rebuilding of many existing layouts and a higher standard for new courses.

The Roaring Twenties decade that followed World War I, then saw the opening of thousands of superb new courses with admirable characteristics. Sadly, that decade was followed by almost a quarter of a century of depression and war dating from the stock market crash in 1929 to the end of the Korean War in 1953. Only a handful of great courses emerged during those years.

By the mid-1950s golf was on a roll again. Still, the efforts of course architects were hampered by low construction budgets until well into the 1980s. Yet despite the problems, course architects got their courses right.

In the last decades of the twentieth century, everything came together. Adequate funds became available for development. The might of modern earth moving equipment was with

OPPOSITE: **Fifth hole, Cape Cod National Golf Club, Massachusetts, USA. (Photo courtesy of Ronald Whitten.)**

us together with the vast knowledge of agronomists and other scientists who produced a new generation of grasses and a host of other products. At the same time, engineers developed miraculous irrigation and drainage systems, together with advanced equipment for maintenance. Moreover, highly skilled and college-trained course superintendents or greenkeepers, as they are proudly called in many countries, continued their dedicated work, which had by then become a science in addition to an art.

A dynamic and talented generation of course architects, trained and skilled in the principles of art, and marshalling all the wondrous new developments and products continues to take advantage of adequate budgets to produce the most magnificent golf courses since the game spread from its homeland. This is a never-ending effort to satisfy our thirst for impressive landscapes together with the excitement, challenge and interest of golf. Surely golf architects in recent years have produced masterpieces.

But who knows? Golf is a game that mirrors life itself. Involving a club, a ball and a hole, it is exciting by itself, and its landscapes enhance that pleasure. Not surprisingly, golfers have long felt that God's creation of the universe and everything in it was incidental to his creation of the Old Course at St. Andrews and other glorious links that absorb the golfer with a sense of well being.

Course architects have long known how to provide golfers with this sense of well being although they did not know why golfers reacted as they did to their creations. Now evolutionary biologists researching ancient landscapes have observed that for tens of thousands of years, our species evolved on the savannahs of eastern Africa. Landscapes there are characterised by short lush grass, scattered trees, focal points, distant vistas, bodies of water and humps and hollows that accentuate the terrain. It seems those savannah ancestors of ours took advantage of these characteristics over millennia to survive, and somehow those landscape features became embedded in our genes. Course architects have created miniature savannahs that provide the sense of awe, well being and satisfaction that arises in each of us when we encounter such terrain and,

most of all, when a club is in hand.

In this volume, Paul Daley, the eminent Australian author of *Links Golf: The Inside Story* (2000) and *The Sandbelt: Melbourne's Golfing Heaven* (2001), has compiled essays by course architects, writers and other golfers concerning the playing fields of the game and their architecture. To say the least, his concept is inspired. It provides a remarkable insight into a remarkable profession and art form that continues to create the most magnificent layouts for golf since the game spread from its homeland.

I think that those experiencing what golf architects have wrought are justified in suspecting that the courses appearing today are in the same league as the glorious natural links. The following essays in *Golf Architecture: A Worldwide Perspective* enhance my statement. They are recommended to all students and lovers of golf, and could add another dimension to their games.

Geoffrey S. Cornish
Fiddlers Green
Amherst, Massachusetts, USA

Acknowledgements

I would like to thank Neil Crafter (SAGCA president) for allowing Geoff Shackelford's essay *Does it tempt?* to be reproduced. The modified essay first appeared as *Into Temptation* in the Society of the Australian Golf Course Architects *Golf Architecture* Journal – issue 5, 2002.

Thank you to John Lindsay and Joe Dora for their time spent reading and commenting upon the manuscript, and to artist Barry King for his outstanding and serene collection of golfing sketches.

Thank you to Wiley and Sons for granting permission to reproduce an adaptation from Forrest Richardson's book *Routing the Golf Course: The Art and Science that Forms the Golf Journey*, Wiley and Sons, New York, 2002.

To Geoffrey S. Cornish for giving us the benefit of his wisdom and years of experience through his beautifully crafted and educative foreword, and Andrew Cunningham from Studio Pazzo, to acknowledge his flair and innovative design.

Special appreciation is reserved for both Linda Daley and Jenny Restarick for their interest, advice, and expertise throughout the project, and to Ronald Whitten for providing many of the wonderful photographic images.

Introduction

Paul Daley

Rarely does the rank-and-file tennis player ponder the intricacies of building better tennis courts. To be sure, the same level of detachment holds true for most sportspeople in regard to their sporting arena, especially when a fixed dimension applies. Yet golf and its golfers are different. Seemingly everyone who plays has an opinion about the golf course. Handicap is no barrier, nor experience. Indeed, some of the most audible armchair architects are those members who rarely venture three woods and a pitch from their home course. Universally, club captains enjoy their share of perks. However, being 'clobbered' on the stroke of teeing-off by the club bore each Saturday—'now captain about that course master-plan'—is not one of them.

Not so long ago, the curiosity of many architecturally minded golfers could be sated purely by making do with reading a glossy magazine feature, or by dusting off an early twentieth-century book on the topic. The curious have in recent years turned aficionado. They seek insight into the architect's mind: to measure their own thought-process; to study an architect's complete body of work; to categorise personal styles; and evaluate golf courses against a set of design principles.

Dedicated golf writers such as Neil Crafter, Tom Doak, Brad Klein, Jeff Mingay, Geoff Shackelford, Daniel Wexler, and Richard Wolffe, have played a vital role in providing an outlet for their expanding audience. It is no coincidence that many of them have gravitated towards golf course architecture, having studied the theory and now busily undertaking the practice. I am honoured that they have seen fit to contribute to this two-volume collection.

Like actors and rock stars, the life of a golf architect seems glamorous, privileged even. I put this to one of our young essayists, and he retorted: 'I don't know so much about that! I'm shacked up here away from home in a dwelling without a light bulb or my trusty computer, and with no end in sight to the project. Thank God, Dave can cook'. Yet what a responsibility it is. Not everyone is cut out for accepting the stewardship of our golf land. Some architects maintain an eclectic output, ever-changing their colours. Some golf course

OPPOSITE: **The shimmering, dune-binding grasses dominate the 467-yard par-5, thirteenth hole at Doonbeg, Ireland. (Photo Larry Lambrecht ©)**

architects undertake the practice for survival, others do it out of sheer pleasure, working hard not to be recognised as championing a certain look. Architect Mike Young, lists the following as the ideal attributes for an aspiring golf designer: 'It's a profession that demands a rare blend of characteristics: the heart of an artist, the mind of an engineer, and the soul of a golfer. These three elements, combined with a relentless desire to achieve perfection are what make an architect successful.' With today's intense competition for work, I would add advanced selling skills to the list.

The essayists in this volume come from a variety of golfing perspectives. Every industry has its establishment, and we welcome the contributors who represent membership of the European Institute of Golf Course Architects, the Japanese Society of Golf Course Architects, the Australian Society of Golf Course Architects, and the American Society of Golf Course Architects—those of the Red Blazer brigade.

The golf course architecture industry encompasses a big brave world, and in truth, architects who belong to societies and institutes are outnumbered by those who don't. Consequently, it was considered important for this collection to canvas a range of both establishment and non-establishment opinions. We welcome all contributors and their perspective on the industry.

Some readers will disagree with the ideas and philosophies espoused by the writers. There may well be a differing of opinion among the architects themselves. If so, I'll take it as a sign that the project has succeeded in stimulating ongoing debate.

European architect, Jeremy Pern, was forthcoming about how to break into golf course architecture: 'you must be in the right place at the right time. But to make a living once you're in the business, depends on talent, luck, hard work, and the absolute certainty that you are totally unemployable in any other field'.

Golf architecture has evolved to such a degree that one can easily ponder how pioneer designers such as Willie Park Jr., Old Tom Morris, and H.S. Colt would view computer aided golf design if still alive today. Intuitively, one senses the term 'shaper' would raise an eyebrow. In the current design era, some see it as a method of ensuring a fat fee, while at the same time reducing an architect's work burden. The speed of modern greens, and a strange device called a stimpmeter, would be cause for concern for the pioneers: allowing uniformity yes, but at the possible expense of stripping away ingenuity and idiosyncratic putting surfaces. Were these groundbreakers alive today, their views on the cookie-cutter syndrome—the mass-produced design stamp—paying little heed to site constraint—would no doubt produce a coarse response. But let's not fall victim to genuflection regarding their status: every industry has progressed, and it would be a dull old world if it hadn't.

A paradoxical situation in golf course architecture should be noted: in spite of a reduction in the available land for building golf courses, worldwide, the number of architects continues to rise. Most pundits will view this situation in a positive light and bask in the increasing popularity of golf. Perhaps it equally reflects the view that the rate of technological advance shows little sign of abating. Architects are mak-

ing a comfortable living, and not just the big-name practitioners. In every corner of the globe, courses are in dire need of upgrading, remodelling, or major overhauling. One movement, a veritable *tour de force*—the restoration movement—is gaining great momentum. By way of comparison, in 1947 at Pinehurst, the American Society of Golf Course Architects (ASGCA) held its first gathering with only ten men present: William P. Bell; Robert White; W.B. Langford; Donald Ross; Robert Bruce Harris; Stanley Thompson; William F. Gordon; Robert Trent Jones Snr.; William Diddel; and J. B. McGovern.

These early adopters worked primarily in North America. Today, golf course architecture spans the continents, and although the local and regional hero still exists, architects are thinking globally. In gaining this international perspective, architects are travelling more frequently than ever. Since the dawn of time, Man has been imbued with the talent, desire and creativity to build things. While most of us felt well satisfied toying with model aircrafts and trains, or Leggo, others dreamed about building things on a grander scale. Hopefully, you too will enjoy learning more about these gifted people, their architectural principles, ways of life, and the professional influences that leave an indelible mark on their own work.

Eighth hole, Pine Dunes Resort, Texas, USA. (Photo courtesy of Ronald Whitten.)

What is golf architecture?

Tom Doak

Great golf architects have come from every background imaginable. James Braid and Jack Nicklaus were professional golfers, and Alister Mackenzie was famously a medical doctor. Charles Blair Macdonald was a stockbroker, Pete Dye an insurance salesman, George Crump a hotel owner, and William Flynn, a greenkeeper. All had a love for the game of golf, but many of them managed to design and construct their first masterworks with almost no formal training for their new avocation. How did they do it? And what is at the root of golf design?

I have many friends and acquaintances who envy the career I chose, though few seem to understand what I do. Some clearly believe they could do it themselves: that golf course design is no more complicated than deciding how one wants a golf hole to play. Others, describing it in the same terms as drawing or sculpture, must never have seen my own pathetic attempts at freehand sketching.

In high school, I was a mathematics whiz, and so I spent my first year of college at Massachusetts Institute of Technology learning that I did not have a burning desire to be an engineer. Advised that landscape architecture was the best academic background for golf architecture, I transferred to Cornell University and learned what I could from drawing planting plans and grading parking lots. Years later, I was asked to take a personality test, which pegged me to a tee, except for the baffling recommendation that engineering would be an ideal career for me. Had I taken a wrong turn somewhere?

Certainly, golf course design is not without its engineering applications: civil engineering for the grading of the course and hydraulic engineering for the planning of the irrigation system. Pete Dye once told me that ninety-five per cent of the job is making drainage look good, and there's a lot of truth to that. Yet I had never really thought of routing holes and shaping them as a form of engineering.

The classic definition of engineering is the application of a system to a specific situation. In golf architecture, this would be the application of the game of golf, with all its complexities and varying appeals, to each individual piece of land.

Another view of the magnificent golfing terrain and scenery at Pacific Dunes. Tenth hole facing north-west. (Photo by Wood Sabold © Bandon Dunes Resort.)

This is precisely what the golf architect must do. One tries to fit golf shots and strategies to the contours of the land. Green sites and fairway landing areas should be put in spots with an appropriate amount of elbow room and surrounding difficulty. Tees are located where the important features will be in view, while affording an easy transition from the previous hole. Fairway contours affect the golfer's stance and the action of the ball after it lands. In the larger picture, we are putting together a three-dimensional puzzle with an eighteen-piece (or perhaps, a seventy-two piece) solution.

Two aspects make the job especially appealing to the engineering mind. The first is that changing one piece of the puzzle will have ramifications for at least one other piece, a fact lost on many critics of golf courses. The critic might believe, for instance, that the fourth hole would have made a better par-3 than a par-4. Perhaps so, but would the third hole have been as good if the green were extended further on? If we didn't want five or six par-3 holes on the course, which of the others would have had to be extended into a par-4, and how

would that have affected the holes around it? Unfortunately, many modern architects have simplified things for themselves by rationalising that golf carts reduce the need for easily connected holes. This is one of the reasons we have less variety of golf holes today, and is the main reason golf takes longer to play. A great example of golf course routing is Mackenzie's plan for the third through sixth holes at Royal Melbourne, at what later became the West Course. If the same holes were built today, many golfers would criticise the fourth hole for its blind tee shot, which even Mackenzie would have admitted was less than ideal. But the routing of the fourth up over the hill made the third, fifth and sixth holes possible, and his addition of bold, carry bunkers at the top of the hill made the fourth both dramatic and unique. Indeed, the fourth may well be the best hole of the lot, although Mackenzie himself probably did not visualise that it would turn out so.

The other interesting aspect of golf design to the engineering mind is that each puzzle is different, and none offers a definitive solution. Apart from the subjective nature of

design, a 200-acre property is so complex, and the rules of golf design so free-form that it is impossible to consider every solution. In fact, few golf course critics seem able to separate the art from the canvas—a sad truth, which makes it more difficult for young designers to achieve recognition for their efforts with lesser properties and modest budgets.

At the dawn of golf architecture, the field was dominated by golf professionals and greenkeepers, only few of whom had any real talent for solving puzzles. In the boom of the twenties, bright minds from a variety of backgrounds were captivated by the game of golf, and a rush of outstanding golf courses was born. I believe the new generation of architects has similar promise. Just as Tiger Woods hits golf shots which Old Tom Morris could not imagine, tomorrow's golf architects will create original and exciting golf holes, as unique as the land they are built upon.

FOLLOWING PAGES: (left) Fifth hole Pacific Dunes, facing south-east. (right) Thirteenth hole facing north. (Photos by Wood Sabold © Bandon Dunes Resort.)

Golf architecture: an artistic endeavour or a feat of engineering?

Graeme Grant

Equipment for planning and construction has advanced beyond the wildest imagination of the early master architect. Not surprisingly, the courses produced resemble engineering accomplishments rather than the artistic creations that have excited our emotions over many years.

Is it that the land available in the early days was superior, or are there other reasons to be explored? There is no doubt that suitable land in readily accessible areas has become more scarce as years have passed, but modern earthmoving equipment is capable of transforming almost any ordinary piece of ground into attractive golfing territory.

Could it be that only lip service has been paid to the often-preached principle of the likes of Alister Mackenzie that the irregular lines of nature be imitated? Has too little time been spent in the field by the architect creating the nuances and features that make the difference in design?

A general belief in the beauties of natural forms exist, but it seems there has been a preference for symmetry and formality on our golf courses. Not only have the modern courses been constructed with clean symmetrical lines, the classic ones have in one way or another been distorted by maintenance and the wishes of committees. There is an innate desire in mankind for symmetry and formality. We like things to be squared or levelled off, evenly spaced or parallel with each other, and we like things to look balanced. If we see a picture hanging at an angle, we feel an urge to straighten it.

The first job for a new course superintendent is to trim and sharpen up the bunker lips to give the course that clean, tidy appearance. He is out to make an impression with his grooming. Apart from striving for a neat and tidy or formal appearance, this grooming can be an effort to make the game fair—to eliminate the chance of an unfair lie in a hazard. It has been said many times before but golf, like the game of life, was never meant to be fair. What were these natural forms that the early masters utilised so well?

In general, they were the things that offered variety, contrast and real sport. A visit to the links lands or a study of the original pho-

OPPOSITE: **Hell Bunker (fourteenth hole, Old Course, St. Andrews) suffering the ill-effects of erosion. (Photo courtesy of St. Andrews University Library.)**

tographs of courses reveal a great deal. The features were generally rougher, more unkempt looking and contained ditches, creeks, burns with eroded banks, sharp ridges and mounds too rough to be mown, indigenous grasses and dwarf plants, stone walls and so on. Mostly, they recognised and copied what is our most common hazard—the eroded bunker. It is here that the greatest move away from nature's work has been made. Everything that could be done has been done to standardise and formalise the construction and maintenance of bunkers. Mackenzie left his bunkers with sand flashed up, the faces in irregular patterns, and with rough or laced edges on them. Harry S. Colt abhorred anything symmetrical, and although different in style to Mackenzie, his philosophy was similar. He states:

> The shape and nature of bunkers can be varied with immense advantage. How often do we see a delightful landscape spoilt by the creation of a number of symmetrical pots, or banks, or humps, made at apparently so much

a dozen! If we have to make bunkers—and no doubt they will be necessary—we can in great measure conceal their artificiality, and in any event we need not make them of a certain stereotyped pattern.[1]

These early architects would turn in their graves if they knew what had happened since their time and the way in which their work has been mutilated such as, for example, at Augusta National. Can there be a more incongruous site than the perfectly circular revetted pot bunkers distorting the natural rugged landscape of the old links? Further, being capable of enunciating the principles of golf course architecture by written word, these people were genuine artists who could either convey their thoughts while closely working with their crew in the field, or undertake some of the construction themselves.

David Owen, in his *The Making of the Masters* (1999), notes competing philosophies at work during design and construction between Chairman Clifford Roberts and Mackenzie. He states:

The correspondence between Roberts and Mackenzie was affectionate but always lively—and it was made especially lively by the fact that the two men had very different temperaments. Mackenzie was an artist. His drawings of the course were sometimes suggestive rather than explicit—because as he explained to Roberts, many of the most important decisions, such as those governing the exact shapes and contours of the greens could not be made until picks and shovels were in hand. Roberts, in contrast liked details. 'What I want you to do,' he wrote in December 1931, 'is to give us something in the nature of your official map, everything drawn to an exact scale, and all the features put down as accurately as it is possible at this time.'[2]

Today it is expected that an architect produce paper plans, computer assisted design (CAD) drawings and specifications so that any construction company—often unknown to the architect—can produce that special or unique course. Although a general impression

ABOVE: **Tenth hole, Pine Valley Golf Club, New Jersey, USA. (Photo by Graeme Grant, 1998.)**

LEFT: **The same hole in its raw 1930s state.**

Double greens are common on the Old Course, St. Andrews, though surprisingly uncommon throughout the rest of Scotland. This photo features the vast shared green of the fifth and thirteenth holes. (Photo courtesy of St. Andrews University Library.)

can be imparted to a shaper, it would be impossible to put on paper the intricate natural edges of, for example, the original Cypress Point bunkers. While precise drawings are necessary for the engineering components, such as drainage, for example, it is obvious that by today's standard, the plans of yesteryear were quite basic and the courses were brilliant.

More than anything else golf course architecture is an artistic endeavour. Somewhere along the line, the true artists have been left in the wake of engineers and property developers unable to spend time in the field creating the small interesting details vital to a special golf course.

In order to shape the ground to resemble the beauty of nature and offer the strategic challenges for golf, it must be worked upon as if it were a sculpture. All the possibilities the land offers can only be properly developed by the architect being on site. However, who among the golf course architects of today has either the capabilities or the time to physically shape the ground and work with the construction crew?

In most cases it is up to the construction crew to interpret the architect's intentions. One of two things can occur here: either a bland set of design features straight off the plan, or a golf course heavily influenced by the constructor's skill and imagination. Many of our courses in Australia are the result of the latter, although credited to the more famous or marketable architect.

Most notably the relationship between Michael Morcom and Alister Mackenzie produced work that was Morcom's style rather than Mackenzie's; that is, the style of the Melbourne sandbelt courses (especially the bunkering). Mackenzie has been given credit for the majestic work at Royal Melbourne and bunkering at Kingston Heath. Is this possible given that he spent no more than one month in Melbourne during October and November in 1926, and the construction at both places was not started until 1927? He made no return visit but left things in Morcom's hands. It was more likely that Morcom and his team decided upon and constructed the subtle features to make everything blend or fit into

Tenth hole at Kingston
Heath, Melbourne, in 1937.
Today, indigenous planting
has filled in the tee-to-
green aspect. (Photo
courtesy of Kingston Heath
Golf Club.)

place. Taking this point a little further, Mackenzie advised in similar ways at a number of courses throughout Australia producing similarly worded reports. In them he would suggest that the details of construction be left in the hands of the secretary and those who had the advantage of receiving verbal explanations of his ideas. How many of these courses have Mackenzie's stamp? Why is the course at Manly in New South Wales not held in the same high regard as Kingston Heath in Victoria?

This same theme applies to Morcom's son, Vernon, who undertook copious amounts of design work throughout Australia, even though the only classics are in Melbourne where he was able to spend time teaching his skills and operating in a hands-on fashion himself. The natural landform of the Grange West in Adelaide is in no way inferior to that of Kingston Heath, but it lacks the artistic bunkering, fairway features and greens of the latter.

Further to bunker construction, we have maintenance that can either support the natural irregular lines and the strategic qualities of bunker placement or completely negate both. Over the years these obstacles have been turned into impotent or meaningless areas of sand because of an unnecessarily high level of maintenance. We have been conned into believing that anything but a consistent, level surface to play from is unfair.

Apart from the money spent, it is hard to understand the logic behind bunker preparation, especially for tournaments. In Britain, the floors are graded so that a ball can finish against a lip and become almost unplayable. However, at the same time, the sand is raked to near perfection. In America, the USGA is now setting things up so that a plugged lie is possible. This has arisen in response to players' preference of finding their ball in the so-called hazard, rather than on the grass outside it. Has a greater distortion of the game been allowed to fester? If the bunkers were simply left alone, and the wind, rain and footmarks were left to determine the lies, these hazards would assume their proper role, and course maintenance expenditure greatly reduced.

Think how far have we come from these two following stories. When told by Norman von Nida some thirty-five years ago, that the bunkers at Kingston Heath looked impressively natural, the greenkeeper remarked they were only appeared that way because of lack of staff! When teaching Peter Thomson to play bunker shots, the same von Nida, knowing bad lies were common, would stand on the practice balls and instruct Thomson to find a way to get them out. So what does the future hold?

One can only hope that with the renaissance of quality literature on golf course architecture, architects, greenkeepers, committees and golfers in general will gain a better understanding of the spirit and traditions of the game, and seek to preserve them for future generations.

A sense of place in course design
Mark Parsinen

Kingsbarns Golf Links, although still in its infancy, has become part of the fabric of one of the great golf destinations in the world, St. Andrews, Scotland. More than 30,000 golfers visit St. Andrews each year. The typical visitor spends at least three days taking it all in. A sense of place clearly resonates for each and every visitor.

People travelling great distances to enjoy a spectacular location like to be reminded of where they are, especially during their recreation. From the first tee on the Old Course to the eighteenth green, the town of St. Andrews with its medieval skyline of spires and recognisable buildings is always in view, sometimes even in play. And when visiting any of the surrounding links from Carnoustie to the others in St. Andrews to Crail, Lundin Links, and Leven Links, one is never in doubt as to where one is. The dune slacks and ridges, revetted bunkers, wispy fescues, gorse, heather, and the immediacy of the sea are ever present in one's golf experience throughout the Kingdom of Fife. The sense of being there is so palpable that most leave with vivid images and recollections that they will cherish for a lifetime.

Herein lies the challenge facing golf course design at destination resorts with spectacular settings and distinctive contextual attributes. The golf course must resonate as much as possible with the attributes of the location and aspects of its spectacular setting. It must not feel generic or common; otherwise, the experience of being away is less fruitful than it could be. Better for the traveller to be reminded of the place they have travelled afar to visit; better yet to be overwhelmed by a sense of place clearly associated with the chosen destination.

From our first day on the property at Kingsbarns, we were overwhelmed with its seaside setting. The distant vistas are uniquely Scottish. To the north across the Firth of Tay lie the often snow-capped Grampians with Carnoustie in the foreground. Prominently set in the vista southward down the coast is Crail, known locally as Balcomie Links. The topography of the property's immediate coastline is striking. It arches, curves, and meanders, punctuated with little bays and promontories. Further, an old sea cliff defines

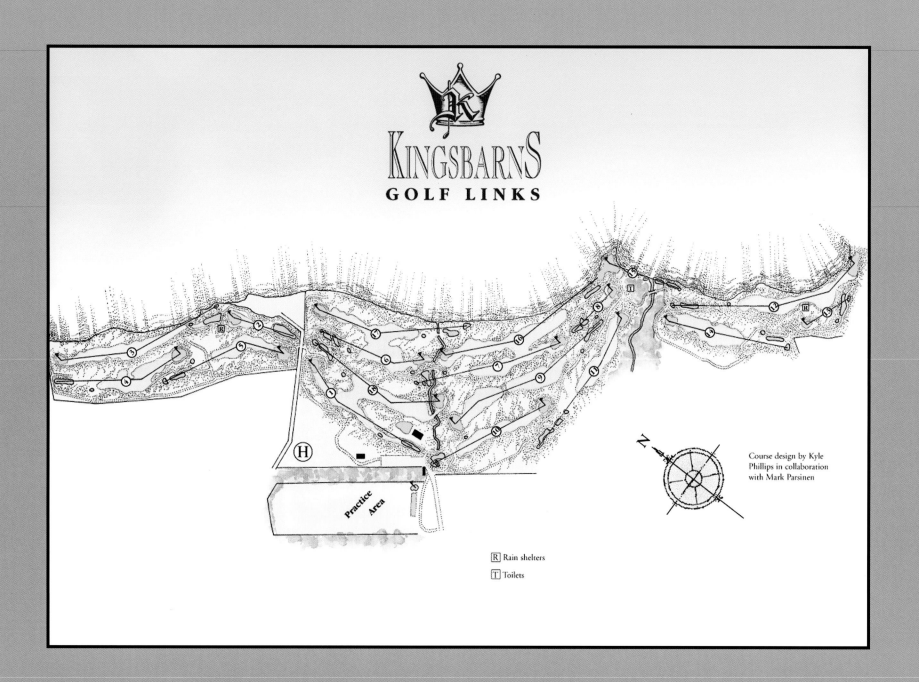

KINGSBARNS
GOLF LINKS

Course design by Kyle
Phillips in collaboration
with Mark Parsinen

R Rain shelters

T Toilets

a step-up from a strip of land along the sea to an inland tier some sixty feet higher in elevation, creating a curving amphitheatre effect. And from virtually every location on the property, one is granted more than just a glimpse of a distant horizon line on the sea. One is presented with the visual immediacy of the North Sea, waves crashing against a rocky foreshore with plumes of white water inundating the senses.

Along with the sensual excitement this opportunity presented, we recognised the obligation to measure up to the profound sense of place central to every links pilgrimage to St. Andrews. With Kingsbarns just six miles away, we knew that critical eyes would be abundant. The property did have its drawbacks, however, perhaps significant enough to explain what has kept others from developing the site in recent years. Historical origins for a nine-hole course date back as far as 1793. Yet the golf at Kingsbarns has lain moribund since 1939 when the course was commandeered for military purposes. For locals, resurrection was not a foregone conclusion. The free-draining linksland soils

Fourth hole, Kingsbarns Golf Links, Scotland. (Photo by Brian Morgan ©)

OPPOSITE: **Kingsbarns course plan. (Plan courtesy of Mark Parsinen.)**

and the naturally occurring fine fescues and bent grasses of the original nine did not extend to the additional land required for an eighteen-hole course. There were other issues as well. The upper tier to the west, and the land to the north and south had been flattened by farming practices of hundreds of years. Further, the inland view to the west from the upper deck was unremarkable, featuring flat farmland, farm animals, barns, sheds, and so on. The view northward and slightly away from the coastal foreshore was similarly modest, as was the view slightly inland to the south. So as promising as certain aspects of the property were, others were problematic.

The negatives, however, brought a certain clarity to our thinking. A 'plan-view' approach to routing; one that focused solely on the existing topography of the 190-acre site would likely fail. The ordinary and detracting visual perspectives to the west, north and south would undoubtedly dilute the visually compelling seaside elements over a round of links golf, thereby eroding a sense of place. To measure up to the site's promise, Kingsbarns would need to resonate from start to finish with a links feel and extraordinary sea views.

To corroborate our direction, we talked with golfers on their pilgrimage to St. Andrews and they graciously shared their perceptions and expectations of links golf. Not surprisingly, they talked about dunes and the windswept look and landscape of a links. They were intrigued with playing running shots under the wind. When discussing favourite holes and courses, however, they revealed what made for a memorable links experience, a notion that we came to call 'sea aspect'. Television is largely responsible for this. Virtually every commercial break during an Open Championship is characterised by a dramatic camera shot which pans from golf course to the sea, lingering there before going to the break. Post-commercial, the sequence is reversed. A lingering view of the sea pans back to the golf course and action. These images have shaped our perceptions and expectations of links golf. 'Sea aspect' has become synonymous with links golf.

Our approach at Kingsbarns was duly affected. We intended to make 'sea aspect' synonymous with Kingsbarns. To accomplish this meant doing away with all compromising visual distractions. We began to imagine a links 'cocoon'. We imagined controlling every aspect of a golfer's visual experience from arrival to departure. Hide the distractions, and focus attention on 'sea aspect' as well as the links landscape so as to keep golfers absorbed in this visual experience. Similar to an engrossing movie experience, we talked of golfers in our 'cocoon' losing themselves in a Kingsbarns links experience. Delivering this vision would be the basis for measuring up to the 'sense-of-place' standard of St. Andrews.

And so the idea of a dune ridge, almost two miles in length to screen visual perspectives inland to the west, north and south was born. Making that screening landform look natural and links-like, however, was a challenge. We spent more than a year studying naturally occurring dune forms under the tutelage of Dr Robert Price whose book *Scotland's Golf Courses* (1989) is the seminal work on the geomorphology of links landforms. A dune is simply not a mound of sand. The dunes of Cruden Bay, for example, are as different to those of Fife as ice cream is to a popsicle. In the end, we created dune landforms that were not merely attributes of individual holes, but were much larger in both concept and scale. Individual holes would actually twist through, around, and over them. Rather than being a single ridge, these dune landforms were conceived to meander throughout the entire site helping to frame arrival scenes on tees, and privacy or intimacy on greens. The specifics, including the look and feel of the dunes, were carved out of the dirt painstakingly in the field. As golfers now find their way through the experience at Kingsbarns, the dunes serve their purpose. Golfers never consider what they cannot see, only what they do see.

In order to control every aspect of our golfer's visual experience from arrival to departure, we had to start at the beginning. We sited the clubhouse well inside the golf cocoon, with parking outside. We set the location of the clubhouse and the grades of one's approach through the dunes to focus visual attention on the eighteenth and ninth greens with the sea and whitewater prominently in view as the backdrop. The existing topography, plus tie-ins to parking lot grades, burn locations, and so on did not make this an easy task. To achieve a natural looking topography and landscape, the pieces of the puzzle had to be assembled with multi-relational cuts and fills that often tested our patience.

The first hole, which pointed north into humdrum adjoining farm fields before turning toward the sea to the east, required a dune ridge to obscure those fields. However, not one so high as to hide what lay beyond—the Firth of Tay, Carnoustie, and the Grampians. From the tee, we also wanted to present the first green with seemingly nothing behind the putting surface but the sea, when in reality several hundred metres of undesirable view actually lay between. To get these various perspectives right was not entirely possible in plan view. Accomplishing interacting visual perspectives tied to distant vistas is best achieved in the field. For one consideration, the tee might best be lowered; for another, lifted. Everything seemed to affect something else, and sometimes confoundingly so. In some cases, tee, green, and fairway elevations, plus dune height and scale had to be modified repeatedly in order to achieve the overall desired result. Much like the opening scene of an engrossing movie, we intended to set the tone of the Kingsbarns experience immediately.

The fourth and fifth holes are examples of adjustments made to our earliest routings to achieve maximum 'sea aspect'. These holes run parallel to the sea atop the slightly inland old sea cliff. To put the sea, which was eastward and to the left more into the active frame of play, we altered the fourth hole by giving it a dogleg aspect. A massive and deep carry bunker on a direct line to the green was added. With a carry of 250 yards into the prevailing wind, it defines the high-risk route along the edge of the old sea cliff. This route not only shortens the hole; it offers an easy approach angle to the green. The bunker is penalising in form and the steep slope to the left over the edge of the old sea cliff is also hazardous. The safe play is to the right of the carry bunker where ample fairway beckons. The strategic decision called for on the tee brings the direct route and sea to the left running along and beyond the green into visual consideration. Equally importantly, if one takes the safe route to the right, the approach angle back to the green puts an ominous optical perspective into the player's shotmaking frame. From this angle, the putting surface appears perilously perched atop the old sea cliff with nothing but the sea beyond. A front-right greenside bunker also complicates releasing shots played short of the green. The bunker must be carried while the cliff edge and sea loom unnervingly beyond the putting surface. In reality, the sea is more than one hundred yards away, but for most players, this hole modification clearly brings the sea more prominently into the experience of the hole.

The fifth hole, which was also altered to include a dogleg aspect, reversed the issues. As a dogleg to the right, it turns away from the sea, but the drive must contend with a fairway that seems to disappear into the sea. The horizon line of fairway constitutes an infinity edge with the sea, and also puts the distinctive clubhouse of Crail, Balcomie Links into the frame. The preferred line to achieve the best approach angle to the green is a line down the left side of the fairway, which appears to be hanging on the edge of the sea although the second hole in truth lies beyond, out of sight.

Modifications to the earliest designs for these golf holes help illustrate the impact 'sea aspect' had on our design philosophy. The first, fourth, and fifth holes at Kingsbarns could have been designed by working solely within the immediate topography of the holes and could have taken the surrounding 'sea aspect' as simply contextual. The resulting holes would have turned out very differently. Our determined focus on 'sea aspect' altered irrefutably the way in which we conceived each and every element of these holes. Trying to bring 'sea aspect' into the golfer's visual shot-making frame as much as possible even changed the way we talked about holes. We stopped drawing things in plan-view and started talking about everything in terms of what the golfer saw, both within the hole and beyond. We began to consider visually unnerving perspectives versus reassuring ones as important to shotmaking.

In fact, we have come to believe that plan-view knowledge of a golf hole may be of some value to a player, but inevitably he must play his shot reacting to what he sees. Great golf holes can be described in terms of 'plan-view' and shotmaking requirements. Yet imagine standing on the sixteenth tee at Cypress Point and trying to explain the hole solely in shot-making terms. I can imagine a virtually identical hole, with the same distances, same bailout option short and left of the green, and hazards of similar consequence in each relevant location, but not an equally great one without the hazards being what they truly are: the Pacific Ocean; the coastal geological rock formations; the sounds of crashing waves; the twisted, wind-bent Cypress trees; and so forth. The visual and sensory elements in the active frame make the hole great.

Contours are an extremely important topic in their own right, and of considerable significance to angle-of-play issues in a links context. Another primary design objective at Kingsbarns involved the study and understanding of how releasing golf shots would behave through contours created throughout the course. What is important here, however, is how prominent their visual interpretation came to be in our design considerations. To make contours intuitively obvious to golfers, we connected them to larger topographical features flowing out of the dunes. Green contours became reflections of larger

topographical forms. Everything important lay as naturally as possible in the larger landscape.

If the Kingsbarns experience delivers ample sea aspect and a links landscape mosaic backed up by superior and interesting shot values, then we (colleagues and friends Stuart McColm, Mick McShane, Kyle Phillips, Bard Reynolds, Walter Woods and Tom Doak who was also a source of inspiration at Kingsbarns) will have succeeded in creating the sense of place central to links pilgrimages to St. Andrews and Fife. We will have also developed an appreciation for a different organising approach to golf course design in destination resort environments with a strong visual sense of place.

The opening hole at Kingsbarns Golf Links. (Photo by Iain Lowe ©)

More affordable golf courses in the twenty-first century

Bill Amick

Golf can be fun and it can be fascinating. It should also be affordable. Affordability, however, is relative, and when applied to golf it is more than just a pocketbook matter. It also means having enough time to play. Aspects of affordability are strongly influenced by the golf courses played. In the years ahead, will more or fewer people wanting to play golf be able and encouraged to do so?

Fees at some courses today bar individuals, couples and families from taking up golf, sticking with it, and playing as often as they would like. How long it takes to complete a round can push away time-pinched workers and parents. Also discouraged can be the impatient. For beginners, and even those who've been playing awhile, the game is tough

for gaining competency. Many beginners, and even highly dedicated golfers quit, especially if holes seem overly demanding to them. This is the intimidation factor of golf. Occasional pars are more motivating than mostly triple bogeys. Golfers who have the time, a sufficient level of skill, and enough money believe golf is great. And to them it is. But in the twenty-first century will the current circumstance of costs continue to turn away large numbers of potential players?

One obstruction to beginners sticking to the game is the dominance of championship courses with par of around seventy-two. These are the courses seen on television for professional tournaments, pictured in publications, and ranked as the top courses. Such

courses require from 150 to 180 acres of usually expensive land that must be forever fertilised, sprayed, mowed, aerated, and all the rest in its maintenance. Enough water for irrigation is required for the prepared part. Most of these courses are meticulously manicured, not essentially for enhancing their playing quality, but for the sake of appearance. Property taxes are paid annually on land and on the improvements. The bottom line for this model is obvious: a lot of money is required for creating and keeping these big courses, which is raised by its players. This is fine for those who can afford the time and money for a round, and also for those fortunate ones with the talent to handle the challenge of these top courses.

Wouldn't it be great if in the future there were other types of golf courses that did not present those affordability hurdles many people face in par-72 courses? As a golf course architect, I look for ways of designing more affordable courses, yet still with those benefits of the less affordable. Like one model for all car buyers, one kind of golf course cannot accommodate all golfers and their situations. I have outlined several other golf course models below. Each would save on course construction costs, flowing on to lower playing fees. Each model would reduce playing time for rounds, and could be designed to fit better the skill level of more golfers than par-72 courses do currently. Some of the models are familiar; a couple are brand new. Most would require no changes in playing equipment. One would require fewer clubs, a different ball that has been on the market since 1985, and some adjustments in the rules necessitated by the ball. Because of their real cost-saving advantages, I believe these courses should receive serious consideration in the future by course developers and golfers.

The more affordable public course model:

The majority of eighteen-hole par-72 courses that opened in the 1990s and continuing into the very early twenty-first century have been less affordable. Ways to make new courses less costly is simple because many public courses have been doing it for a couple of centuries. They are not trendy, upscale courses. They are comparatively short, easier to play, plainly constructed, and not so intensively maintained. They have much lower green fees, are faster to play unless crowded, and are not so discouraging to golfers lacking high playing skills. These courses can truly be termed more affordable eighteen-hole courses.

The more affordable par thirty-six course model:

Much the same can be said about nine-hole courses with a par of around thirty-six. Lots of these exist in rural areas and near small towns. A widespread prejudice is that a nine-hole course is not a legitimate golf course to be built in urban and suburban areas, even though available land there is usually scarce and expensive. Naturally, these locations are where most people live. Nine-hole courses could help people in populated places find an acceptable home course. Properly positioned pairs of tee markers and two cups per green, with a colour of flags for each nine, could add interest to the second nine holes played at these courses.

The more affordable smaller scale accompanying course model:

A smaller golf course alongside a par-72 course is an established concept and the two courses can nicely complement each other. The smaller could be labelled the executive par-3, or Pitch and Putt course. These could have eighteen, nine, or even fewer holes. They could be compact or Cayman models described below. Pebble Beach has a Pitch and Putt course named the Peter Hay Course. Augusta National has its nine-hole par-3 course, and Pine Valley a short course, all indicating the appeal of small second courses accompanying famous first courses. In fairness, in these cases, saving money was probably not a motivating factor. In Scotland, some high-profile regular courses also have a wee course, including Turnberry, Gleneagles and North Berwick. The latter opened its children's course in 1888. A course with reduced playing difficulty, allowing for quicker rounds and taking a limited amount of land, may have been the main reason for each of those and others in the birthplace of golf. Smaller second courses can be looked upon as what beginner's slopes or trails are for starting skiers. According to the National Golf Foundation, shorter courses are so popular in Florida that they comprise close to nineteen per cent of the State's 1261 courses. Of the par-72 type courses in that state, nearly ten per cent have smaller courses.

An accompanying course has fewer demanding holes than those on the bigger course. This instantly appeals to beginners, families with children not ready for a longer course, some couples, and short hitters. The concept is also attractive when utilised as an area for experienced golfers wanting to practice their short game, for golf teachers giving on-course instruction, persons with disabilities, and for someone who wants to walk but

is not allowed to on the main course. It is particularly useful while waiting for a tee-time to become available on the main course. Smaller courses provide for a variety of golfers closer to their scale of game and at comparatively low additional costs to owners already with a par-72 course. A second course is often put on unused land and maintained with little extra equipment and ground crew. Usually, no other buildings or parking lots are required. A second course can be something like adding an extra room or porch to a house. At a membership club, the accompanying course could even be open to the public for its extra revenue and as a service to the community.

The more affordable compact course model:

Many touring pros regularly boom their tee shots over 300 yards, which to them has turned traditional par-4 holes into a drive and short iron approach shot. With modern high-tech balls and clubs, nearly all par-5 holes are reachable in two, sometimes with middle-iron second shots. Par-5s demand the most land, are costly, and time inefficient in terms of the three types of golf holes. Putting the earlier challenge and balance of golf into new par-72 courses would necessitate much longer holes totalling somewhere near 8000 yards for golf's top performers. Doing that would require more land, further increasing their construction and maintenance costs, plus making playing time for rounds even longer. These are not in the interest of golf for any level of play and for affordability. The golf ball could be reduced somewhat in its length capacity, which would return the value of classic-length holes, and eliminate the need for longer, new courses. However, this is not likely to occur in the near future.

Courses of a different configuration could match up to the current ability of touring pros and to low, middle and high handicap amateurs without having to change any equipment, rules or procedures. Holes could fit the distance for each kind of golfer's hitting ability, and ideally all golfers would use similar clubs for the same hole. This is accomplished by a mix of holes and multiple tees placed to accommodate the vast difference in hitting length of golfers. Then at the beginning of their round, each golfer only needs to select the tee markers suited to their game.

Other than tradition, there is nothing sacred or magical about the composition of holes that give us golf courses with a total par of around seventy-two. A model compact course would reduce the par average per hole, and the number of holes in a course. It would require a smaller amount of land, involve less construction, and reduce fairway size, playing time and green fees. Such a model would be a mixture of par-3 and par-4 holes of varying lengths, and golfers would use all the clubs in their bag during the round. Not only are par-5 holes by far the biggest land grabbers, they are the hardest holes to spread the tees sufficiently to cater for golfers of varying strengths and abilities. Having twelve instead of eighteen holes, further cuts the demand for land and cost. A driver could be hit up to six times during each round. Compact courses would actually give a more uniform distribution of the clubs used by each golfer, instead of paying lip service to this cliché. Significantly less time would be consumed during a round, shortened again, because there would be no stopping at the turn

HYPOTHETICAL COMPACT COURSE SCORECARD

Yards given first. (Metres in parentheses.)

HOLE	PAR	A	B	C	CLUB(S) TYPICALLY REQUIRED
1	3	104 (95)	93 (85)	73 (67)	Pitching Wedge
2	4	403 (369)	362 (331)	282 (258)	Driver+7 Iron
3	3	186 (170)	168 (154)	130 (119)	4 Iron
4	4	470 (430)	423 (387)	329 (301)	Driver+5 Fairway metal
5	3	141 (129)	127 (116)	99 (91)	8 Iron
6	4	425 (389)	383 (350)	298 (272)	Driver+5 Iron
7	3	231 (211)	208 (190)	162 (148)	3 Fairway metal
8	4	328 (300)	295 (270)	229 (209)	Driver+Sand Wedge
9	3	209 (191)	188 (172)	146 (134)	2 Iron/7 Fairway metal
10	4	380 (347)	342 (313)	266 (243)	Driver+9 Iron
11	3	164 (150)	147 (134)	115 (105)	6 Iron
12	4	448 (410)	403 (369)	313 (286)	Driver+3 Iron/9 Fairway metal
Totals	**42**	**3489 (3191)**	**3139 (2871)**	**2442 (2233)**	

for refreshments. These reductions would better fit the concentration span and energy limits of some golfers. As for all new courses, principles of good golf course design should be followed in laying out the holes of compact courses.

A scorecard of a hypothetical compact course for amateur golfers is given above. For simplicity's sake only three sets of tee markers are given here. More sets would accommodate a greater range of golfers. Tee markers 'A' are based on those who hit their driver approximately 250 yards, 'B'– 225 yards, and 'C' – 175 yards.

The more affordable Cayman ball course model:

Cayman courses are played with the distance-limited Cayman ball. Beginners and not-so-skilled golfers find the Cayman ball easier to make airborne, while still demanding most of the skills of regular golf. Not only is Cayman golf a great way for someone to learn what golf is about, but experienced golfers can also find personal and competitive pleasure from playing it. Each golfer must only remember that all other participants are similarly restricted in their distance, and the game is quite dissimilar to what they are familiar with. It is widely accepted, and indeed proven, that playing the Cayman ball will not ruin a golfer's regular game, so such a fear or excuse against it is not valid. Golf is always a series of judgements and adjustments.

Because of its lightness, the Cayman ball is safer in terms of both people and property than errant shots with a heavier and faster travelling golf ball. Undeniably, its benefits allow Cayman holes to be designed closer together in addition to being considerably shorter and narrower than regular golf holes. Combined, these features make Cayman courses only a fraction the size of conventional golf ball courses. Since the holes are

HYPOTHETICAL CAYMAN COURSE SCORECARD

Yards given first. (Metres in parentheses.)

HOLE	PAR	A	B	C	CLUB(S) TYPICALLY REQUIRED
1	3	62 (57)	58 (53)	53 (48)	Wedge
2	4	232 (212)	218 (199)	199 (182)	Driver+7 Iron
3	3	114 (104)	107 (98)	98 (90)	3 Iron
4	4	220 (201)	207 (189)	189 (173)	Driver+9 Iron
5	3	92 (85)	86 (79)	79 (72)	7 Iron
6	4	268 (245)	252 (230)	230 (210)	Driver+3 Fairway metal
7	3	103 (94)	97 (89)	89 (81)	5 Iron
8	4	202 (185)	190 (174)	173 (158)	Driver+Wedge
9	3	80 (73)	75 (70)	69 (63)	9 Iron
10	4	254 (232)	239 (219)	218 (199)	Driver+3 Iron
11	3	128 (117)	120 (110)	110 (101)	3 Fairway metal
12	4	243 (222)	229 (209)	209 (191)	Driver+5 Iron
Totals	**42**	**1998 (1827)**	**1878 (1719)**	**1716 (1568)**	

scaled down, Cayman courses are considerably easier to fit onto odd-shaped sites and unusual contours. Greatly reduced land requirement, construction cost and area to be maintained are affordable advantages of this enjoyable golf-like game also played on grass.

The chart above illustrates what a Cayman ball course scorecard could look like.

Not everyone can afford the sit-down time, the menu prices, or has cultivated the taste for fine restaurants. Not even connoisseurs want to dine that way at every meal. Neither does one size golf course fit all golfers. The present par-72 course will remain as the dominant membership, upscale daily-fee, and resort model in the foreseeable future. However, other models do exist. And the market for them includes young people without much money for recreation, and those of any age coming into the game: parents wanting to play golf with their children; active retirees with restricted resources; busy people short of time, but still desiring an invigorating outdoor not-too-strenuous activity; off-work league players; occasional golfers on vacation or in events at conventions; and students learning golf in schools. No doubt, there will be many other golfer-candidates who, for whatever reasons just aren't comfortable at the costlier par-72 courses.

Are egos ruining the golf business?

Steve Burns

Unfortunately when building new golf courses, sometimes the egos of golf course developers and golf course architects get in the way of sound business practices and common sense. In their quest to build the next 'top 100,' or 'best new' course, developers often end up spending way too much money to build their course. As a result, they end up only temporarily owning a course that can't possibly generate enough revenue to service its huge debt. After a season or two, the developer is often forced to sell the course at a loss. Usually, by the second or third owner, the course has been discounted enough from its original cost to turn a profit.

It is not uncommon to hear of daily fee courses that cost $7-10 million to build, not including the clubhouse or other facilities. If this is in Las Vegas or a similar area, where year-round play and/or green fees of $150 or more are common, this may be a good investment. However, these construction numbers are often found in areas where the average green fee may be only $20-30. If the developer borrowed $10 million at ten per cent, the course has to accommodate 40,000 rounds at $59 for green and cart fee just to break even, let alone make any money. In the Midwest, with roughly a 200-day golf season, that's a very expensive, very busy course. If the course attracts only 30,000 rounds, which is more typical, the charge needs to be $78 to break even. No matter how nice the course is, it is just too tough to generate enough rounds at a high enough cost to make any money when the course cost this much to build. Following the same pattern of overspending, courses in the high green fee areas sometimes cost $20 million or more to build, so they still aren't as profitable as they could be, although this is sometimes offset by the hotel or casino revenue and/or the expensive real estate developed in conjunction with the course.

As the golf magazines generally don't consider construction cost when evaluating courses, many of these courses do win a lot of the awards and recognition. It only makes sense that a $10 million course will be nicer than a $3 million course—all other things being equal—but is it really that much nicer? Generally, these high-priced courses also have very high advertising budgets, as the owners

desperately need to attract enough golfers to pay the bills. The awards, however, serve as little consolation to the developer who is losing money and is forced to sell the course at a loss.

Golf is a strange business, sometimes based too much on emotion than common sense. Not infrequently, architects fail to discourage this over-spending. An architect who follows this practice hasn't really done his client any favours. Unfortunately, as the profitability of the course isn't one of the award criteria, the architect wins praise from the magazines. This favourable publicity leads more clients to the architect's door, where they will ask for a course just as good or better than the architect's last award winner, and the whole over-spending process is repeated again.

Fortunately, for the less emotional, this foolishness doesn't have to occur. There are hundreds of golf architects in practice doing their jobs properly, building quality courses that are inexpensive enough to succeed. With a good feasibility study, good management, and no major changes in external conditions, there is no reason for a course to not be profitable. A well-built golf course, with nice

lakes and bunkers, USGA greens construction, full cart paths, generous irrigation and drainage, and a decent amount of earthwork, can be built in most areas of the country for $2.5-3.5 million, not including non-course items like buildings. This basically holds true anywhere but in the desert and similar areas where the extremely complex irrigation systems alone often cost well over $1 million. Quite often, given a decent construction site, these courses can even win some awards. For example, the Cobblestone course, near Fort Wayne, Indiana, was built for less than $2.5 million, yet *Golf Digest* ranked it the "8th Best New Affordable Public Course of 1999." This category includes all the public courses opened that year that cost less than $50 to play. The first place winner that year was built on an ideal site in Central Florida. With the natural hills and sand, they built the course for less than $2 million. The Fox Meadow course in Medina, Ohio, was built for $3.4 million including $250,000 for trees in the mostly open site. It only missed making the *Golf Digest* list of the 'Ten Best New Private Courses of 1996' because walking wasn't allowed. The two bonus points this cost them put them 1.8 points behind the tenth place finisher. Regardless, Fox Meadow is successfully selling homes from $350,000 to over $1 million, and competing favourably with a couple of other similarly priced developments that have $9-10 million golf courses. The Hawks Nest course, near Wooster, Ohio, is on several lists of the top public courses in the country. It cost around $2.9 million including roughly $100,000 for on-course restrooms and a waste treatment plant.

The conscientious architect will determine what the client's real motives are, when establishing a construction budget. Although the client may say they want a top ten course, at whatever cost, it still should be the architect's job to help the client understand what that really means. The client should know that a high construction budget may result in his top ten course being unprofitable. Some clients may truly not care what the course costs. If this is the case, it's fine to spend the big money, but in most cases, some sort of budget should be set and adhered to, even if it's a fairly generous one. It's not right for the

architect to take advantage of a client by building a monument that will bring praise to the architect and bankruptcy to the client.

The 1990s was a decade of strong growth in golf course construction, particularly of upscale daily-fee courses. Much of this construction was in response to the growth in golfers, and rounds played, in the 1980s and early 1990s. However, as rounds have levelled off, many market areas are now over-saturated with courses, and course owners are having a harder time making a profit. In some markets, particularly resort areas, all green fees have gone up in reaction to the many new expensive courses being built. One of the reasons for this levelling off of rounds may be the fact that these expensive courses only appeal to a limited portion of the population. As the average cost of a round of golf goes up, fewer golfers can afford to play. Although there is a definite place for high-end courses, there also is a need for more mid-range and inexpensive courses to develop the new golfers that are needed to keep the golf business growing.

Third hole, Hawks Nest Golf Club, Ohio, USA. (Photo by Steve Burns.)

By accident or design?

Donald Steel

If musicians and authors receive royalties in perpetuity on the sale of their works why not golf course architects? Their creations are every bit as long lasting and worthy. However, as with Amadeus Mozart or Ian Fleming, architects would probably end up wealthier in the grave than on the ground.

Pleasure takes many forms, but measuring the delight that golf courses provide is the biggest pleasure of all. What's more, there are no rules, not even guidelines, to help shape judgements. Beholders of beauty rightly apply their own interpretation, but it is a sobering thought that with two of the world's most celebrated courses, nobody knows who to credit for their design. In these cases, distributing royalties might be tricky.

Nevertheless, it is naïve to believe that the Old Course at St. Andrews and Old Prestwick simply evolved. Man must have lent a hand. Was the making of the Road Hole as easy as many would have us believe? Somebody knowledgeable must have placed the tee box, devised such a devilish green, and routed the fairway so tortuously. And can you really believe the Road Hole bunker was formed from a natural hole in the ground? Nor does it seem any more rational to claim that the original twelve holes at Prestwick, on which the first dozen Open championships took place, weren't planned. The schemer must have had a warped sense of humour and logic with the bewildering crossfire of holes that became more an example of what not to do in archi-

tectural terms. Bernard Darwin, golf's most celebrated writer, was certainly an eloquent advocate of leaving well alone. When the course was extended by the removal of a wall behind what is now the third green, he wrote, 'I still want on a charger, the head of the iconoclast who took it down'.

Darwin belonged to the 'leave well alone' school of thought, a sentiment he echoed again when change was afoot in the early days at Royal St. George's: 'confound their politics, frustrate their knavish tricks!' he wrote, 'Why do they want to alter this adorable place? I know that they are perfectly right, and I have even agreed with them that this is a blind shot and that an indefensibly bad hole, but what does it matter? This is perfect bliss'.[3]

By the beginning of the twentieth century, architects had begun to lend a coherence to their designs by studying what makes a good golf course, and which demands are reasonable to ask players to meet. They lent thought, imagination and sophistication to a process that quickly became an art form. However, architects through the ages could only couple their design to the playing equipment of the day. As equipment has changed, so too has design.

When you consider photographs of golfers in tight fitting jackets wielding rudimentary hickory shafted clubs and hitting a feathery ball, it scarcely seems the same game as witnessed today. The most revolutionary change came with the advent of the rubber-cored ball, a situation that provoked that respected figure, John Low, to rant, 'the game of golf has been waging war with the inventor. The one aim of the inventor is to minimise the skill required for the game'.

It was no wonder he thought the game had gone to the dogs. In the 1904 Open championship at Sandwich, the first rounds under seventy were recorded, and the winning score

lowered to a then unthinkable 296. Soon after steel shafts were introduced to Britain, Henry Cotton set the golf world on fire with opening rounds in the 1934 Open of sixty-seven and sixty-five.

Gene Littler, the famous American golfer who made the game look so classically simple, defined golf in terms of the swing as 'a game of constant adjustment'. By the same token, courses have for over 100 years had to adjust to the changes brought about by the manufacture of clubs and balls. Generally speaking, clubs have undertaken these adjustments willingly, either because there was room enough for expansion on land within their possession, or it was possible to acquire extra land. Now, saturation point has been reached nearly everywhere.

Change has involved considerable cost to clubs, a fact largely disregarded, but nobody would want to return to hickories and guttie balls even if they required greater skill to handle. There have been other factors that have led to improved skills and lower scores, namely, greenkeeping techniques, personal fitness levels and improved teaching. However, three important riders must be added.

First, modern courses built with all the mechanical aids are no superior to the masterpieces produced by hand, horse and a hundred men, even though course conditioning is far more advanced. Second, insistence by modern tournament professionals and organisers that the playing of thirty-six holes in a day is not their ideal, is confounded by some portly amateurs who think nothing of playing two rounds without caddies—invariably with a hearty lunch in between. Third, it is acceptance of the value of good teaching, as much as the teaching itself, that has launched the transformation in coaching standards and results.

Where heavy machinery has been of assistance in building new courses, is in allowing unpromising ground to be converted by moving mountains, draining swamps or reclaiming land from the sea. If earthmoving is the only way forward, it is reason enough to adopt this method. Many new courses represent engineering miracles, but they don't come cheap. The cost has ultimately to be picked up by the golfer.

Irrigation and the urge to set a stiff challenge has led to the emphasis in design shifting to the aerial route for shots seeking out small optimum landing areas. At the same time, this has spawned the fashion for long carries to greens, frequently over water. Margin for error has become fractional. From the days when players carried four woods and a wedge, they now opt for one wood and four wedges.

This state of affairs has come about in the mistaken belief that hard, fast greens have to be defended by collars of thick rough and every new course must possess championship credentials. Compounding the architect's difficulty has been the lack of clear guidelines by authorities over the future trends for balls and clubs. In turn, this state of affairs underlines the dilemma of architects tending to play safe by making their layouts longer should 7500-yard courses become the norm. However, against that benchmark, ninety per cent of all courses will be obsolete.

Reverting to Darwin, who struck a chord long ago that still resounds in reference to the term 'championship' course, he states:

I am not thinking of any particular course but I hear this foolish phrase constantly used. Most courses are not fit for a championship, never will get one and nobody wants to see one there. Then, why in the name of goodness should we set up this nonsensical standard and then spoil our courses and break our backs in trying to live up to them?

Certainly, the best approach to combating power is still a site of high, natural quality where the golf course blends effortlessly with the landscape, and the strategy behind the play offers several options on every hole including around the green. Faster running courses are a more potent force than those watered to death, a dictum followed most faithfully by the marvellous sandbelt courses of Melbourne.

Given good land, there should be no question of major reshaping of the landscape in order to accommodate the course. It begs the question therefore how much does the picture owe to its frame? Serious attempts have been made in certain parts of the world to recreate the Old Course at St. Andrews, either in whole or in part, even though copies are unrecognisable without their surroundings.

How recognisable, for example, would the coastal stretch at Turnberry be in a barren wilderness a hundred miles from the sea, or how distorted would Pine Valley appear if it became part of Palm Desert? An equally fascinating flight of fancy is conjured up when applied to architects. A hundred artists can paint the Eiffel Tower, and you can take your pick of the best of them, but the design and building of a golf course is entrusted to one person. We shall never know how different Royal Melbourne would have been if it had been in the hands of Harry Colt. And would Pete Dye have designed something more dazzling at Augusta than Alister Mackenzie? How would Robert Trent Jones have fared if he couldn't have moved dirt, or would Donald Ross have become a slave to building water hazards everywhere, if born a hundred years later?

All architects are products of their time, but altering layouts involves a responsibility not experienced by musicians or artists.

Nobody dares to tamper with the *Mona Lisa* or rewrite Beethoven's Ninth symphony. Delicate touching up or special arrangements are common place, but changing the fabric of a golf course means dabbling with the copyright. The only way for a contemporary architect to salve his conscience by so doing is by imagining himself as a reincarnated Mackenzie, Tillinghast or Colt.

These great men would recognise the need for revision, although they might not fathom or approve why it had become necessary, even though nearly all alterations over the years have been prompted by the desire to keep pace with the advances in the manufacture of clubs and balls. It is a relentless march, and the truth is that many clubs haven't been able to keep pace. This is not the platform to enter that debate.

However, there isn't much doubt that the easiest, cheapest and best way would have been to control the ball, as has happened once or twice in history. The American Society of Golf Course Architects (ASGCA) was concerned enough in 2001 to write to the United States Golf Association expressing their fears

that 'the onus of adjusting to technology is still falling on the golf courses'. Every week, there are examples of once mighty par-4s being reduced to a drive and a sand wedge, or once famous tournament or championships courses relegated to obscurity because they are no longer long enough to test a world-class field.

One example. In winning the 2001 US Masters, Tiger Woods took the bunkers right out of play on the seventy-second hole, leaving himself a second shot of just seventy-five yards after an uphill drive. Contrast this with Tom Watson hitting a drive and a 2-iron, on the flat, to the seventy-second hole at Royal Birkdale to secure his fifth Open title in 1983. Even allowing for Birkdale's eighteenth being sixty-five yards longer than Augusta's finishing hole (until recently), there is no doubt which episode provided the greater theatre or required the greater nerve and skill.

Time alone will be the judge whether the ball should have been throttled back or will continue to be hit further. You wouldn't bet against the latter, but at least one distinguished club is making a comeback. Royal

Liverpool (Hoylake) has been restored to the Open championship rota after a spell in isolation dating back to 1967. When Roberto de Vicenzo, one of the finest of all golfers became champion, the attendance for the week was less than it is now for a day. Changes to England's second oldest links involved the release of space to aid positioning of grandstands and crowd movement as well as a critical review of the bunkering, teeing grounds and other playing characteristics.

It is a strange twist that, having sat on the sidelines for so long, Hoylake could be made the most challenging of all the Open courses. However, it is not everyone who sees change as progress. James Braid, one of the Great Triumvirate and professional at Walton Heath, was distinguished enough as an architect himself to be miffed not to have been invited by his club to advise when change to the New course was suggested eighty years or more ago.

When an exuberant member later asked, 'Jimmy, what do you think about the improvements to the New?', he rephrased him acidly, 'you mean the alterations?'

Reality check: the art, the science and the permits

Jeremy Pern

Eighteenth hole, Golf Club du Chateau de Vuissens, Friburg, Switzerland. (Photo by Jeremy Pern.)

OPPOSITE: **Eighth hole, Golf and Freizeitpark (Diamond Course), Tullnerfeld (near Vienna), Austria. (Photo by Jeremy Pern.)**

The human brain is probably the most complex structure that exists in the known universe, and what we have done with it over the past 100,000 years is what distinguishes us from other organisms. We have learned to think about the environment in which we live, and to construct ideas about how it has evolved. Magic and religion provided the principal source of these ideas until Galileo and fellow scientists started to pull back the curtain on reality. Science has been described by E. O. Wilson as 'the organised systematic enterprise that gathers knowledge about the world and condenses the knowledge into testable laws and principles'.[4] But gathering that knowledge requires seeking things undiscovered and unseen. Like an artist, the scientist requires imagination and vision in addition to rigour and objectivity. 'The ideal scientist thinks like a poet and works like a bookkeeper.'[5]

Art has been described as the means by which people reach out to others in order to transmit feeling. Art exists in many forms, most of which fall into distinct groups that are relative to space and time. Sculpture, painting, and many of the visual arts exist only in space, while music exists only in time. Both art and science transmit information and both seek elegance to create order out of a confusion of detail. What makes great science also makes great art—an understanding of the possible, combined with a realisation of the probable. The matrix of creativity is what has gone before and what is yet to come. Art and science in their purest forms are the opposite sides of the same coin; one cannot exist without the other.

And what has all this to do with golf course architecture today? Not much, but it has

Sixteenth hole 'The Rocket', Golf and Freizeitpark (Diamond Course), Tullnerfeld. (Photo by Jeremy Pern.)

OPPOSITE: Seventh and sixteenth holes, Golf and Freizeitpark. (Photo by Alex Kramel.)

everything to do with golf course design. Design is a process not a product. Golf course architecture is concerned with creating an object in an environment conditioned by space, time, economics and law, whereas golf course design is concerned only with space. The art of golf course design and the practice of golf course architecture are now two very different things. Design modifications imposed by forces beyond the control of the architect are now so extensive in most European golf course developments that the role of the architect during the pre-construction phase resembles that of a shepherd herding his rowdy and unpredictable flock towards a hardly discernible and distant goal.

A significant proportion of the millions of golfers around the world have given serious thought to designing a golf course. Every golf club has several members on their committee whose dream is to be allowed unfettered access to the opportunity of creating a golf hole. But there are only several hundred men and too few women who make their living exclusively from golf course architecture around the world.

The single biggest event in golf course development in Europe since the game was conceived in its present form has been the movement to regulate planning and development of the environment. In most European countries until the mid-1980s building a golf course involved little more than a design coupled with a declaration of intent that a course was going to be built and a few months later work started. The finished product usually bore more than a passing resemblance to the initial design.

Today, things are different. The legislation in place in most European countries means that a golf project takes at least three, most likely five, and not unusually ten years to go from the initial idea to construction. This time frame does not just apply to large-scale housing or resort developments, but also to modest golf facilities.

The developer needs only three essentials to start the construction process—the land, planning permission and money. As a result of centuries of inheritance divisions, European land ownership is a complex issue. The land bank of a golf project invariably changes in size and shape between initial ideas and the start of construction, with all the resulting modifications to the design of the course.

The planning process in different European countries is broadly similar. The initial phase involves a change of use permit, from say agriculture to leisure. This outline permission is usually based on outside criteria—regional or local planning issues rather than site-specific issues. The architect is involved at this stage with, among other things, land selection and evaluation, draft routing, traffic flows, sewage processing, water consumption, power requirements, project economics, cash flows and visual impacts. Once the change of use issues have been successfully dealt with, the design work begins.

The architect draws up the detailed plans, and in concert with a host of consultants, starts becoming involved in planning negotiations and impact studies. There are consultants for everything: ecology; flora; fauna; traffic; forestry; agriculture; water supply; treatment and quality control; fisheries; archaeology; local history; and so forth. The consultants are often paid by the client in addition to working for the administration or local planning department. They may also be paid by both, yet work for neither. There are battles fought between consultants themselves and fiercer often than those between the developers and the authorities. The agricultural lobby is invariably opposed to the ecologists, who may be at loggerheads with the forestry people, who usually have difficulties with the landscape specialists, while the water authorities dither in a frenzy of uncertainty.

In a hasty effort to align themselves with European directives, many legislative bodies have rushed through a host of politically correct environmental regulations. This useful regulatory information is essentially misunderstood, differentially applied, or selectively ignored by the planning bureaucracy. There are few, if any, procedural precedents for the planners, resulting in much to-ing and fro-ing in pursuit of the planning permit.

When the permit eventually arrives, the initial business plans drawn up by the client will have suffered the passage of time. The slings and arrows of a global recession, a rise in fuel prices, interest rate hikes, a new golf

course next door, a reduction in the number of housing plots, the cancellation of the motorway exit project, and a new runway at the local airport involving a minor, but irritating modification to the flight path, may all impose design changes to deal with the economics of reality and the reality of economics.

If one ignores the awesome clerical grind of permit acquisition and examines the nuts and bolts of course design, the single most important element is the course routing. Good routing relies on observation, instinct and a genuine understanding of landscape, coupled with an intelligent imagination and an ability to visualise the construction sequences at this conceptual stage. Visions of the impossible are no good to anyone.

Like the conductor of an orchestra, it is the architect's role to optimise the potential of the resources available. Not everything can be drawn on a plan, and much can be improvised on site to the benefit of golf course quality, providing the budget, permits and timetable are respected accordingly.

To golfers, the aesthetics of design and the playing characteristics of a golf course are sub-jective, whereas construction details remain more of an objective science. Water will always flow downhill just as grass always needs food, water and air. The science of golf course architecture resides in finding solutions to technical problems related to geology, agronomy, botany, civil engineering and the physics of the game itself. Once struck, a ball will behave in predictable ways depending on its velocity through the air, wind speed and direction, topography, and the characteristics of the surface along which the ball travels after landing. Admittedly these factors are all dynamic and interrelated, making accurate predictions difficult, but they can be assessed objectively. What happens immediately before the ball is struck is an altogether different equation involving motor-neurone skills, brain synapses, physical fitness, anatomy, ironmongery, sociology, human behaviour and psychology.

Although consensus exists as to what is more or less beautiful, it is in the unexpected nuances and subtleties of 'arrangement' that the beauty and the playing characteristics of a course can be most successfully understood and enhanced. Therein lies the art. The prin-ciples of golf course design are common and shared. The conservative nature of a highly codified participant sport, dependent upon a large, expensive organic playing field has seen to that. So where does the distinction lie in golf course design? And what of the future of the art and science of golf course architecture? The answer to these questions is found in the simple truth that where we all share princi-ples, we each have distinct and different responses to the creation and revelation of detail. A golf course is a highly specific and functionally defined artefact. Artefact design, like biological design, evolves through incremental change over time. The best courses, those most fitted for their purpose, are preserved with affection by their users and multiplied through imitation by their admirers. Bad design is not sustainable, as it is rapidly replaced through redesign or renovation.

Dr Alister Mackenzie, in his book *Golf Architecture* (1920) defined the terms of golf course design and the role of the golf course architect. He claimed that a golf course architect, if not actually an artist, should possess both an artistic temperament and an education in science. His book is full of pithy observations concerning golf, golfers, and golf course design and construction. His comments are as valid today as they were when his book was first published, but with one notable omission. He made no mention of the environment and planning permits. These are the challenges of the contemporary golf course architect.

Many golf course architects today seek to emulate the work done by the likes of Mackenzie, whose qualities are to be admired and respected, not fawned over as emblems of a rosy past. Our predecessors enjoyed the art of design as few of us in Europe can today. Now we have to heed the constraints of political correctness that ensures conformity in the misguided name of science, thereby shackling the art of our wonderful profession.

Eleventh green, Golf and Freizeitpark (Diamond Course), Tullnerfeld. (Photo by Alex Kramel.)

BELOW: Opening hole, Golf Club du Chateau de Vuissens, Friburg, Switzerland. (Photo by Jeremy Pern.)

Japanese golf courses: a brief overview

Hisamitsu Ohnishi

Japan still has much to learn from Europe and the US in terms of aesthetics and the game's underlying architectural principles. We must also learn ways to design courses that help make golf more enjoyable. This should include creating fast greens with shapes and slopes suited to the newly developed turf. The introduction and maintenance of the newly developed, third-generation turfgrass is another important challenge for us.

In 1901, a four-hole golf course—Japan's first—was built on top of Mt. Rokko, about 1000 metres above sea level, by Englishman A. H. Groom. So began the history of Japanese golf, which celebrated its 100th anniversary in 2001.

In 1932, Hirono Golf Club was opened, followed in 1936 by Kawana Hotel Golf Course (Fuji Course), both designed by Englishman, Charles Alison. Today, they are considered Japan's most prestigious courses. Not surprisingly, all Japanese golf courses have been strongly influenced by Great Britain, the birthplace of the game.

In 1957, the Canada Cup was held at the Kasumigaseki Country Club, designed by a Japanese architect and opened in 1929. Torakichi Nakamura and Koichi Ono won the event, and triggered a golf boom in Japan. By this time, Japan had 116 courses, and the total golfing population was 1.83 million—a mere two per cent of today's golfers. Of the 116 golf courses, only ten were designed by foreign architects.

A total of 1287 courses opened between 1958 and 1979. Of these, ninety-one were designed by foreign architects. Architects of this period included Joe Crane, Peter Thomson, and Ching-Ce Chin, who designed nineteen, thirteen, and sixteen courses, respectively.

By 1984, a total of 1353 courses were constructed. Of these, only ninety-nine courses were designed by foreign architects. The Fujioka Country Club and Nambu Fuji Country Club, designed in 1971 by Australian Peter Thomson, and still considered one of the finest golf courses today, represent those

OPPOSITE: **Eighteenth hole, The Cypress Golf Club, Japan. (Photo by Brian Morgan ©)**

infrequent courses designed by non-Japanese architects. One of the unique features seen in many Japanese architect-designed courses is the use of two greens: one incorporating korai grass for summer, and another, bent grass for winter. The two-green system was considered necessary to allow play throughout Japan's four distinct seasons.

From around 1985, Japan saw the opening of many new courses that were designed by famous foreign architects, including Jack Nicklaus's twenty-two courses, Pete and Perry Dye's twenty-two, and Robert Trent Jones's nineteen. Of the 947 courses opened in Japan from 1985 onwards, 207 have been designed by non-Japanese architects. Most of these courses adopted the one-green system that prevails overseas. And, reflecting the economic bubble years in which they were built, many of them come equipped with luxurious facilities.

Of the courses constructed between 1957 and 1984, those designed by Seiichi Inoue are especially well known and highly acclaimed. One of the characteristics of his courses is that they are all built on excellent terrain. Upon closer inspection, however, one finds that some may require conversion to a one-green system. Building cart paths and other improvements may also become necessary.

The prerequisites of a good course are beautiful natural elements and a design that makes the most of them. Fortunately, Japan is blessed with abundant beautiful nature. Two-thirds of the land is covered with forest, rarely seen elsewhere in the world. Since most of the remaining flatland had been turned into farms, many golf courses were built in mountains and forests. This, and the enforcement of rigorous development restrictions, has made it extremely difficult to build good courses in Japan. It is highly unlikely that outstanding courses can be constructed from now on.

Japan still has idle farmland whose area would correspond to about 10,000 golf courses. The possibility of making this land available for use as golf courses is the subject of much controversy. The issue is something the entire golf industry must consider seriously, including what role golf courses should play in Japanese society and what forms they should take.

One can see the problems of the courses built prior to 1985 with the clarity of hindsight. With the increase in corporate golf from around 1960, courses geared to business use increased. This resulted in courses lacking in design philosophy, with an increase of shallow and therefore meaningless bunkers, and a preference for relatively flat courses. As many of the courses are located in mountainous areas, 'playing four'—a rule peculiar to Japan—has become quite common in the case of a carry over a valley or the like. Local rules such as moving a ball by a length of a club have become rampant, neglecting the game's fundamental tenet of playing the ball as it lies. In many cases, course owners insisted on having their own personal tastes reflected in course design instead of leaving it up to professional architects.

As a result of the above, most high quality golf courses in Japan are either those made under the direction of Charles Alison, or the ones opened after 1985.

Of the courses designed by Japanese architects, the twenty or so courses designed by Seichi Inoue, are reputed highly. All his courses

excel, particularly in terms of the selection of sites and the routing of the eighteen holes.

There are some outstanding golf courses in Japan. Otaru Country Club, opened in 1974, and designed by Kokichi Yasuda, is one of the finest courses in Hokkaido. Despite its seaside location, the course has large trees that separate the respective holes. The original course was opened in 1928 with three holes, and was subsequently remodeled into a one-green system after the 1991 Japan Open.

Kasumigaseki Country Club (East Course) opened for play in 1929. Its co-designers were Shiro Akaboshi and Kinya Fujita. This course was the site of the 1957 Canada Cup and the 1995 Japan Open. Situated on a gently sloping hillock, the course is separated into respective holes by tall trees. The only problem is that it still uses two greens.

Hirono Golf Club opened in 1932, and was designed by the famed architect, Charles H. Alison. Built on a moderately undulating terrain near Kobe, the birthplace of Japanese golf, it is truly one of the best courses in Japan in all aspects, including, the layout and the diversity of its eighteen holes.

Kasumigaseki Country Club (West Course) opened in 1932, and was designed by Seiichi Inoue. A hilly course with moderate undulation, it was remodeled in 2000 into a one-green system by Taizo Kawata.

Another Charles H. Alison course, Kawana Hotel Golf Course (Fuji Course), was opened in 1936. This is a splendid seaside course overlooking the Pacific Ocean with substantial ups and down terrain. Although being primarily a winter course, it nevertheless uses the two-green system of korai grass. Conversion to a one-green system is much anticipated. The course is the permanent venue for the annual Fuji Sankei Classic, where the seventeenth hole is used as the eighteenth, and that hole as the first.

Tokyo Golf Club opened in 1940, designed by Komyo Otani. Built on a gently rolling hill, it was the venue for the 2001 Japan Open, and draws much praise for its excellent layout. The only drawback is the use of the two-greens system.

In 1953, Oarai Golf Club, designed by Seiichi Inoue was opened, and by common consent, it is Inoue's finest work. Surrounded by numerous pine trees, the course is highly challenging. No stranger to tournaments, Oarai has hosted a number of major events including the 1998 Japan Open.

The Phoenix Country Club opened in 1971, and was designed by Gokichi Ohashi. With its coastal location, Phoenix is known for having staged the 1971 Japan Professional Golfers' Championship, and it was here where Masashi Ozaki captured his first career victory. As the venue of the annual Dunlop Phoenix, the course has been visited by many renowned players: Jack Nicklaus; Tom Watson; Ernie Els; and David Duval, to name a few. The only drawback is that it has spare greens.

One superb golf course is Nambu Fuji Country Club, which opened in 1974, and was designed by Peter Thomson. His layout takes full advantage of its natural scenery. The design also reflects Thomson's golfing expertise as the five-time winner of the Open Championship, as well as his extensive knowledge of Scottish courses. This course has hosted the Mitsubishi Gallant tournament in 1978, 1983 and 1992.

Taiheiyo Club (Gotemba Course) opened in 1977 and was designed by Shunsuke Kato.

One particular honour was being selected as the 2001 World Cup venue. A close-up view of Mt. Fuji provides a breathtaking backdrop to the course. Conversion to a one-green system is currently under way.

American designer, Robert Trent Jones designed Pine Lake Golf Club in 1985. This course became the first full-scale, one-green course of bent grass in Western Japan. In 1987 the Mitsubishi Gallant tournament was held here. The ordeals of the co-leaders who hit their balls into a pond—one after another—made the course famous throughout Japan. This is an excellent layout on difficult terrain.

Horai Country Club, a Robert von Hagge design, opened in 1990. The course is beautiful, but highly challenging even for tournament professionals as evidenced during the 2000 and 2001 Japan Tour Championships.

Jack Nicklaus designed the Hokkaido Classic Golf Club in 1991, a superb course built on a magnificent Hokkaido landscape.

My design of the Cypress Golf Club, which opened in 1992, is surrounded by steep mountains on three sides with cypresses, cedars, firs, wild cherry, and other huge trees separating the

Nambu Fuji Country Club, Japan. (Photo courtesy of Justin Trott.)

holes, and the course impresses players with the grandeur of its natural beauty. No stakes or fence posts are used to mark the out of bounds or hazards. This reflects the design concept of creating as natural a course as possible with minimum artificiality.

Land-based design and the modern aesthetic

Kelly Blake Moran

The intensity of modern life has a profound influence on our thoughts and actions. Sometimes we act superficially by following what we are told, and sometimes we act in ways that are individual, more truthful to who we are spiritually. Land-based design and the modern aesthetic seeks to describe the qualities of the experience that produce a modern golf course that has a deeper moral or spiritual purpose rather than a faddish superficial manifestation of design.

Ultimately, the personality of a golf course is revealed to all who play it. I played the home course of my youth over a period of thirteen years, and almost daily for three years. I can walk that course in my mind, and recall much of it in intimate detail even though I am 1700 miles and twenty years removed from the last time I played it. This personal encounter, this face-to-face intimacy with the land and its natural and man-made elements, is the best means by which to know the truth about it. After all, what is more truthful to you than your own personal engagement with something that you really care about.

If the best judgment of a golf course comes from a lengthy experience with it, then it follows that the same is true with the terrain before it becomes a golf course. This should be the basis of all design disciplines that work with the land. Architects, landscape architects, engineers, and land planners—for that matter people on local planning commissions, zoning boards, and boards of supervisors—should all spend much greater time considering the land before ever formalising their design concepts, and land use regulations. Sadly, it appears that most designers perform their best when making the land fit their traditional design standards, and the standards set by the local, regional, and federal government agencies.

The concept of land-based design is not original, since it seems probable that many of the old designs that we enjoy the most came from people who took the time to become acquainted with the truths about the land prior to its conversion into a golf course. Land-based design and the modern aesthetic is an approach to finding new, fresh ways of adapting the landform into a golf course.

ABOVE LEFT: **Future site for the fifth hole, Heritage Golf Club, Pennsylvania, USA. (Photo by Kelly Blake Moran.)**

LEFT: **Fifth hole tee-shot, Heritage Golf Club. (Sketch by Kelly Blake Moran.)**

© KELLY BLAKE MORAN GOLF COURSE ARCHITECTS, INC.

TEE SHOT
#5
HERITAGE
GOLF CLUB

Why should we listen to the old traditions handed to us by past generations when we can walk on the land under the same sun, see all of its beauty, and have our own thoughts about it and how it should be treated?

At the outset, the architect should wander the land to discover what makes it special. This entails not looking for areas to make prototypical holes, like the Redan hole, the Alps hole, as classicists like to do. Instead, land-based design means that through the personal encounter with the land, and the effort to unravel its secrets, golf holes will emerge as opposed to being imposed on the landscape. Through this process, the golf holes are formed by the personality of the land, and its God-given beauty becomes self evident to the architect.

The inexperienced person can usually only visualise a golf hole on the land after it has been transformed into fairways, bunkers, and greens. The trained eye sees all that when looking at raw land. In fact, the trained eye sees more, and probably sees the hole at its finest before it is converted into the more popular form of a golf hole. This concept can be compared to seeing the skeleton, much like the finest artists did when they would visit morgues. There, the artist could envisage what was underneath the skin, and how the bone structure and muscle made the form of the body clothed in skin. This process helped them convey a more realistic version of an arm or a hand, because they knew more about how it was formed from the inside to the outside. Should not the golf course architect have such intimate knowledge about the latent features of the land before it is clothed with the manifest features of a golf course? Learning about the land helps the architect know what is most appropriate when shaping the features.

Man-made imposition is required to insert greens, tees, and bunkers into a landscape. The form these features take can be unique if the form giver is thoroughly familiar with all the fine qualities of that land. If the architect knows the land, and this is the basis for developing the routing of the course and the course strategy, the course will be beautiful.

But let us not forget that golf is a game; beauty is only one element of designing a golf course. The history, purpose, and skill required to play it must be of first priority, which means the architect must develop a strategy shot by shot, hole by hole, out and in. Arguably, the beauty of a golf course emerges for the player upon the realisation of a personal connection; that is, his strategising is carefully allowed for and acknowledged by the architect.

As the architect spends more time walking the land with eyes wide open, and with a clear mind and purpose directed toward strategy, recognising the land's natural features greatly assists in isolating elements to challenge the skill and mind of the player. If there is a basic principle for finding strategy on the land it is this: behold the entire landscape in front of you, and consider the widest range possible for how the hole can be played. In other words, do not think in terms of one fairway, 100 feet wide, materialising through the landscape; instead, consider the panorama as the only limitation in terms of the number of ways the player can journey to the green. If possible, a worthy exercise might be to tee it up and play the raw land. This would probably be the purest form of battle against the natural elements, and it might impress

ABOVE LEFT: **Future site for the fifth hole, Old Wales Golf Club, Pennsylvania, USA. (Photo by Kelly Blake Moran.)**

LEFT: **Fifth hole tee-shot, Old Wales Golf Club. (Sketch by Kelly Blake Moran.)**

© KELLY BLAKE MORAN GOLF COURSE ARCHITECTS

TEE SHOT
#5
OLD WALES GOLF CLUB

upon the architect the magnificence and sanctity of the natural land, and the sheer joy it gives to the game.

The critical first impressions gained from walking the land over several days are the hardest aspects to keep hold of in the final design. This may be the biggest challenge a land-based architect faces. Much of the modern way of doing things conspires against this approach, so it requires vigilance and a staunch belief that for all the advancements in modern art and architecture, the most modern of taste and beauty is still found in the natural world. The more the natural world is infused into the man-made world, the more beautiful and meaningful are our designing efforts.

Once the architect is ready to begin designing the course, usually months before construction begins, the translation of the architect's ideas based on what is seen is best accomplished by hand, sketching three-dimensional ideas onto paper. This moment is probably the most truthful moment in the design of a golf hole. Truthful in the sense that the architect is at that moment more connected to what is the very best way to play a golf hole on the land before

them than at any other time in the design process. This does not disregard the importance of refinement back at the office. However, the experience on the land, that moment when suddenly the design is self evident, that moment when the architect experiences the most intense sensation that the idea being held in their mind's eye is the right one, that revelation should be given the highest priority when the refinement process begins back in the office where the architect is separated from the actual place and experience of the site. Being on the land looking for golf holes requires the architect to leave behind preconceived paradigms, and the forces of other people's thoughts. It requires letting the land tell its story, and should result in an intense and gratifying improvisation going on between the architect and the land. This approach is about the here and now.

Although we must sometimes alter the natural terrain for the game, it is best to try to predict the impact of that embellishment; that alterations and impositions can make the terrain look deformed.

Everything about the golf course should have an organic appeal that can only result

from the intense engagement with the land well before the construction crew arrives. Walking the land continually makes the architect aware of the simple economy of nature. There are no superfluous elements that interrupt its natural grace. The real challenge is in discovering what is most prominent about the land and making those prominent elements the organising structure for the routing plan and the strategic design. Even if the land is almost totally devoid of what some consider beauty, as long as the course illuminates the best of what little it has to offer, and presents a smart strategy that challenges the player to think their way through from beginning to end, then it is the most beautiful course to behold. This is why strategy must come first, and physical beauty second, for golfers are too smart to be fooled by something that is beautiful yet does not excite the imagination when it is engaged in play. The golfer determines the beauty of the golf course by how captivated they are by the way the course plays.

Translating the mechanics of land-based design into written form is not easy. It is not readily explainable, nor should it be for fear that it might be codified and thus become devoid of life. Throw out the books by the old masters and their heirs, throw out the magazines, throw out the opinions of the most ardent spokespersons for classic, modern, post-modern, and all the other movements. Go to the land, look and listen for her wisdom, beg for her insight to be made known to you. What is land-based design and the modern aesthetic? I cannot tell you. You must go outdoors and find it for yourself.

Fifteenth hole, The Harvester Golf Club, Iowa, USA. (Photo courtesy of Ronald Whitten.)

The evolution of golf course design
Christoph Städler

Since the earliest reports about the game of golf, dating back to the fifteenth century until far into the nineteenth century, golf courses had not been built but discovered. In Scotland, the cradle of golf, the so-called links land—which is the unarable belt of sand dunes between the ocean or river estuaries and the fruitful hinterland—proved to be ideal as golfing grounds. The golfers looked for areas where the grass grew as close and even as possible, called them greens, and put a hole into them. In the early days, tees did not yet exist: according to rule one of the thirteen rules of 1745, the tee-shot had to be played from within one club-length of the previous hole.

At first there was also no ruling about the number of holes for a golf course—it varied between five and twenty-five. St. Andrews initially had eleven holes running behind each other along the coast (out), and in order to come back to the starting point (home), the same holes were played in the opposite direction. Under this arrangement eleven holes became twenty-two. Until the end of the eighteenth century, this counter play was held on the same fairways and to the same holes on the greens until the increasing number of players necessitated creating parallel fairways and the famous double greens

In 1764, the Society of St. Andrews, the future Royal and Ancient Golf Club decided to combine the first four holes, and consequently the last four to two new starting and finishing holes, thus reducing the number of holes to eighteen. When the Royal and Ancient took the leadership of the game of golf in the early nineteenth century, this purely coincidental number became the standard.

Until the late nineteenth century, golf holes were simply laid out by reasonable routing; there was no construction work involved. The game of golf was played over completely natural terrain; the well-drained links with their fine, crisp grasses offered optimal conditions.

The early style: penal design
When the game of golf spread in the nineteenth century, more terrains with less suitable soils were used as golf course sites. Sometimes earth movement equipment was necessary although it was normally kept to a

OPPOSITE: **Heroic design at Senne Golfclub Gut Welschof, Schloss Holte-Stukenbrock, Germany. (Photo by Christoph Städler.)**

minimum because it was often inadequate and expensive.

At that time, the supervision of golf course construction had generally been executed by a golf professional or top amateur who believed that the topped shot was the worst shot. The ball of those days, the featherie, was rather difficult to fly high and long, and topped shots were often running the same distance as an accurate shot was flying through the air. In order to punish such shots, these first golf course designers ordered the construction of steep, ugly earth walls and huge bunkers that blocked the line of play for all shots except the most perfect. This penal design principle remained predominant until the first decades of the twentieth century. Even the introduction of the guttie ball, around 1850, and of the first wound ball, the Haskell ball in 1902, which blessed the game with better playability and larger ball flight distances, did not herald the foreclosure of penal design. Only the hazards were placed at farther distances.

Around 1900, many new golf courses emerged in Great Britain, America and on the European continent, and along with them grew the demand for professional golf course architects. Some of them, under the leadership of the Englishman, Harry S. Colt, felt that the traditional form of penal design was too severe. They softened it by taking the hazards out of the direct line of play, and by moving them to the sides of the fairways. However, it was still penal design because the bunkers had the purpose to punish slices and hooks, but at least they gave a chance to the average golfer to reach the green unhindered with short but straight shots.

Although penal design was gradually replaced by other design styles in the following decades, until today, many famous and notorious golf holes were built in penal style simply because penal holes are often particularly spectacular and dramatic in their extreme contrast between success and failure. However, such holes have the disadvantages that small target areas or forced carries make them frustrating, or virtually unplayable for too many golfers, and that they dictate only one possible way to play the hole.

The modern style: strategic design

In the years between 1911 and 1937—the Golden Age of golf design—more and more golf course architects began to apply a different design philosophy. This was derived from the famous Old Course at St. Andrews where there is not a single hole which dictates only one possible line of play or playing strategy. Along the way, there are countless hazards of different degrees of difficulty to overcome that demand a conscious decision about the best playing strategy on each shot. The essential attraction of the game lies in the courage to carry hazards, or to pass them as closely as one dares in order to make the next shot shorter and easier. The freedom of choice to weigh up between risk and reward epitomises the strategic design philosophy, which gradually superseded the penal design.

The architects that postulated the strategic design philosophy recognised that it was against the target of gaining a broader popularity for the game of golf, when inaccurate shots were punished too severely by deep bunkers that allowed only short recovery shots. Therefore, they developed the guideline whereby the supreme aim of golf architecture was to make the course a stern test, and an interesting challenge for good players, without being exceedingly demanding and dis-

couraging for the weaker players—a guideline which is still valid today. From it they derived that the hazards, following the principle of 'risk and reward', should be placed in the vicinity of the landing area of the tee shot which offered the best angle of play for the following shot. Thereby, the player should be encouraged to play on position, similar to a billiards player. The architects realised that strategic design could be executed in a more striking manner by angular-shaped holes. That is, by placing hazards into the inner angle of the landing area of such a so-called dogleg hole.

The most challenging style: heroic design

Along with the growing popularity of water hazards, a new design style emerged which stood in between the severe penal design and the moderate strategic design: the heroic design. It confronts the player with a penal hazard, but this does not have to be crossed for better or worse. The player can either take a safe but longer route around it, or he can bite off as much as he dares from a diagonal hazard. That is why this classic variant is also known as bite-off-design.

ABOVE: **Modern penal design at Golfclub Schloss Westerholt, Herten-Westerholt, Germany.**

LEFT: **Early penal design at Wentworth Golf Club, Surrey, England. (Photos by Christoph Städler.)**

Heroic design is spectacular. It provokes the better players to evaluate the reward of a successful shot higher than the risk of failure. So it offers 'risk and reward' to a stronger extent than strategic design: the higher the risk, the higher the reward. Since heroic design is both an extraordinary challenge for better players and fair to circumvent for weaker players, it is very popular among both players and architects. Hardly a championship course has been built in many years that doesn't have at least two or three heroic holes.

The contemporary trend is for a design mix with strategic dominance. Both the strategic and the heroic design demand from the player an assessment as to how close he dares to pass the hazards in the landing zone of the tee-shot in order to reach the best position for the consecutive shot. Thus he must plan his strategy from the green backwards, basing the plan on an honest estimation of his own capability. Strategic design builds a sharp contrast to penal design, which gives the player no real alternatives, apart from passing the penal hazard with the shot at hand, or to lay up first before crossing the hazard. Either way, he can't avoid the consequences in case of failure.

When discussing penal design, you have to distinguish between penal holes and penal hazards, which are often incorrectly regarded as identical. A deep pot bunker in the middle of a broad fairway is a penal hazard within a strategic hole, whereas shallow bunkers at both sides of a straight fairway qualifies as a penal hole.

Difficult hazards, which a player may regard as penal, are the essence of the game of golf, especially at strategic holes offering sufficient room to play around them. To exaggerate the point: holes with strategic design may well have penal hazards in contrast to holes with penal design if the hazards are reasonably fair for an average player.

Some holes cannot be assigned to a certain design style because they contain elements of two or even three styles. A good example is the notorious seventeenth hole of the Old Course at St. Andrews, where the drive offers a heroic abbreviation across the diagonal out-of-bounds at the Old Course Hotel, while the shot to the green demands strategic play to avoid the extremely difficult penal pot bunker at the left edge of the green and the road and wall behind it.

The vast majority of the golf holes built during the last three decades demonstrate strategic design. However, the best courses don't have eighteen strategic holes, but contain some holes of the other design styles too. A well-known example is Amen Corner at Augusta National: eleven is a strategic hole; twelve is a penal hole; and thirteen is a heroic hole.

Under the influence of the architectural avant-gardist Pete Dye, the penal hole has regained some popularity. In particular, this is shown at his seventeenth hole of the Tournament Players Championship Course at Ponte Vedra, Florida, with its nerve-racking island green, which became notorious worldwide and inspired hundreds of other architects. Although such holes normally are beyond the capability of most amateurs, their spectacular look quickly gains them a high degree of fame. They also have good marketing value as signature holes.

Penal holes of the extreme kind, which punish each shot except the perfect one with the maximum penalty of 'stroke and distance', are highly questionable. They only offer two possible results: success or total failure. Fairer, and strategically more varied, are holes that force the player to judge how close he dares to pass the hazard. The higher the risk, the higher should be the reward; that is the essence of strategic design and, even more, of heroic design. On a well-designed golf course, most of the holes should be equipped with sound and fair strategic and heroic features, because this determines to what degree a course is both challenging and fair.

The history, theory and folly of roughs

Dr Michael J. Hurdzan

Roughs are those areas of grasses cut higher than fairways and bordering them like a fur collar on a coat. They have become a common form of hazard on golf courses: perhaps too common, to the point of ruining the game. A look at the history, theory and folly of the rough might serve to refocus our thinking on their purpose, and restore some vital elements such as strategy back to the game of golf.

First, the folly. There seems to be an attitude among organisations holding golf tournaments for the need to defend par, the honour of the golf course, or the tradition of their competition. These bodies, fretting that a competitor might post a score of perhaps twenty under par or better, and that this would somehow diminish the value of their championship, may think that having a deep rough would protect against such an event. The most obvious overuse and abuse of rough was once seemingly the sole purview of the US Open. However, at Carnoustie in 1999, the practice was extensively employed, and even Augusta National started to grow rough to repel 'Tiger attacks'. William 'Hootie' Johnson, Chairman of Augusta National, said, 'These young men are hitting the ball a long way. We [Augusta National] felt we could no longer let them swing from their heels'. Jack Nicklaus added, 'Now Augusta National looks like a US Open Course'. Rough for tournament play is one thing, but many golf courses and country clubs are trying to grow US Open style roughs for everyday play.

The theory of rough is that if a competitor is not sure with his shots, such that they can't keep them within the narrow confines of the manicured heaven of the fairways, then his ball may come to rest in the unmanicured purgatory of the rough. And just like purgatory, rough isn't easy to escape from. Typically the fairways are twenty-eight to thirty yards wide and mowed at half an inch with perhaps a 'friendly' rough of one and a half to two inches high grass, while the rough is mowed at four to six inches high. 'Real' rough is usually classified as 'jungle'. At many competitions, the rough has been so fertilised and watered that forecaddies are required to spot the ball when it lands, and place a small flag by it to ensure it won't be lost to the competitor. The player is then expected to make a thrashing shot out and get on with his game. There is virtually no hope of hitting a decent shot.

The difficulty of rough for the golfer is trying to get the clubface on the ball to impart backspin when it is nestled like an egg in leafy green vegetation. Competitors have injured wrists and backs trying to hack their way to freedom. When a ball is struck with virtually no backspin, it's commonly called a 'flyer' because it travels farther on a lower trajectory. Perhaps these shots should also be called 'runners' because it more aptly describes how the ball reacts when it hits the ground. The misery caused by rough for the golfer is compounded by today's penchant for ultra fast greens. This means they are flatter, with little or no frictional resistance to roll because of the micro-fine mowing height of greens, and with no grain, making it virtually impossible to stop a shot even with lots of backspin.

A shot from the competitive rough to the modern green is more the result of luck than skill. In fact, one only needs to look at the hot, new lofting irons, the utility woods that promise the ability to dig out the golf ball and give high trajectory shots that stop quickly. Golf balls designed with dimple patterns to produce high, soft shots are also an innovation in golfing equipment for coping specifically with rough. Many club-fitters are dissuading customers from buying 2, 3, and 4-irons, and substituting them for more utility woods and wedges to handle flat, firm greens and deep roughs.

In my fifty-year association with the game, I can't remember a person saying, 'gosh, I love hacking golf shots out of ankle deep rough'. Honestly, I don't expect to hear that in my next fifty either. Shots out of the rough are no fun, and can even be downright discouraging, and this isn't why we love and play the game. You might ask, 'but isn't that the purpose of a hazard, to impose a penalty on a wayward shot?' Of course it is, but when it is overused it will destroy any strategic qualities the golf course might offer, and simply makes it a penalising golf course.

In speaking again about Augusta National, Jack Nicklaus said, 'It has changed the nature of the golf course. The Masters has always been a more difficult golf tournament than any other; open fairways with hard, fast greens. Bobby Jones wanted it to be a second shot course'. Adding to the debate, Ben Crenshaw said of the Year 2000 Augusta roughs, 'I would say what it has done is to make the course less interesting. This course does not play like it did before [the added rough]. It was the most vastly interesting course I had ever seen because it was not dictated where you had to put your drive. There were some spots where you wanted to be in the rough'.

The Old Course at St. Andrews has wide landing areas with virtually no rough. It offers multiple avenues between the tee and green, which is the essence of strategy. Sure, there is a fair amount of gorse and areas of long grass, but these are not formalised on either side of the fairway like a noose around a condemned man's neck. Not only is there no design creativity in simply ringing a fairway with rough. It is boring, artificial, slows play, and puts a premium on mechanically hitting straight shots instead of allowing golfers to invent creative, recovery golf shots.

I trust I have sufficiently established the theory and folly of rough. To further illustrate my case, I believe it is instructive to look at its history.

Some believe that golf was a game first played by the Dutch on ice, and later by Scots on linksland, mostly in the late fall to early spring when native grasses were short and dormant after a season of grazing by livestock. In the spring and summer, grasses were at their optimal growth, and since no mowing was done, the entire golf course or 'green' looked like rough, making it easy to lose the expensive, featherie golf balls.

At some stage in the second half of the 1800s, the game became popular enough that efforts were made to keep summer grasses shorter, first by increasing the herd size of grazing animals, then by using men with scythes and sickles, and still later by horse-drawn mowers. Each of these progressions resulted in more precisely controlled turf heights, and more discrimination about where they should occur. Obviously the animals didn't care whether they were grazing on a tee, green, fairway or rough, and so they nibbled everything to the same height. The guys with the scythes and sickles were a little more cerebral about

what they were doing, though not much. Their job was to cut all the grass, probably once or twice in the late spring or early summer, and probably to the same height. If you have ever cut large areas with these tools, you can understand the imprecision and difficulty involved.

The horse-drawn mower not only improved the speed and efficiency of mowing, it also improved the precision with the reel and bed knife that was adjustable for height. However, this also added to the expense of course maintenance, and inconvenience for golfers. Probably some general manager or club secretary wanting to save money gave the mowers instruction to cut only certain areas and to let other areas grow. This miserly move was the

Sixth hole, Atlantic City Golf Club, New Jersey, USA. (Photo courtesy of Ronald Whitten.)

Golfer in deep rough at Dennis Highlands Golf Club, Massachusetts, USA. (Photo courtesy of Ronald Whitten.)

genius that gave golf the feature of the rough.

When golfers complained about losing golf balls in the unmown grassy areas, they were probably told then, as now, 'Well that's part of the game, and you must simply learn to stay on the fairway'. Also, the compromise of being able to play golf in warm weather seemed worth the inconvenience of longer grass just off the fairway. Soon, rough became accepted as part of the game. My estimation is that this trend took place around 1875. By the early 1900s, when mowing machines powered by internal combustion engines were starting to be introduced, rough was an integral part of the golf course and became an accepted form of hazard.

Although contemporary golf course architects commonly use rough as part of their design strategy, fairways were usually fifty to seventy yards wide to give the golfer plenty of options about choosing the best line to the green. A major principle of design strategy was that individual and daily decisions should be encouraged as to how to attack any given hole location based upon factors of wind, dryness of turf, personal strength, and the most prudent and proper balance of risk and reward. One day might favour a drive to the far right of the fairway, and the next might suggest a line to the far left on that same hole. Golf was reinforced as a thinking person's game that required inventing and hitting creative golf shots.

This wonderful form of golf is still found on many historic links. However, sadly it has been lost on most modern courses. Strategic golf has been choked to death by rough, drowned by irrigation, and buried by trees. Allow me to explain.

Wide-open fairways with some bordering rough became a hallmark of golf courses with unwatered turf. By necessity, the rough had to be pushed back to allow for the run of the ball

once it landed on baked summer ground that was covered by dormant grasses. Then starting in the 1920s, and in full swing by the late 1940s and early 1950s, fairway irrigation became a normal golf course fixture. Typically, the irrigation pipe was a single line placed right in the middle of the fairway. However, sprinkler heads only threw out water effectively to about sixty per cent of their total precipitation pattern. This meant a sprinkler head rated to throw ninety degrees, only provided significant water out to fifty-four degrees, with the remaining area outside the radius only getting a fraction of the core. Moreover, this meant that the greenkeeper had to either over-irrigate the inside fifty-six degrees to properly reach the outside thirty-four degrees, or more commonly he would properly water the inside and hence underwater the outside. So now the middle 108 degrees of the fairway (fifty-four degrees either side of the irrigation pipe) was lush and green in the summer drought, but the rest of the turf was more brown than green.

At this point, a logic emerged: since we can now irrigate the fairway, the ball doesn't run as far as it used to before irrigation and if we let the grasses beyond the irrigated area grow higher they won't be so brown; then we'll simply move the rough in closer to the centre of the fairway. This reasoning slowly reduced fairway width from between fifty to seventy yards, to around thirty-five or forty yards. Since rough requires less upkeep than fairway, the golf course management could also reason that narrow fairways would help contain spiralling maintenance costs.

Where environmental conditions of a site permitted tree growth, the next step in the evolution of rough was usually for a group of skilled golfers, albeit amateur arborists, to reason that if each hole was framed by trees this would make the golf course even more attractive. And what better place to plant them than in the rough, usually near the interface of fairway and rough. These well-meaning, but usually uninformed folk, either planted the wrong species, or they didn't allow for the mature height and width of the tree canopy, or both. Soon, shade and competition from tree roots made growing turf grasses under these trees extremely difficult, and the usual solution was

to again narrow the fairway by letting the turf under the shade or drip line to grow taller. Finally, since around 1960 fairways have narrowed to the point where there is no room for a truly strategic golf experience. Hence, most golf courses today either accidentally or intentionally, are of the penal style of design. The design concept of 'risk and reward' is almost non-existent except on links that haven't suc-

cumbed to the perversion and folly of rough.

If golf course management or a golf course architect wants to establish or restore the most exciting brand of golf, that of risk and reward, then efforts should be made to once again produce wide fairways. Push back the rough lines, cut down the trees, and use rough as a hazard as sparingly as possible. The game will be the better for it.

Sixteenth hole, Broken Top Golf Club, Oregon, USA. (Photo courtesy of Ronald Whitten.)

Lessons from St. Andrews

Jeff Mingay

Following decades of natural evolution and redesign, it can be difficult to believe the majority of the world's best inland golf courses are derivatives of the Old Course at St. Andrews, Scotland.

Golf courses have an annoying tendency to shrink. As time passes, trees are planted and grow to infringe on former lines of play, threatening turf health. Fairways become thinner, and putting surfaces recede toward their centres. Furthermore, during the past fifty years since the popularisation of comprehensive fairway irrigation, over-watering has been rampant.

The Old Course represents the ideal, primarily because its blatant width and consistently fast-running character caters to golfers of all abilities. At St. Andrews, better players are presented with a cerebral test as well as physical examination. Each shot must be played with the next in mind, and the influence of ground contour must always be considered. All the while, less skilled golfers are provided with ample space and a helpful bounce to enhance their recreation.

Narrow, slow-moving golf courses are comparatively uninteresting. They permit mindless golf and allow accomplished players to rely on mechanical swings and exact yardages rather than demand thoughtful and creative play for success. Worse still, restrictive and soggy layouts are terribly difficult for mid-teen, and high-handicap golfers who benefit from some lateral forgiveness. These golfers gain with a few extra yards off the tee and some assistance with running the ball along the ground onto the greens. Yet today, we still find many aged layouts in this unfortunate condition.

Prior to the 1950s, when fairway-watering systems became the rage in North America, greenkeepers let nature take its course. During the typically rainy springtime, courses were predominately green in colour and played comparatively slow. But throughout the arid summer months, the golfing landscape was beautifully textured, and courses played appropriately firm and fast. Moreover, there was no debate about fairway width. Greenkeepers simply gang-mowed from tree line to tree line, and fairways on most courses

A self-explanatory message for golfers seeking to practise their putting at the Old Course. (Photo by Paul Daley.)

averaged sixty to eighty yards across.

However, those first, rudimentary watering systems were installed in a single row down the centre of each hole corridor. With the new-found ability to water from tee to green, maintenance expectations changed and fairway width was strictly determined by the range of the sprinkler head regardless of design intent. Total fairway acreage on many first-class layouts was reduced by nearly half as a result and,

inevitably, the character of those golf courses was markedly altered.

Ironically, a new era in golf architecture was ushered in around 1950 as well. In preparation for the 1951 United States Open, Robert Trent Jones was commissioned to refashion the Oakland Hills South course in suburban Detroit, Michigan, specifically to counter the abilities of the day's best golfers. Trent Jones transformed a wide, multi-dimensional, Donald Ross layout into the golfing equivalent of a torture chamber. Fairways were narrowed significantly, and tee-shot landing areas were pinched with sand bunkers at calculated distances from the tees.

The great Ben Hogan, who opened the tournament with an uncharacteristic seventy-six, decided to retire his driver for the last three rounds of the championship in order to keep straight and to stay short of Trent Jones's fairway 'traps'. Hogan subsequently improved his scoring with each consecutive round, firing a remarkable sixty-seven in the fourth to claim a two-stroke victory over Clayton Heafner. Nonetheless, the stoic champion was not an admirer of Trent Jones's work at

Oakland Hills. Hogan averred that the course lacked strategy from the tee. The fairways were so narrow, the only place to aim was down the middle, and thus it was not possible to drive into an advantageous position from which to approach the greens.

Ross's golf architecture never promoted defensive play from the tee. Instead, he encouraged golfers to play boldly and intelligently in their efforts to reduce the length of the ensuing shot and 'open up' the green for the approach.

The strategy of a golf hole is dictated by the design of its green complex. Its predominant slope and orientation combine with surrounding hazards to suggest a preferable angle of attack depending on the location of the hole on any given day. For example, if a flagstick is tucked behind a greenside bunker at far right, it is imperative to approach from the left side of the fairway, particularly if the course is running fast. Otherwise, getting the ball close to the hole becomes that much more difficult.

Trent Jones's ideology contrasted with that of Ross and his contemporaries from the interwar period, affectionately referred to as the Golden Age of golf design. Ross's work was essentially an adaptation of links characteristics and principles onto inland sites. His goal was not to build the most difficult golf courses, only the most interesting.

To this day, the infamously penalising Oakland Hills South course design presents golfers with but one option hole after hole. It is a golf course with a definable place in the history of golf, but does not represent the ideal in course architecture.

Golf design has come full circle in recent years. Today, students of the art have the facilities to look back over a century of past works, to ascertain which philosophies and styles worked well and perhaps most importantly which did not. The consensus among a new breed of contemporary architects who have made a study of the history of their profession is that golf courses are more interesting, more enjoyable, and also more complete tests of skill when appropriate width and more consistently firm and fast conditions through the green prevail.

The practice of narrowing fairways and thinning hole corridors with trees to thwart

low scoring has proven futile. Another failure has been over-watering turf for the sake of vanity. Instead, golf courses should be arranged and maintained to force the best players to be thoughtful and creative in order to score low and, at the same time, to cater to the enjoyment of mid-range and high-handicappers. History suggests that a wide, fast-running layout, in the image of the Old Course at St. Andrews is the ideal.

A rainbow scene at St. Andrews. (Photo by Gary Prendergast.)

Penal, strategic and heroic design redefined

Forrest Richardson

Accuracy, carry, and length. According to golf architect, William Flynn, this is the order of importance in designing individual golf holes. One of the youngest to be commissioned to design a golf course—nineteen in 1909—this was his advice in later years.

When you combine these ingredients into different recipes—maybe a little more accuracy here, but not so much length there—you wind up with holes of abundant variety and merit. The idea of balancing accuracy and length is a fundamental principle of golf course design, and vital to any well-crafted golf course plan.

The traditional classifications of golf holes in terms of their play are penal, strategic, and heroic. How useful are these descriptions? Aren't all golf holes strategic? Isn't it just that some involve more strategy than others? Strategy can be evident even in its absence. In my opinion, strategic is no more a useful description of a golf hole than it would be of a war. Strategy is a constant. It is part of the game regardless of what lies ahead of the golfer.

That said, I now confess to having encountered a few golf holes that required no strategy at all. Faced with this stark experience, one has a completely open invitation to reach the green in a carefree manner with nary a hazard, bump, or tree in the way. It has always haunted me that the presence of a field-like expanse, a landscape devoid of hazards, is what makes such holes so terribly frustrating. Could it be that their lack of strategy was their strategy? Certainly, understrategised holes are sometimes neither penalising nor heroic. Therefore, I coin such holes 'open', as that is exactly what they are: open to a golfer's own method of attack, or open for the golfer to fall apart in response to their relative ease.

Rather than embracing the traditional classification, a better way to approach golf holes is to think of the individual strokes that make up their strategy. The following modified terminology permits golf shots to be accurately classified, and therefore it enables golf holes to be more accurately labeled with respect to strategy. In my book, *Routing the Golf Course* (2002), I presume strategy to be a constant. It refers to the individual shots planned into holes, rather than the entirety of the holes themselves.

This redefinition of strategy produces a design formula. By combining the five types of golf shots demanded by golf holes: penal, heroic, detour, lay-up, and open—among par-3, par-4, and par-5 holes—280 design variables may be created, rather than the traditional three. A tee shot may be heroic in nature, while an approach may present a detour, and so on. Infinite possibilities come into play when all other variables are added to the equation, such as alignment, length, hazards, and more.

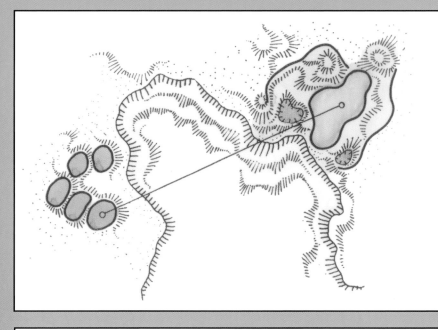

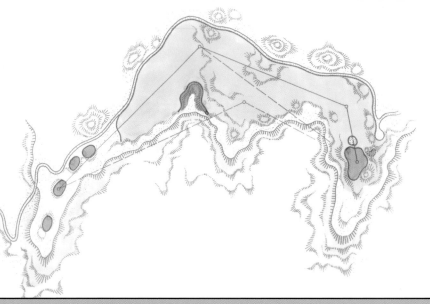

LEFT: The *penal* shot requirement is such that it must outdistance a hazard, or be caught in its grip. In this example, a par-3 plays across a canyon with little room for error.

BELOW: The *heroic* shot is a matter of choice, but mostly of courage. Does one play boldly and reach the green, sooner? Or is it prudent to aim to the right or left, to avoid a negative outcome? Heroic shots are invariably over, or by, hazards from which recovery is bleak. In this example, the hole is heroic for the entire journey—at the tee the decision is how much to bite off; with the second shot the choice is again presented. This hole also portrays elements of lay-up and detour holes, proving that classifying golf holes is not as accurate as classifying individual golf shots. (Sketches by Forrest Richardson.)

Penal Design

A golf shot that presents no alternative route to avoid a hazard or feature is said to be penal. The word comes from the Latin *poena*, which means 'fine' or 'penalty.' Penal golf design is thought to have been a standard of early golf course design, but perhaps this is not so. Only sometimes did hazards completely obscure the path to the hole. In fact, on many links and even early designed courses, holes described as penal were played by way of alternate routes devised by golfers who refused to believe there was no way around the impediment. They devised their own routes to the hole and, in the process, invented what has become known as strategic and heroic design or, in our new vernacular, detour, lay-up, and heroic design. Penal holes are not in favour in today's golf world. An obstacle that requires playing across is not as appealing as one where the golfer has choices to go around. Nonetheless, a place remains for penal design, as it provides a change of pace during the golf round.

The most workable condition for penal designs is when the design will not unfairly penalise the higher-handicap golfer. The penal design can also be a good choice where there is no other way—that is, when a natural hazard of remarkable interest presents itself such that routing must get across it and the opportunity of drama cannot be ignored. A gorge 150 feet wide is a good example. The hole might just lead to the shot of a lifetime, and for most golfers a carry of this length is achievable. Penal design requires careful planning though and should only be administered in small doses.

The classic example of a penal shot is the very short par-3. This is significantly more palatable than the same forced carry designed short of the green on a par-4. In this instance, the higher-handicap golfer may attempt a long iron or fairway wood to reach the green by virtue of his position off the tee. To necessitate a penal approach in this instance is reason for criticising the penal school of design.

Heroic Design

Heroic shots are those that must carry over an obstacle in order to gain a favourable position, and where there is ample room to hit around the obstacle. Golfers can incrementally adjust the shot to aim either more over the obstacle, or more away from it, depending on the level of excitement desired. At times we've all admired the 'hero' who clears the hazard or obstacle in its greatest dimension. The classic example of heroic design is the shot over a diagonal hazard that extends into the golf hole. The expression 'bite off as much as you can chew' is often associated with heroically designed holes and shots. Again, all holes and shots are strategic.

Detour Design

Detour shots, unlike heroic shots, offer distinct pathways around obstacles. The choice is deciding whether to deal with the obstacle or hazard. This is not to say that heroic and detour design principles cannot be blended; in many instances, they are. If, for example, a lake presents a heroic opportunity, there may also be a wide and slightly longer fairway route to the hole along which the lake is taken almost completely out of play. In this case, the golfer faces shot options that are both heroic and detour in nature. This adds

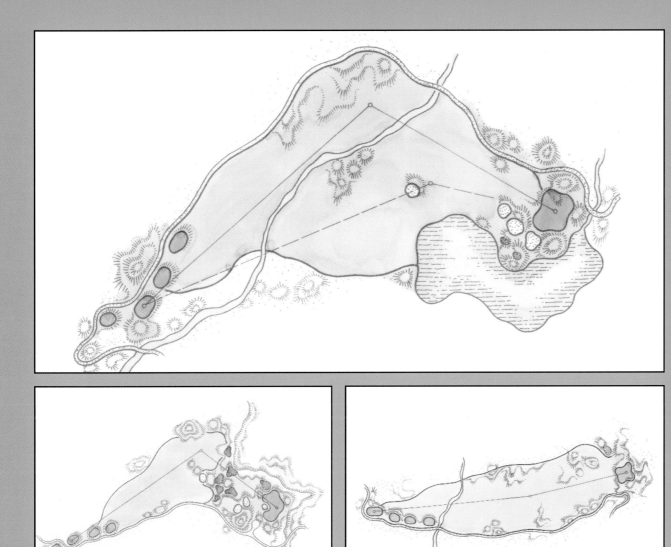

LEFT: The *detour* shot presents golfers with multiple-choice. Here, the wise play is left of the creek, or right. The left-sided route produces a distinct approach, different from the path to the right. Detour shots produce detour holes, and yet, there are other shot types at play: lay-up and heroic opportunities also exist.

BELOW FAR LEFT: The *lay-up* shot describes a shot requirement that usually calls for the golfer to hold back on distance, and play to a safe haven. Frequently though, golfers disregard their instinct and blaze away. In this example, the area fronting the green is so broken and confusing, there is no point in entering it. And so, the tee-shot calls for a lay-up to a choice fairway position. A hallmark of great lay-up shots is that they don't just demand restraint, but also demand selection of where the lay-up comes to rest. For the better players and long-hitters, such a hole may well induce a heroic shot in an attempt to outwit the notion of a lay-up.

LEFT: The *open* shot is the easiest of all. Not just to negotiate, but also to dream-up, design and build. There is not much strategy present; hit away and keep the golf ball relatively close to the preferred line. There are no obstacles, except the golfer's mettle. (Sketches by Forrest Richardson.)

further to the 280 variables noted earlier. As the name suggests, detour shots are shots around. Split fairways and isolated hazards sitting almost in the middle ground of a hole create detour options from which the golfer must choose—and the more the merrier. In golf, detours are good. They prompt thinking and problem solving. They bring out the best in golfers without requiring reliance on length.

Lay-up design

A lay-up shot can be decided with free will by the golfer, and may be invoked at any moment in the round, even on penal, heroic, and detour shots. However, the hallmark of the true lay-up is force. The design condition that forces a shot to be played well short of a full shot cannot be considered either heroic or a detour. The lay-up shot is not always appreciated, but it is nonetheless a part of the game. It can be brought about by playing conditions or through the use of a particular set of tees. That extremely penal lake fronting the green can require a lay-up shot when the wind is howling and the tees are back, but this is only a tempo-rary condition. The lake fronting the green is meant to be carried, and is therefore penal in nature on any other day. The reason that forced lay-up design is not well liked is because it takes the gambling element out of the golfer's arsenal. If a shot is forced to be hit short, there is no real decision, only restraint. Aside from the possibility of a heroic shot by a skilled golfer to clear the obstacle that has caused the lay-up condition, tantalising options are all but eliminated.

A lay-up design is probably best deployed on shortish par-4s at the tee shot. This interruption of brute force, when used sparingly, can be an interesting diversion. The best of all worlds is the lay-up shot that involves a degree of heroic and/or detour playing. Lay-up design, in these cases, brings even more decision making into the picture. Obviously, it has little use at par-3 holes, but great examples of par-3s where a lay-up area has been provided, do exist. The most famous example that embraces this design is the sixteenth hole at Cypress Point Club. In reality, this Mackenzie hole is a heroic, detour and lay-up design all wrapped into one.

Open Design

Open design typically presents as luck-lustre fairways that are not encumbered by hazards, twists, obstacles, or anything else. The object is just to get there. That such shots and holes exist in golf is no reason to design more of them. To create abundant shot requirements that are completely open in their design is to go against the origins of golf and its point. When used, open design strategy should be reserved for appropriate points in a routing. Examples include leading up to a particularly difficult penal shot on a hole, or for starting holes of a round.

The new list of penal, heroic, detour, lay-up and open may take some time to get used to, and I fear it is more cumbersome than the old terminology. But the old is neither accurate nor complete. Golf's playing board is among the most magnificent of all sports and games. To more adequately define its strategy—that ever present quality—we need this redefinition.

Technology and the game of golf

Bobby Weed Jr. and Chris Monti

Golf is a game of tradition, a game for the ages, a game that no player has ever mastered. Common sense indicates that technological advances in equipment should preserve the game's future by making golf more enjoyable for the masses. With such a legacy at stake, the question must be asked: is the impact of modern golf equipment eroding the integrity of the game?

The balance between preserving golf's integrity and encouraging a free market in the manufacture and selection of golf equipment has been an on-going battle throughout the past century.

Consider the following from golf architect, C.B McDonald:

There is a consensus of opinion among first class players that the time has come to check the excessive length to which the golf ball can be driven. Ball makers are vying with each other in producing balls of ever-increasing driving capacity, and as most of the best courses have now been stretched to their utmost limits, it is obvious that holes and courses are speedily being ruined as tests of the game. Green committees and golf architects have been struggling for some time to maintain the normal rate of scoring by multiplying hazards, by rendering the approaches to holes more difficult, and even by increasing the difficulties to putting, but it is clear that a point has been reached at which such devices are destroying the balance and character of the game which makes it enjoyable and worth playing.[6]

Such thoughts are reminiscent of many articles and letters featured in recent golf publications. In reality, they originate from a petition sent to 152 of Britain's top amateurs in 1912. One hundred and forty one golfers replied, agreeing that the Amateur Championship in Britain should be played with standardised golf balls.

Like those amateurs, everyday golfers feel a special connection to the game that other sports do not offer. No matter their age or ability, many golfers can play the same course with the same equipment as the best players in the game. Today's advancements in equipment threaten that connection. In agreement, the USGA states, 'the fundamental element that success at golf—for the very skilled, the moderately skilled and beginner—should come from improvement in swing fundamentals, mental discipline, and practice instead of from technological innovations.'[7]

Responsibility to maintain the integrity of the game is shared between golfers, golf course architects and manufacturers. Significant precedents exist where the latter have been forced to adjust to new rules and parameters that preserve the way the game is played.

The past few decades have witnessed a rapid increase in the distance that the golf ball travels. Without question, improvements in the club, shaft and ball are the main reasons that players are capable of achieving incredible distance from the tee and through the green.

While the manufacturers may market to the masses, the higher handicap golfer actually benefits the least from the new equipment. A beginner starts on the ground floor regardless of the technology being used, while the player with developed skills can gain greater advantage with his equipment. This difference has resulted in a greater disparity in skill levels between high and low handicappers than ever before.

Many of today's manufacturers disagree. They claim that modern technology has been able to benefit the weaker player without damaging the integrity of the game at the highest level. They point to consistent scores on the Professional Golf Association Tour over the past twenty years as strong evidence that championship golf has suffered no ill-effects from the longer flying golf balls.

Despite the claim, the damage may not be provable. One of the inherent charms of golf is that two players of varying ability can play a golf course and be tested equally on the same range of skills—short game, long game, driving, putting, and so on. Always, golfers weak in one area could compensate with strength in another.

With 400-yard drives today nearly a reality, distance is far too important for the skilled golfer. The range of skills required to be a top-level player is narrower than it was years ago. Being a long hitter is more critical than mastering other aspects of the game. A player who crushes it off the tee has a distinct advantage over the crafty shotmaker.

Today, young players grow up swinging with their full strength, knowing that modern equipment will keep the ball from going too far off-line. In the past, the best players learned to throttle back, skilfully using their power when it suited them. Slowly, physical ability is replacing mental agility as the prime determinant of golfing success.

This turn of events represents a fundamental shift in the character of the game. By destroying that which makes golf an intriguing challenge, we may in turn destroy future interest in the game itself. This concern has caused many of today's 'thinking' professionals to request that mental skill be reinjected

into the game because the overall challenge has diminished.

Parallels with other sports exist. Tennis participation was at an all time high in the mid-1970s, when it was played with finesse and strategy. The emergence of composite frames and oversized rackets, designed and marketed specifically to make the game easier for the masses, turned tennis into a power sport that has lost much of its following. To many, the finesse-oriented play of the women's golf circuit is more popular than the power game that the men play.

Indy-style racing also met a similar fate. The Indy Racing League's (IRL) 'one-engine rule' favoured finesse, strategy and driver ability over the Championship Auto Racing Teams (CART) idea of 'spend as much as you can to go as fast as possible'. After an initial defection, many drivers are returning to the IRL, where savvy and skill are paramount. Individual ability, not team budget, determines success.

Modifying equipment is part of the solution. Due to technological advances, golf course owners and operators are adding additional length, and rethinking strategic design.

They bear the sole expense of defending their layouts. It is ironic that manufacturers do not bear any of the responsibility to upgrade the courses that their technology is rendering obsolete.

Some golf courses can no longer host events, and suffer a decline in prestige that can be measured in real dollars. New courses are becoming longer and require wider corridors, consequently adding to the cost of construction and maintenance. These costs are ultimately passed on to the paying golfer—the one who is supposed to be benefiting from modern equipment.

The burden has not always been the golfer's. Periodically, the ruling bodies of the game have modified the parameters that determine conforming equipment to help preserve the integrity of the game. Regardless, today's manufacturers respond in shock when rule changes are suggested. Precedent was set far before many of these companies began production.

The golf ball alone has gone through a number of dramatic changes. With the introduction of the Haskell ball in 1898, not fully accepted until the early 1900s, the debate began over how to adjust ball specifications to preserve the game's traditions. The USGA, at various times, has specified a 1.62 inch, 1.62-ounce ball; a 1.7 inch ball with no weight restriction, and a 1.68 inch, 1.55-ounce ball. In 1932, there was a consensus agreement on a 1.68 inch, 1.62-ounce ball that is still the standard. In Great Britain, the smaller ball remained legal until it was banned at the Open Championship in 1974. It was eliminated outright in 1990.

Donald Ross, the legendary designer and a charter member of the American Society of Golf Course Architects (ASGCA) voiced his own opinion about the process of ball legislation in a letter to James Tufts of Pinehurst, North Carolina in 1923. He wrote:

My personal view is that the standard ball should be a floater. I do not believe it is possible in any other way to control the manufacturers from continuing to make a ball which will fly as far as the present one. A floater will control the distance absolutely on the long hitter, would not take a yard from the distance of the average players who really are the supporters of golf, and the average man would find it a much easier ball to pick up through the fairway. It would be more durable, reducing the cost of the game to some extent. In fact, altogether, I think it would be a very desirable change.[8]

Ross's letter foresaw today's controversy and legitimises the role of the golf course architect in the debate. The architect must get involved, not only to defend the great layouts of the past, but also to protect today's hallmark designs from suffering the same fate in the future.

The architect's role is central. No one is better situated to be an advocate for the golf course than the golf course architect. They must lobby for equipment changes, but not stand idly by waiting for them. Every aspect of course design should be rethought, modified and updated to insure that the golf course remains the heart of competition. Traditional strategic design that allows golfers to carry as much of a hazard as they wish, confers powerful players the double reward of both a shorter approach and a better angle into the flag. This must be altered, since distance is already its own reward.

More importantly, architects must devise innovative ways to challenge the great players without rendering the golf course unplayable for the novice player. Perhaps there should be fewer par-72 layouts that include longer one and two-shot holes.

Options and variety create interest, and must be apparent in the course design. Testing a player's mental ability with an odd feature or dramatic hazard is paramount. Creating short game intrigue around the green is a great test of decision-making. Architects cannot succumb to simply adding length to preserve the challenge of a golf hole. History has proven that this is not a sustainable solution.

While maintaining free enterprise among manufacturers in the design and production of golf equipment is a tradition of the game, the control over the parameters in which that production takes place must be absolute for the ruling bodies of golf. The fate of golf's value and integrity is inherent in that control.

More than ever, the effects of equipment advancement is making its presence felt and eroding the game's traditions. Inaction today is complicity in the deterioration of the game tomorrow. By working together for the integrity of the game, golfers, golf course architects, governing bodies, and manufacturers can ensure that the golf course will remain the competition for players of all abilities.

Re-designing the glass ceiling

Line Mortensen

'Oh, so you must be the new secretary!'
'No, I'm here to re-design your golf course!'

Historically, golf course architects come from various educational backgrounds, some highly unrelated to the job of architecture. One thing they all have in common is an interest and love for the game of golf. Thousands of men and women all over the world love the game of golf, but its old traditions are sadly still biased against women, which explains why so few women are involved in the business.

Some of us cannot even remember when women would not be expected to have certain jobs or qualities because of their sex. It is therefore a bit of a surprise suddenly to discover that the fact that you are a woman still means something different in the world of golf course architecture.

Nonetheless, things are changing. By reaching more countries and more people than ever before, golf is not only expanding, but also undergoing generational and attitudinal changes. So even if, up until now, there have been many reasons why there are so few female golf course architects, it is something that seems likely to change in the years to come.

The reason why there are so few women involved in golf course architecture today is in many ways the familiar story about women not being attracted to so-called technical jobs, and about how difficult it can be to be among the first women to make a career in a male-dominated industry. But it is also the story of a profession very closely connected to a game and its traditions, and when it comes to golf one of these is, sadly, that women, like children, are not always welcome on the course. The old-fashioned *'No dogs or women allowed'* barriers may be coming down slowly, but they still exist. As a female golf course architect, not being allowed to set foot on some of the finest courses cannot be excused by an appeal to tradition.

There is no doubt that golf used to be a game reserved for the middle-aged white male. This group of golfers is still very dominant in golf today, but in many countries things are changing, and women and children are now also queuing up to take up the game. For those countries, such as my own,

Denmark, where golf did not seriously start until the 1970s, golf is a new game with no traditional restrictions on who can play, and how and when. Why do young Swedish women dominate the world of women's professional golf these days? Perhaps it is because golf in Scandinavia is a family game, and here thirty-one per cent of the golfers are women. The golf tourist industry is also helping to close the gap between the number of male and female golfers. For those golf clubs, tour operators and other businesses in the green fee market, every golfer is a potential client regardless of age, sex or race.

However, the gap between the number of male and female golfers still certainly exists. Only fifteen per cent of golfers in the UK are female, while the figure rises to around twenty per cent in the US, and twenty-seven per cent on average for continental Europe. The connection can easily be made: the more traditional a golf nation is, the fewer female golfers—and architects—there will be. This is something you cannot fail to notice when having been brought up in a country where thirty-three per cent of golfers are women, you work

Mortensen at work, attending to a drainage issue. (Photo courtesy of Gaunt and Marnoch Golf Course Architects.)

in the UK where there are very few women golfers and where old traditions are working against women's involvement in the game.

There seems, however, to be a general tendency for more women to be taking up golf. In the US, around forty per cent of all new golfers are women—a definite indication that change is on its way in the global golfing market. It is therefore reasonable to assume that the role of women in the golf design business will also change in the years ahead. So what is it like to be a woman in this business? As one of the few, I'm often asked this question. Overall, like most golf architects, I feel privileged to be practising in what is a fascinating profession.

Being a woman in this industry is not an issue for about a third of the time. Sometimes it can even be an advantage. Given the rarity value of women golf architects, most people seem to remember you. For about half of the time, gender is a sensitive and exhausting issue. Lots of clients do start with the assumption that you are anything but the architect, and that as a woman, you cannot possibly know much about golf. Male golf architects

will be asked: 'What's your handicap?' I frequently get asked: 'Do you play golf?' In the all-important task of gaining the respect of clients, contractors, greenkeepers and others, female golf architects undoubtedly face additional burdens compared to their male competitors. For the most part, these burdens are not insurmountable. It must be acknowledged, however, that as the expanding golf tourism market takes the game to new corners of the globe, so there remain countries where a female golf course architect would never stand a chance of getting the job done because of different cultural and religious perspectives on women and their role in society.

The history of women's involvement in golf design is inevitably very limited. The Golden Age of US golf design was a very male-oriented era, yet Marion Hollins—one of the leading women golfers of her day—played a vital role at one of the all-time great courses, Cypress Point. Reportedly, it was Hollins, and not Alister Mackenzie, who took out her 3-wood to demonstrate to doubters that the carry, on the sixteenth hole, as a par-3 was possible.

Little seems to have happened since Hollins made her mark in the history of golf course architecture. Perhaps, this is due to golf's strong traditions. Golf course architecture does lag behind other male-dominated industries when it comes to the number of women involved. In other industries where women were traditionally under-represented, the problem now is often that there is a 'glass ceiling' blocking women's promotion. In golf design, the problem is not a glass ceiling but a 'glass door' that has prevented women even gaining access to the profession. It is difficult to find more than ten female golf course architects in the world. If there are more, then they are hiding very well for some reason.

In the American Society of Golf Course Architects (ASGCA), only five of the 146 members are women (three per cent participation rate compared to the twenty per cent women's participation in US golf noted above). Neither the Japanese Society of Golf Course Architects (JSGCA) or the Society of Australian Golf Course Architects (SAGCA) have any women on their member lists. And when the European Institute of Golf Course

Architects (EIGCA) started its professional diploma in golf course architecture in 1997, there were no women within the Institute. However, since the introduction of the course, four women have graduated and found work in the industry. Yet, they are still only representing around five per cent of the total EIGCA membership.

Obtaining a professional diploma in golf course architecture does perhaps enhance women's access to the golf design industry. Working to get the diploma raises one's profile and enables students to make contacts in the design industry. Furthermore, the diploma is a recognised sign of competence and quality, which undoubtedly is helpful when as a woman you are trying to overcome the extra barriers in such a traditional and male-dominated industry as golf design.

As a female golf course architect, you are often asked if you design differently from male colleagues. It is known that one of the reasons why Alice Dye joined the ASGCA in the early 1980s was to try to pave the way for more women in the industry. She thought, for example, that there was a huge need and potential for women to be involved in the placing of women's tees. Perhaps we as women do pay more attention to where the forward tees are going but, besides that, it will be hard to spot any difference between the way male and female architects are designing their courses, especially as there is still a paucity of practising women architects .

Overall, women face a difficult task in establishing themselves as golf course architects, but changes within the golfing world and, specifically, in the golf design industry, suggest that the number of women golf course architects may rise in the future. Perhaps a distinctive female-style of golf design might even emerge in the next ten or twenty years, but don't count on it. Regardless of gender, each golf course architect will strive to have their own unique style of golf design.

Designing in the field

Rod Whitman

A golf architect requires a great deal of flexibility throughout the design process in order to attain the desired look, feel and playing character of a golf course. While drawn plans serve as a purposeful guide, a blueprint they are not! After all, a world-class golf course cannot be created on paper at a drafting board in a downtown office. An architect's most critical work is done in the field, throughout construction.

The routing is the most important aspect of golf course design. The sequence, variety and flow of holes will inevitably determine the quality of golf on any given site. Therefore, a golf architect must spend many hours prior to and throughout construction walking the land visualising golf holes in order to make the very best use of a property's natural attributes. An initial routing plan may be quite detailed, even though the specified locations of putting greens, tees and bunkers will often deviate from that initial drawing as new opportunities present themselves to the architect in the field.

Reading the classic texts, it becomes clear golf course design has long been a fluid process. In his landmark *Golf Architecture* (1920), Dr Alister Mackenzie states: 'The designer should not be tied down too closely to his original plan.' Although referring directly to 'unexpected changes in subsoil' and so on, which results in the necessity for changes to an original plan, Mackenzie's statement also applies to the need for artistic and strategic alterations. The golf architect determines when these changes are necessary as a course evolves from a concept into reality.

Mackenzie's one-time partner, the English architect, Harry Colt, provided similar advice in his book, *Some Essays on Golf Course Architecture* (1920). He opined that, 'when the framework has been decided upon, the placing of the bunkers will be the next consideration. It is no doubt desirable to postpone the construction of some of the bunkers until the course is in playing order.' Although this method is rarely, if ever, employed today, it is a reminder of the need to remain flexible throughout the design and construction processes.

US based architect, Pete Dye, for example, is notorious for spending countless hours

Ninth hole, Wente Vineyards, California, USA. (Photo courtesy of Ronald Whitten.)

on-site throughout the construction of his golf courses—tweaking contours and improving upon the placement of hazards in an effort to achieve the best possible results. He once told me, 'I don't change things; I merely develop them.' In Pete's mind, in-the-field alterations are essential to the design process.

Today, many contemporary golf architects spend far more time in the field than in the office, particularly those of us influenced by Pete Dye. Like all of the master golf architects, including Mackenzie, Colt and Dye, I too prefer to rely on my own creative and artistic instincts rather than detailed construction plans. From the initial conceptual planning stages through to opening day, there is always opportunity to improve upon initial ideas and concepts, if provided the necessary flexibility.

View from behind Tenth Tee, Opening Day Exhibition Match featuring Bobby Jones · · · Sept. 8, 1929

Alister Mackenzie's inspired use of ground contours

Todd Eckenrode

Picture the tee shot for the tenth hole at Augusta National during the annual playing of the US Masters. Regardless of whether a player's natural shotmaking pattern is a fade or draw, everyone stands on this tee and envisages working that ball from right to left. If they do, they are rewarded with a caroming kick off the right to left and downhill slope of the fairway. Their ball rockets forward, leaving them with a much shorter distance, and level lie in their approach to the green. The concept of this slope, this ground contour, is so profound that it almost forces the modern tour player to recognise this strategy, and engage in the lost art of shot-making to try to utilise its inherent advantages. This is certainly not the only instance of such thinking in the

designs of Alister Mackenzie. For a man who served as the consulting architect for the Royal and Ancient Golf Club, St. Andrews, his appreciation for the values of the ground game was probably unmatched.

My exposure to Mackenzie's legacy has been most intense at his 'big three' in California: Pasatiempo Golf Club; the Valley Club; and Cypress Point Club. Growing up and learning the game at Pasatiempo certainly exposed me to Mackenzie's genius, and perhaps his most personal work. It also greatly shaped how I learned to play the game, acquiring shot-making skills I probably wouldn't have learned elsewhere. Both of these facets were furthered at the Valley Club, as I played collegiate golf at Santa Barbara,

and longed for Mondays—our day to visit this jewel. I am least exposed to Cypress as far as number of rounds played, but its unmatched uniqueness and overwhelming quality have led to a never-ending study.

In studying all three gems of golf architecture, I gained an appreciation for Mackenzie's affinity for slopes, or contours, and how he utilised them in building strategies into a variety of shots on some of his best golf holes. The manner in which he utilised the sloping terrain on tee shots certainly provided some insight into his thinking. Interestingly, at Pasatiempo, some of the more profound slopes affecting tee shots have progressively become out of play, and easily carried by the longer hitters. This is in part due to the uncontrolled specifications

OPPOSITE: **A photo taken in 1929 of the par-5 tenth hole at Pasatiempo Golf Club, California, USA. A heroic tee-shot, shaped from right-to-left over the farthest point of the barranca, would bound to the top of the crest. Of note is the wide landing area, and alternate routes of play. (Photo courtesy of Pasatiempo Golf Club.)**

This fearsome bunker at Pasatiempo's sixteenth hole was far easier to avoid if the tee-shot could be played from right-to-left, or alongside the ravine to the left. Such a shot could take advantage of a dramatic slope in the fairway running toward the green, thereby shortening the hole and opening up the approach. Mackenzie considered this hole his favourite par-4. (Photo courtesy of the Brooks collection.)

on equipment, but also to a couple of design changes that happened in the 1940s to the second and tenth holes. In the original design, both played as par-5s with tee shots crossing the entry road to the club. Although the second hole is still regarded as one of the finest on the course as a modern day par-4, it was a much more interesting hole then. The landing area for tee shots on this hole is now an area of rough, a fairway far below the apex of a prodigious drive. Originally, a pronounced right-to-left slope affected the ball after the tee shot had landed. A sufficiently strong drive could

carry a slight crown in this slope and take advantage of a downward slope towards the green. This presented the player with an option to have a go at the green in two—as the approach favours a running shot coming in from the right—or lay-up in a good position from which to attack this very challenging approach to the green. A weaker tee shot would simply bounce to the left after failing to gain benefit from the downslope. This scenario lengthened the hole and increased its challenge, as the second shot had to be played off a strong slope and visibility to the hole was lessened.

The tenth hole is a fearsome tee shot to this day, but was even more so in the original design. Yet it was indicative of Mackenzie's belief that 'there should be heroic carries, but always an alternative route'. The deep barranca that must be carried is certainly the stand out feature that catches your attention. A more subtle aspect to the strategy of the hole, however, would have been the slope of the fairway beyond this chasm. A strong drive up the right-centre, with a nice draw to its flight, would have had the velocity to bound up to

the top of the crest. From here, options and temptation would have greatly increased the interest of the hole as the player could take a shot at the green in two, or position a lay up to the right to avoid the bold bunkering fronting the left side of the green, thankfully recently restored. A tee-shot towards the left side of the fairway, where the slope is significantly steeper and facing the tee, would have stopped dead in its tracks. This would have left an uncomfortable blind second shot played over the crest with little to orientate the golfer as to the direction of the green. Today's play, with the tee significantly forward and the hole played as a par-4, has its own strategies with regards to the slope beyond the crest. However, it does not present the range of options originally intended, and is best played more defensively.

Other holes on these noted courses where slopes greatly affect the strategy of the hole off the tee are the Valley Club's tenth, and Cypress Point's eighth holes, though in very different ways. The former offers golfers the opportunity to gain advantage due to the contouring, while the latter example demonstrates how

Aerial photo of Pasatiempo (1931). The clubhouse site is approximately in the centre of the picture, with the outward nine to the left, and the inward nine to the right. Play crossed the entry road twice on the second and tenth holes, both par-5s then. (Photo courtesy of the Fairchild aerial photography collection at Whittier college, C-1437, A: 7.)

Eleventh hole and green
at The Valley Club,
California in the 1930s.
Mackenzie makes great
use of the hill and
sweeping tie-in to the
green. (Photo courtesy of
The Valley Club.)

slopes can serve as a defence of the hole, leading the golfer into potential peril. At Valley Club's tenth hole, a well played fade off the tee, down the left side can take advantage of the bounding slope to the right, gaining the most yardage running down the hill, and eventually settling in a level area on the right side of the fairway. From this position, your play is much easier as the options increase; your ability to execute is significantly increased by having a more level stance. The tee shot at Cypress Point's eighth hole is unique for America: a frightening carry over the dunes, with a fairway that falls away from the turn of the dogleg right. A heroic carry over the right side, or a well-played fade off the tee, affords the player a shorter approach, a more level lie, and enhanced visibility to the green for the second shot. A bail out to the left off the tee catches the slope running away, significantly compounding the difficulties from there on. Interestingly, all of these featured holes, apart from the last, were par-5s. Perhaps Mackenzie was merely adding to the variety of shots presented for tee shots on these holes. More likely, however, he was utilising these slopes to give a possible advantage to the player who didn't merely bash away brainlessly on the long holes. Perhaps he was playing on people's tendency to overswing when teeing-off on long holes, and testing their mental ability to avoid this tendency. Regardless, the player who could grasp the strategies brought about by the natural contours, and perform shots with accuracy and shotmaking, could gain the advantage here.

A look at the approaches to the greens at these three courses adds insight to Mackenzie's thinking as well, and his belief in the influence that natural contours should have. Most of the front approaches to the greens at these three courses are open, at least to one side or from one strategic angle, encouraging an option for shots to bounce in. Pasatiempo typifies this feature less than the Valley Club and Cypress Point due to the many carries of the barrancas or ravines—it's

The approach
to the sixth hole at The
Valley Club in the 1930s.
A powerful drive (played
at 295 yards from the
'long' tee) could skirt the
flanking bunkers and
reach the green.

Photo taken from the fifth
fairway at The Valley Club.
Mackenzie and Hunter
encouraged a running
approach as the method to
attack this mid-length
par-4. (Photos courtesy of
The Valley Club.)

interesting how often and varied these were utilised on the back nine—and the softer conditions that can prevail in the wet months. Side slopes were often utilised as well, such as at the Valley Club's eleventh hole, a wonderful par-3. This hole offers the opportunity to run a ball up the front approach, or to carry the front left greenside bunker and utilise the natural right banking slope. Mackenzie's attention to the effects of these approaches was not lost, and the details and subtleties never ignored. As Robert Hunter, Mackenzie's partner in that era noted:

> There is no portion of a golf course which requires more care at the time of construction, and more attention later in the up-keep, than the area upon which most approaches to the hole will land. What decisive and subtle influences may be made to work upon the ball at just this point![9]

Modern conditions altered the original intent of many of these playing characteristics. Common belief in long rough surrounding the green complex, and the propensity to irrigate, heavily emphasised the advantages to an aerial attack more than one along the ground. A look at old photos of all three of these courses shows the green complexes maintained in a fairway cut, with a shaggy and rugged look to the bunker lines. What an infinite variety of shots would be required in such circumstances, instead of the tendency to merely grab the sand wedge and flop a shot out of the heavy rough. Not only would the tighter lies dictate that more 'shots' be played, but a level of playability is also added in such circumstances. The contouring in the immediate surrounds could be utilised more in playing shots that bank and kick, or defensively as backstops. The contours would be utilised as Mackenzie intended, thereby affecting play. Playability would be particularly enhanced when shots are required down the significant slopes of many of Mackenzie's greens. The combination of long grass surrounds and today's green speeds have rendered recovery from behind many of his greens a terrifying experience prohibiting aggressive play. This was certainly not his intent in such a general way.

Thankfully, the importance of the ground contours and their effects on how the game is played, along with many other facets of Mackenzie's genius, are being widely recognised both within and outside these wonderful golf clubs. The restorations are underway, and the results are fantastic. The broad concept of returning conditions of respective golf courses to 'firm and fast' is at least beginning on a greater scale, and I sincerely hope this will be furthered. The game of golf must have been so fabulously fun and interesting in the Good Doctor's day.

The value of Pitch and Putt courses

Dr Ramon Espinosa

Golf attracts new players day by day, as can be easily seen by checking the growth rate of the number of federated players in each country. In Spain, for example the number of players in 2000 increased by fifteen per cent over the previous year, and the upward trend continued in 2001, with another increase of twelve and a half per cent in federated players.

If we extend this finding to other countries, we will probably see that the tendency is growing everywhere, and nowadays much of this increase in the number of players is due to the proliferation of the short form of golf, known as Pitch and Putt. These facilities have brought this marvellous sport closer to the majority of the population. Therefore, we consider them to be the nurturing ground of future players.

The only difference between Pitch and Putt and ordinary eighteen hole golf is in the playing distances. In essence, the game is the same as the long game of golf.

The design, construction and subsequent maintenance of the courses require the same care and study as their big brothers. The difference is that as they are smaller, these expenses are reduced enormously, and the final prices to be paid by the player become really attractive.

These facilities are true player factories, as they are normally visited by persons wanting to play golf for the first time. In this respect, they are ideal as players are not overawed by the dimensions of a big course, and can play without getting in the way of more experienced players. In any case, experience has shown us

The 'innocence of youth' swinging freely at the Waverley Public Pitch and Putt course, Mulgrave, Australia. (Photo by Shannon Morris, courtesy of Leader Sport.)

One of the key points of Pitch and Putt is that it should always be close to an urban centre, allowing experienced players to access the facilities quickly and practise golf in their free time, without having to spend an entire morning on the course. Nine holes of Pitch and Putt can be played in just under an hour.

The advantages of Pitch and Putt are many from the golfer's point of view: it is not necessary to be a member of a club or to fork out large sums of money; green fees are low; and it adapts perfectly to the creation of new players; and it helps sharpen the short game. Consider that sixty-five per cent of all strokes played on a golf course are played in the final 100 metres. This is where the three clubs used in Pitch and Putt are most used. Young children can find golf courses discouragingly large so the distances of Pitch and Putt are perfect for them. And people who are not members of a club can access these facilities much more easily.

From the point of view of the promoter, the advantages are also apparent: the facilities do not require a great area of land (an attractive Pitch and Putt course can be built on seven

that once players learn to play well, they tend to graduate onto full-length golf. Pitch and Putt facilities, therefore, are used by three clearly defined types of player: beginners; players with not much time; and experienced players who want to practice their short game.

In accordance with this player profile, a Pitch and Putt course must have a practice fairway long enough to see the flight and roll of the ball (250 metres); a large putting green of at least 500 metres square; an apron; a practice bunker; and, of course, at least nine holes with distances of between forty and 130 metres. These facilities include all the possibilities of a normal golf course, making it possible to practise all the important golf strokes.

hectares); no large investment in construction is required; and earnings are high due to the continuous flow of players. The location of the course heavily influences this factor.

For these reasons, Pitch and Putt has continued to grow since it was invented in Ireland in the 1930s. It has become so popular that many normal golf courses now include these facilities, acting as an escape valve for moments of maximum occupation, competitions and, of course, to practise golf without holding up play. People can play without the pressures of a large course.

The greatest inconvenience of these facilities is, as we have already hinted, getting players enthusiastic enough about Pitch and Putt to want to play over and over again. Several factors are involved in encouraging longer-term commitment including proximity to a populated area and attractive design. With this form of golf, namely Pitch and Putt, only three clubs are used: pitching wedge; sand wedge; and putter.

It is necessary, therefore, to have an attractive design where the holes, in spite of being of similar distances, are different from each

The 54-metre ninth hole at Waverley Public Pitch and Putt course. The screen aids with the protection of players on nearby holes. (Photo by Peter Johnson.)

OPPOSITE: A general panorama of the Waverley Public Pitch and Putt course. (Photo by Peter Johnson.)

other. This can be achieved using the same technique as a normal golf course, using lakes which influence play, bunkers in different positions to induce different strokes, trees in strategic places, humps requiring different stroke angles, moved greens, and so on. These factors also contribute to increased safety which must be kept very much in mind as many players at these facilities are beginners. Therefore, a well-placed bunker, a lake in a strategic position, or any of the mentioned items may help to avoid accidents. In short, we believe that these facilities are necessary to give golf a boost, and are true player factories.

Stop making sense!
Gil Hanse

In nearly all of the design disciplines there are sets of rules, formulas, or equations that serve to guide designers and set standards for their industry. There is often a structural reason to make sense of why a formula or rule has been applied to the design. In the moulding and use of the natural landscape for a game, the need to follow a strict set of rules should be almost non-existent. The use of natural landforms to create interesting and creative golf holes should not be held to any formula. If a rule must be stated, it should be that no rules apply to the use of a landscape to create the playing grounds for golf. The golf course architect should be creative in utilising natural features to dictate the strategy of the course. Inherent in the unique character of every site, are unique golf holes just waiting to be discovered. Is this not the true challenge of golf course architecture, to build fresh and innovative holes that derive their beauty, playability, and interest from their natural surrounds?

It is amazing to consider that the greatest model for the world of golf course architecture—the Old Course at St. Andrews—is remarkably free from man-made concepts. It relies on the folds of the ground and the natural rises and falls to dictate strategy, beauty and interest. The Old Course also presents the greatest argument against making sense of golf course design. It is a golf course where there is no prescribed route to play the course on a regular basis. Due to the vagaries of the land forms and the conditions, the Old Course never plays the same whether over a course of two rounds or two thousand. The width contributes to a myriad of possibilities in selecting lines of play and angles of attack. The flexibility in its set-up, based primarily on the size of the greens, allows for creative golf. And this is surely the most enjoyable form of the game to be found.

I have had the great fortune of travelling over nearly all the great golf courses of Scotland, and I am very often asked which I find the most interesting and worthy of a visit. Prestwick, Cruden Bay, North Berwick and the Old Course very often head up my list of favourites. Not because they are the greatest tests of golf, but rather, because they offer a glimpse at the boundaries of acceptability. These courses make great use of their natural settings, and present holes that are unique to all of golf: blind par-3 holes; holes with walls in front of the green; double fairways and greens; and wildly undulating greens are all components of these designs. These holes certainly push the envelope of design, and should serve to liberate the minds of golf course architects from the encumbrance of conformity. If courses of this type can be appreciated and studied, then innovation and interest can again become a part of any architect's arsenal when designing golf courses.

It is not my intention to sponsor a form of architectural anarchy. I believe that there are certain formulas that work well in the design of a golf course. Dr Mackenzie laid out his thirteen principles for golf course design, and George Crump certainly designed Pine Valley with a framework for the types of shots he wanted played on his course. Designing with balance in the shot requirements is certainly a key component in the design of any course. Proper balance in direction, length and strategy should make up the components of golf holes on any well-designed site. The creative golf course architects can usually find these characteristics in the existing landscape of most sites. However, it is better to use what the land gives you than to re-arrange the site in order to find this perfect balance in the design. At Rustic Canyon, in Moorpark, California, we designed a golf course that possesses five one-shot holes, and five three-shot holes. This is not the perfect balance that most architects strive for. However, in our opinion, this layout yielded the most natural of golf courses. To have wrestled with the natural features in order to have a more uniform and 'normal' layout would have meant conforming to the very idea of formula that I am speaking against. Every site has its own unique flavour, topography, and vegetation. The golf course architect should exhaust the possibilities inherent to the site to accomplish the goals he has in mind for the shot making on the course. Unfortunately, the opposite has become the norm in modern golf course architecture, where the architect feels at ease with creating the design without much regard for the lay of the land. Architects often choose instead to

subjugate the natural characteristics of the site through earthmoving, as opposed to embracing these features and incorporating them into the design in fresh and creative ways.

We have very often run across these types of situations, and rather than take a bull-dozer

The brilliant, but non-sensical thirteenth hole at North Berwick, Scotland. (Photo by Gil Hanse.)

to a natural contour we have tried to work them into the design of our golf courses. At Inniscrone Golf Club, in Avondale, Pennsylvania, the ninth hole provides an example of using the natural landscape to dictate the strategy of the hole. A natural ridge existed across its fairway at approximately 310 yards from the tee, with the high side of the ridge occurring on the right side of the hole and tapering off to the left. A well-placed drive to the precarious left side is provided with a

clear view of the green on this 434-yard hole, while a drive hit to the safe right side faces a blind shot to the green. Cross-bunkers set into the ridge provide points of reference, allowing the golfer to use them as an aiming point. The further that the golfer moves from right to left, the less of a visual hindrance there is into the green. The ninth hole plays as fresh and different on a day-to-day basis as any hole in the world. Depending on the accuracy of the drive, and the location of the hole, the psychological impact on the golfer changes dramatically from round to round. It truly is a psychological hazard in that whether you are to the right or left, the playing surface and the distance of the shot can be the same. Obscured vision is the main difference: a difference with which most modern golfers are strangely uncomfortable. As a result, the use of this natural landform makes for a beguiling hazard that ensures that this hole will never grow old.

With its lack of structural constraints, and its greatest examples evoking character and natural interest, golf course architecture should promote the most dynamic concepts and daring designs. There are many in the

profession who would claim that my insistence on designing courses that use existing natural vegetation and existing topographical features constitutes a formula of my own. While it may all be a matter of semantics in the end, I would contend that the promotion of the individuality of each site would serve to break the mould from the preceding site. This 'formula' lends itself to creating the most interesting golf course designs, those that are free from the limitations that have been imposed on the field by our own profession. When we stop making sense, and use the land in creative and imaginative ways, we may find that the limitations of our field will disappear.

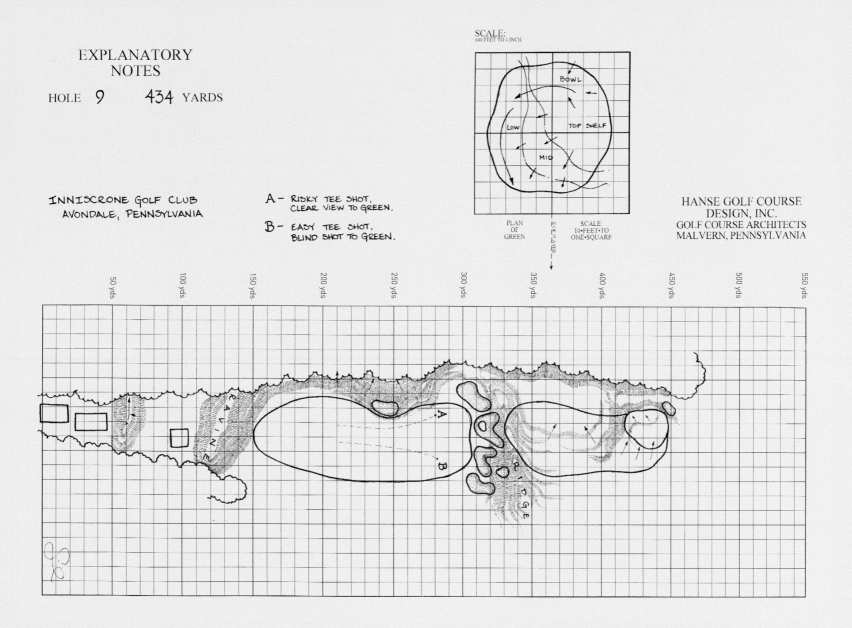

EXPLANATORY
NOTES

HOLE 9   434 YARDS

INNISCRONE GOLF CLUB
AVONDALE, PENNSYLVANIA

A — RISKY TEE SHOT,
CLEAR VIEW TO GREEN.

B — EASY TEE SHOT,
BLIND SHOT TO GREEN.

SCALE:
100 FEET TO 1 INCH

BOWL

LOW   TOP SHELF

MID

PLAN
OF
GREEN

SCALE:
10·FEET·TO
ONE·SQUARE

HANSE GOLF COURSE
DESIGN, INC.
GOLF COURSE ARCHITECTS
MALVERN, PENNSYLVANIA

50 yds   100 yds   150 yds   200 yds   250 yds   300 yds   350 yds   400 yds   450 yds   500 yds   550 yds

Rock rolls into golf design

Thomas McBroom

In golf course architecture, bedrock has generally been treated like a bad family secret: best covered up and forgotten. When rock is encountered on a site, it is generally used as fill to help create high points such as tees or mounding. This is used to dramatic effect, for example, at Highlands Links in Cape Breton, Canada, where Stanley Thompson rolled boulders into the fairways and covered them with grass to create a mogul look.

Historically, rock has not had a place in golf, except perhaps for a boundary wall or to provide an accent around a pond. Most golfers don't conceive of rock when they think of golf courses. Golfers will accept that an errant shot may catch a slope and run into a bunker or water; or that they might lose a ball in a pond, heavy rough or bush. It's the penalty for hitting a bad golf shot.

But using rock either to provide definition, as a hazard, or to protect a green, just doesn't compute for most golfers. The game is difficult enough without getting wild bounces off rock.

However, it has been my experience that rock can provide great beauty, character and strategic nuance in golf design, especially where it is an indigenous and dominant element in the natural landscape. Rock can be used to accentuate the harmony between the course and its surroundings, and can help the course to look right and feel comfortable as though part of the land, rather than an imposition on the land.

The key to using rock is that it cannot restrict the ability of golfers to play the game. If intelligently incorporated into a golf hole, it will not come into play unless there has been an abysmal shot. However, if rock interferes with shots that range from marginal to excellent, it is likely a poorly designed golf course.

I've developed some expertise with rock through my work on four courses in the Canadian Shield region of Canada: Deerhurst Highlands, Le Géant, the Lake Joseph Club, and Rocky Crest Golf Club, which were designed in that order. At each course we progressively brought rock more into the design.

The Canadian Shield dominates the central and northern sections of the provinces of Quebec and Ontario. Unique to Canada, the

Canadian Shield is renowned for its hundreds of freshwater lakes, pristine softwood and hardwood forests, and granite bedrock.

In the Muskoka region of Ontario, rock outcroppings are the signature characteristic of the landscape, which can have dramatic and irregular form, sometimes with rounded edges, other times sharp angles, or flowing lines with pink and blue colouration. They can be ruggedly beautiful, especially when the sun glints off the layers of quartz and mica rippling through the rock's surface. Granite can be quite lovely compared to the lava rock that is characteristic to courses in Hawaii, but lava rock is not prominent because it is usually flat black and foreboding in appearance.

In the past, most golf operators have avoided building in areas dominated by rock—dig down a few feet anywhere in Muskoka and you hit rock. Until recently, there wasn't machinery that was capable of handling the hard formations. And few owners could afford to build courses in locations such as Muskoka because the growing media must be imported to the sites. There's just no topsoil. At Rocky Crest, 26,000 truckloads of

The opening hole at Lake Joseph Golf Club, Muskoka, Canada. (Photo courtesy of Thomas McBroom.)

sand were brought on to the property.

The Canadian Shield provides a brilliant canvas upon which to design golf courses that have great natural beauty and distinctive character. At my Muskoka courses and in the Mont-Tremblant region of Quebec, I took my cue from mother nature and incorporated the rock into the designs. The rock is indigenous, so it looks right, in the same way that desert courses use the topography to frame and accent holes.

My first design experience on the Canadian Shield was in 1988 at Deerhurst Highlands in Muskoka with Bob Cupp, an accomplished architect based in Atlanta, Georgia. The rock is not prevalent near playing areas, but we incorporated vertical rock faces into the design, especially on the tenth hole which features a 100 foot wall running up the right side of the fairway from an elevated tee deck. Deerhurst Highlands was the first golf course in Canada to use rock so dramatically.

After Deerhurst, it occurred to me that there were many more ways to use rock in golf design. At Le Géant in the Mont-Tremblant mountain region of Quebec in 1994, we used rock to show turning points in doglegs, though the rock is well back of the playing areas. We used rock faces as backdrops for a few greens, and we set some tees into rock faces. While incorporating rock into the design was unusual, the owners of Le Géant agreed to the idea because the feature looked so natural, and it didn't interfere with playability.

In 1995, at the Lake Joseph Club in Muskoka, I continued to experiment with the granite outcroppings to take greater advantage of their beauty. It occurred to me that as golf architects, we had it backwards: instead of covering up the rock we should uncover it. Thus, in strategic areas we began to peel back earth from the rock. Where the formations were particularly attractive, we cleaned them with high-pressure hoses and left them exposed.

We used the rock mainly in the foreground between tees and the landing areas. From the tees, the rock provides a dramatic look that can be compared to Scottish links where the back tee and fairway are often separated by about sixty to seventy yards of whins. But at Lake Joseph, there are no intimidating carries over rock from the forward tees.

This was exciting because it represented a novel use of rock as an aesthetic element, but it also proved to be cost effective. On Canadian Shield courses, you must fill in spaces between the rocks to provide relatively smooth turf conditions. The exposed rock decreased the amount of sand required, which was welcomed by the developer. Lake Joseph proved to be a hit as both a member course and as a resort course, which told me that while the use of rock was progressive, it was not only accepted by golfers it was warmly embraced.

When we began work on Rocky Crest in 1998, we decided to push our rock experiment further. Rock became one of the primary themes along with abundant wetlands and regal pines. While the rock was mainly used in the foreground at Lake Joseph, we exposed more at Rocky Crest throughout the course.

We used rock to define turns in doglegs. On the first hole, a rock ridge runs along the outside of the turn, but on the fifteenth and eighteenth holes, the rock formations are found on the inside of the turn. On the seventh hole, a three-shot par-4 for most players, the area to the right side of the green is exposed rock, rather than a bunker, but there's plenty of room between the rock and green. A large outcropping of rock lies in the middle of the sixteenth fairway, about 320 yards from the tee. It acts as a target for most players. For the longest hitters, it becomes a strategic element to consider.

The most extreme use of rock is found on the sixth hole, which became the focus of many debates during construction because it is clearly pushing the envelope of golf design. We deliberately exposed about three acres of granite between the back tee and the landing area. This could be called a heroic forced carry, but it's only 180 yards from the tee to the bent grass fairway. This yardage range is well within the grasp of skilled golfers playing the gold (back) tees on this 569-yard, par-5 hole. The four other tees are angled to reduce the carry to a manageable distance, and players on the forward deck have no carry to concern themselves with.

From a cost perspective, the increased use of exposed rock cut down on the expense of importing sand to the property. However, it also had another benefit. With the abundance of natural features such as wetlands, hummocks and rock, there are only thirty-five bunkers at Rocky Crest, which means lower maintenance costs. And most golfers don't miss bunkers! A number of greens have no bunkers because the course didn't need them to create strategic challenge or visual enhancement.

When Rocky Crest opened for play in Spring 2000, it was well received by its members, resort guests and media, and most people noted the unique use of rock in their comments. As an architect with more than sixty courses under my belt, I never heard a new course create a buzz like the one generated by Rocky Crest. And rock was the key.

At Rocky Crest, I wanted to celebrate our natural Canadian features, and the best way to do that was to show off the spectacular beauty of the rock. I am proud to say that our work in the Canadian Shield represents a progression in the approach to rock in golf design

Incorporation of rock into course design at the sixth hole of Rocky Crest, Muskoka, Canada. (Photo courtesy of Thomas McBroom.)

OPPOSITE: The fourteenth hole at Rocky Crest. (Photo courtesy of Thomas McBroom.)

that has influenced a number of other courses. In looking back at how we advanced our thinking in the use of rock, it is clear that we helped establish a distinct Canadian style that reflects the great beauty, diversity and character of our native land.

Immaculate perfection

Ronald W. Fream

The 2002 US Masters tournament at the newly elongated Augusta National Golf Club clearly demonstrates the unsurpassed and unequalled ability of Tiger Woods's golf game. There is only one Tiger. Indeed, there is only one Augusta National. Its singular existence is often overlooked and unappreciated by avid golfers, golf club green committees, and club members.

During the past ten years or so satellite television, cable access and expanding worldwide coverage of the Masters tournament have circled the globe. As an international traveller I often hear people wistfully say, 'why can't our course look like Augusta?' The unmitigated perfection of Augusta opens the potential for new standards at other courses. Augusta con-

tinues to raise the bar, a situation causing much envy and thoughts of emulation by other golf clubs. In reality, Augusta is an ideal that for most cannot be met.

The basic fact is that Augusta National is Augusta National, as worldwide television portrays its magnificence for all of two weeks a year. Early April is the most advantageous part of the spring growing season in the south-eastern section of the United States. An immense year-round effort is directed into achieving these two weeks of perfection. Other courses attempt to duplicate the appearance of unrestrained luxuriant turf and abundant flowering trees and shrubs, but must face the fact that an immaculate condition is extremely expensive to realise.

When examined from a cost-efficiency standpoint, trying to emulate Augusta brings more harm to many courses and golfers than it produces luxuriant turf. Augusta sets an unrealistic model to follow. It requires a well-educated golf course superintendent, seemingly unlimited maintenance funds (in excess of $1,500,000 per year), a crew of volunteers, experienced back-up superintendents, a year round staff of about forty (that increases in the lead-up to the tournament), state-of-the-art equipment annually, and limited numbers of rounds of play. It also begs for nearly ideal weather conditions in the spring. With such resources, what course couldn't yield exceptional results? The cost of these resources is then reflected in prohibitively higher membership dues.

The clubhouse at
Augusta National Golf
Club, Georgia, USA.
(Photo by Ronald W.
Fream.)

The fairway view to Augusta's tenth green site. (Photo by Ronald W. Fream.)

OPPOSITE: View to Augusta National's thirteenth green complex, from second shot landing area. (Photo by Ronald W. Fream.)

The south-eastern Georgia climate helps too. The basic fairway turf of bermuda grass can easily be over-sown with fine leaf rye grass in late September or October as the bermuda enters dormancy. The rye grass flourishes in the cool winter weather under intense maintenance. The creeping bent grass greens are at their best in early spring before the onslaught of summer heat and humidity. Subsurface heating coils help bring early season growth to some of the greens ahead of nature's schedule. It has been said that cooling tubes beneath

some of the greens help prolong the quality of the bent grass when the heat and humidity arrive towards the end of April. At Augusta, member play finishes by the end of May, and will only resume when the cooler autumn temperatures arrive in October.

To achieve stimpmeter speeds of twelve or even thirteen for the Masters requires the super dwarf varieties of creeping bent grass and special mowers with extremely thin bed knives, often involving double cutting. Even so, the height of cut for Masters week (approximately one-eighth of an inch) cannot be maintained throughout the golf season, as the grass would die. Achieving these speeds requires intense focus on the greens, with many practices beyond simple mowing. With fewer than 10,000 rounds of golf a year, and restricted play leading up to Masters week, traffic over the course is modest. Limited annual play greatly reduces the cancerous effects of induced compaction through golf traffic that causes turf deterioration.

Courses that must withstand 40,000, 60,000 and 100,000 rounds of play a year cannot compete with Augusta's regime. Tropical locations

where bent grass will not grow, must deal with bermuda grass cultivars or paspalum turf on the greens. Trying to achieve Augusta-like greens speeds on bermuda or paspalum is impossible, even with the new tifeagle hybrid bermuda grass variety. Bermuda grass cannot be cut as closely as creeping bent grass. Trying to shave down these greens seeking ever-faster stimpmeter readings leads to deterioration in the reliability of the turf and the quality of the putting. The speed of Augusta's greens are faster during the Masters week than at any other time of the year. The mowing heights are raised the Monday following the tournament.

The image of immaculate perfection on the fairways, and now a little semi-rough 'second cut' along with tees and greens, is as much due to superb management of fertilisers and micronutrients as it is of mowing. The fairway and tee top turf of perennial pye grass responds well to measured amounts of various fertiliser and micronutrient feedings. Not every course can afford the price of intense micronutrient supplements and nitrogen-phosphorous -potassium fertiliser programs. Mowing each year with brand new equipment that is

carefully adjusted helps. Mowing fairways in one direction with a 'fleet' of triplex greens-type mowers (six or eight moving in unison) with grass catchers, presents that lush look. Most golf courses cannot afford to replace all their primary and expensive mowing equipment every year or to utilise six or more triplex for simultaneous fairway mowing.

The spectacular floral show around some of the more popularly televised holes reflects a favourable matching of climate, season and horticulture. Not all those flowers are blossoming every year. If nature is off schedule, the dogwoods will not be in bloom. However, with help from hot houses or cooled greenhouses, the timing of azalea flowering is regulated. Overnight delivery and placement of masses of flowering shrubs can occur at Augusta.

With relatively few rounds of golf being played and caddies on hand, there is no need for cart paths to mar the view. Maintenance pathways are well removed into the surrounding pine forest and out of spectator view.

Being set among mature pine trees, isolated from public roads and the commercial intrusion of resort facilities or residential housing, an exceptional tranquillity exists around the course, making it seem more private than most others.

The smooth appearance of the tidy pine needles under the native pines and around the recently planted trees is not a gift of nature. Not all those pine needles began their existence on an Augusta pine tree. Considerable effort is required to make that pine needle soil cover look pristine.

Augusta National is a wonderful course. It is unfortunate, however, that too many aspire to those playing conditions on their own courses. Since most public courses and country clubs must earn a profit or break even, it is essential to tailor one's own ideals and objectives to the financial realities available, as increased maintenance costs must pass through to the user.

Too many indicators show that escalating fees are discouraging new players, and limiting the play of average golfers in numerous markets. The number of new players has declined in markets where costs are high. Play on affordable courses has increased, as the frequency of repeat play at courses with higher green fees has dropped off. Decreasing the amount of play by excessive cost is only desirable at a few select and noted courses. An experienced superintendent has several avenues of action available if given a reasonable budget to improve the appearance and quality of the course.

Some owners and operators want average or marginal maintenance results, and in some markets those are acceptable. Not every course must strive to produce the perfect ten of Augusta National. Most golfers would be pleased with conditions equating to seven or eight on the Augusta scale. For high traffic, modestly-priced courses, a five or six on the scale, combined with smooth puttable greens, would produce the most favourable revenue stream.

The basic objective for most profit-oriented courses is a sustainable turfgrass quality that meets or exceeds the local competition within the range of market-driven green fees. Without price moderation, the game will not prosper.

Improvements in green speeds and in the appearance of the turf can add an extra competitive edge that helps the course rise above

The well-contoured surface of Augusta's fourteenth green. When running at a stimpmeter speed of thirteen, the green is lightning fast. (Photo by Ronald W. Fream.)

local rivals not offering these conditions. These efforts can translate into increased revenue for the course operator. Members appreciate improved levels of turfgrass quality as scores can go down with better turf. The management of each individual course is responsible to set a reasonably attainable standard. What is good for Augusta is not necessarily good or practical for everyone else.

A golfer's view from the Augusta's seventeenth tee. Eisenhower's pine tree on left defines the holes and dictates the tee-shot strategy. (Photo by Ronald W. Fream.)

Updating old courses: restoration or renovation?

Simon Gidman

Restoration means 'to bring back to a former state.' Is this really a serious option for our older courses? One only needs to look at some of the early plans of these courses to realise that they often played as 6000 yard courses, occasionally less, with hazards placed at 170–190 yards from the tee and landscapes that were often immature and undeveloped. Golf club members, I would suggest, do not want to go back to those times.

Bear in mind too that many of our older courses have gone through a number of reincarnations. How far back would one go before settling upon which layout to restore? Would St. Andrews go back to the pre-1850s, when it was played on the same route going out as in? I doubt it. Would Shinnecock Hills, one of the greatest of inland courses, revert to pre-Toomey and Flynn days? Again, one hopes not. These are perhaps absurd examples, but the point needs to be made that golf courses have evolved since they were first created. They are living landscapes that change in response to the demands of equipment, the ambitions of the membership, and the popularity of the game. Whether or not they have evolved in the right direction is quite another matter. However, I do not know of any of our surviving older courses that have remained unaltered.

If a golf course stagnates it dies. Pinehurst No. 2, one of Donald Ross's greatest legacies, has holes some of which he altered as many as three times. Not many of us have clients so willing to accept constant change, but Donald Ross knew that his course had to adapt both to his own ideas and to developments within the game. I doubt that Pinehurst would have been the great course it is today had Ross not made those fundamental improvements. This was a case of renovation rather than restoration.

Indeed renovation is nothing new. One only has to look at the careers of some of our earliest architects like Harry S. Colt, Alister Mackenzie, Herbert Fowler and Willie Park Jr., to realise how much remodelling work they undertook. Colt, for example, started his career in golf as secretary at Sunningdale Old Course—originally designed by Park Jr.—and spent his early days moving bunkers, adding trees in strategic places, and creating other features on the course. Mackenzie was remodelling Royal St. George's, Lahinch and Blairgowrie; Fowler reworked Ganton, Royal Lytham and St. Annes, Royal North Devon, and so the list goes on. These modifications came about partly in response to the need to create a full eighteen-hole golf course, but more often as a result of major improvements in golf equipment and dramatic changes in the philosophy of the game as it moved from the penal to the strategic schools of golf architecture.

On the question of strategy, history and equipment generally, it is interesting to note the effects this has had on modern design. In the past, great emphasis was placed on the location and angle of approach bunkering. Golf was played with the 1.62 inch ball to firm, non-irrigated greens, and to ensure that a ball stayed on the green it was critical to play short and allow the natural contours of the approach to direct the ball toward the flag. Accurate driving to a certain opening in the fairway, and equally accurate second or third shots to a point on the approach, was the hallmark of a good golfer. Hence, the value of the approach bunker. This approach to golf strategy is less relevant these days. Golfers of all handicaps now expect to hit a ball through the air directly onto the green and for the ball to stay on that green. Thus the modern approach to designing greens is to angle them away from the centre line, and to protect the surface with more hazards both to the front as well as sides of the green. This is an example of modern target golf as opposed to the strategic golf of the past.

However, many of our older courses have an abundance of approach bunkers well short of the green. They don't often come into play these days, but they do set up the approach to the green beautifully. And whatever we may say about the exact location of bunkers, who could forget Ross's timeless comment: 'There is no such thing as a misplaced bunker … it is the business of the player to avoid it.'[10]

Every architect has their own view on this issue—but my own? Well, much will depend on each hole and the strategic influences of the hole. However, on principle, I prefer to retain the original concept and framework. By all means, move the bunkers forward and narrow the green approaches slightly, but the spirit of the original design should be retained. I suppose my answer to the question of renovation is: what would Colt, Fowler or Abercromby have done to their courses had they the chance to remodel their own creations 100 years later?

When one visits these established, properly designed courses, it always surprises me how well they have stood up over the years. While the fundamental principles of golf design have not really altered, these old green complexes are mostly as challenging now as when first built, and the location of hazards around the green still demand thought and precision. Equally, the layout of the golf holes rarely needs to be changed in a Braid, Colt, or Simpson layout unless perhaps it is due to development encroaching close to the boundaries of the course.

So golf is a game that has changed and evolved, and therefore restoration of these old courses to their early designs is rarely a viable solution. Renovating an old course to its original style—now that is an entirely different matter.

and other hazards have been expunged and others put in for no obvious reason. As a result, many of our older courses lack design continuity as every participant attempts to leave their own, often ghastly, stamp on the course. What a course needs is unity, not a jumble of ideas and statements. When renovating, above all else, these 'carbuncles' as Prince Charles might have called them, need to be re-assessed and invariably removed.

To date, I have concentrated on golf courses with some kind of architectural heritage and the issues related to the remodelling of these courses. But there are many older courses with no such heritage. These courses, though by no means all, tend to have certain inherent weaknesses, sometimes due to poor layout. Occasionally, one still comes across holes that cross each other. However, more often it is due to the simple problems such as small greens, bunkers that do not challange, and mounding that needs modification. Nonetheless, a wholesale approach to change is still something to be avoided. These courses may not be of architectural significance, but they are of enormous importance and affection to

Like all creative people, these early architects had certain styles and traits which characterised their courses. Yet when one visits many of these courses, it is remarkably easy to detect the amateurish additions made over time. Changes inspired by personal taste rather than course philosophy, often leave a course bereft of its original strategy. Bunkers

members. The little nuances of the course, the strange shapes, the grassy hollows and knolls, are all significant. This, after all, represents the character of the course.

From both an agronomic and architectural viewpoint, changes need to be made. The greens will invariably be clay-based and often closed for parts of the winter, unlike their new, recently built neighbours. Tees will be too small, bunker faces worn and sub-bases not drained. From an architectural viewpoint, basic golfing principles and shot values may not have been addressed at all in the original layout or simply need to be reviewed. Trees, planted many years previously, now encroach onto the playing surface casting shade and leaf litter, and how often does one find these golf courses lined with totally alien planting—a mass of dark pine, larch, cupressus and poplar with little thought given to long term indigenous planting. Despite these inherent weaknesses, the charm and character of the courses are all-important assets. Members want their courses upgraded, the specification of greens and tees improved, hazards moved to a more appropriate position, occasionally a little more excitement added, and they might even want a little water incorporated to add to the heroic nature of the course. More than anything, though, members want the character of their course retained.

Marrying the two principles is a difficult though not impossible task. Green sizes can be enlarged to adapt to current volumes of play, but still be relatively small; bunker shapes and designs can maintain their uniqueness, but be better placed; and grassy hollows, swales and mounds re-incorporated, yet retain their historic style. Despite the awkwardness of some of these features to maintain, it is surprising how rarely maintenance problems are cited as a cause for renovation. The odd mound or deep-sided ditch might be removed, but on the whole the club will have lived with these features and tend to accept and even enjoy these strange oddities.

In Britain, the development of new golf courses in the late 1980s and 90s has not only helped to satisfy the demand in popularity of the game, but has made existing golf clubs reassess their own courses. Enlightened members, appreciating that they have been the beneficiaries of the previous generation's foresight, are often conscious of the need to pass on to the next generation of golfers a product that will endure for the next 100 years. They know that unless they adapt and improve their own course, in time it will fall by the way side. As a result, many of these clubs are taking the positive step in renovating their course.

These older courses represent a wonderful and valuable golfing heritage, whose maturity is a feature frequently envied by newer golf clubs. This heritage needs to be carefully adapted to the modern demands of the game, improved but not obviously modernised, renovated but rarely restored.

Learning from Donald Ross

Bradley S. Klein

More than a few modern golf course architects have tried to make a living by literally trashing the past. In their view, the game's classical designers—Alister Mackenzie, A.W. Tillinghast, Donald Ross—did work that might have been interesting in its day, but by modern standards, is no more than quaint and out-of-date. From this standpoint, the task of the contemporary architect is to improve upon the weaknesses and limitations of the past by updating and modernising. Blind shots are bulldozed and rendered visible. Severe slopes are softened. Cross-bunkers that are 'unfair' are eliminated. Length is added.

Too often in this manner, interesting ground features are sacrificed in the name of maintenance, fairness, or simply to accommodate an imperative for greater distance. The game's traditions get lost in the process. Moreover, what gets easily dismissed along the way is that the classical designers were in many cases imaginative in their use of land. To presume they were suffering from budgetary limitations or the absence of massive earth-moving equipment and thus had to settle for inferior landscape work is to misconstrue their understanding of the design process. These factors also cheat today's golfers of a certain aesthetic and strategic genius that has enduring value, and that has never been surpassed. A close look at one such designer, Donald Ross, reveals the origins and evolution of that vision. It's a vision of course design worth preserving and restoring.

Tools of the trade

Emigré Scotsman, Donald J. Ross (1872-1948), remade the North American sport's landscape in the first half of the twentieth century. At his death in 1948, he left behind a legacy of 400 golf courses that he designed or re-designed. His legendary creations include Pinehurst No. 2 in North Carolina, Seminole in Florida, Oakland Hills outside Detroit, and Salem, north of Boston.

Ross was born in the north Scottish coastal town of Dornoch. On the crumpled dunes land he grew up playing one of the world's purest links, Dornoch Golf Club (it became 'Royal' in 1906, after Ross left). As a young man he took up 'the keeping of the green.' After a year of apprenticeship at St. Andrews, under the tutelage of four-time British Open champion Old Tom Morris, he returned to his native Dornoch as golf professional, club maker and greenkeeper. In those days, there was no rigid division of labour for golf professionals, so Ross became adept not only at maintaining the grounds, but also as a player and club maker.

He was making an adequate if unspectacular living. All that changed when an American professor on pilgrimage to the sport's holy land invited him to come to the New World to help spread the game's gospel. Ross arrived in 1899 to run (and then re-design) the Oakley Golf Club west of Boston. The next year, he landed an assignment with the Tufts family on a property in North Carolina's sandhills called Pinehurst.

Eventually, he designed and re-built four courses at the Pinehurst resort, none with more love and care than the No. 2 layout. Drawing upon his extensive background in turfgrass management, he revolutionized southern greenkeeping practices when he oversaw the transition of the putting surfaces at No. 2 from oiled sand to bermuda overseeded with

ryegrass that would hold up through the winters during the peak of the golf season. The work was completed just in time for the 1935 PGA Championship. The result was devilishly quick dome-shaped greens and a sense of impending doom for any wayward shots. With virtually no modification in length or playing character (except for speed of the greens), the course has withstood the onslaught of modern playing technology extremely well. When it hosted the 1999 US Open, the players praised its diverse shot-making demands. Only one contestant broke par for the week—winner Payne Stewart, who finished one under par for seventy-two holes.

During his summers, Ross started designing and building courses throughout New England. Eventually, his practice spread into the midwest and down the southeast coast. He maintained long associations with design colleagues J.B. McGovern and Walter Hatch. Ross had satellite offices in North Amherst, Massachusetts, and Wynnewood, Pennsylvania, and maintained his own seasonal summer office, first in Massachusetts and after 1925, on Rhode Island.

Using land

Modern architects are often criticised for doing too many courses at once and not making enough field visits per job. Yet in the 1920s Ross was working on twenty to twenty-five courses at a time. Of all the courses that bear Ross's name, either as original designs or as renovation projects, one-fifth of them he probably never even saw once. With fully half of all the courses he did, he visited only once or twice. Given the constraints of train and car travel in those days, repeat visits were difficult to arrange. Though Ross was a voracious traveller, he did much of his design work from his office atop the clubhouse at Pinehurst, or from one of his seasonal offices up north. He often worked from topographic maps. Once he had his routings, he might follow up with a field visit, then write simple but sharply-worded hole-by-hole instructions that his veteran associates knew how to implement. Befitting his roots in match-play golf, his routing plans contained reference to yardage but not to par. He was evidently more interested in creating holes that would challenge golfers during a match rather than

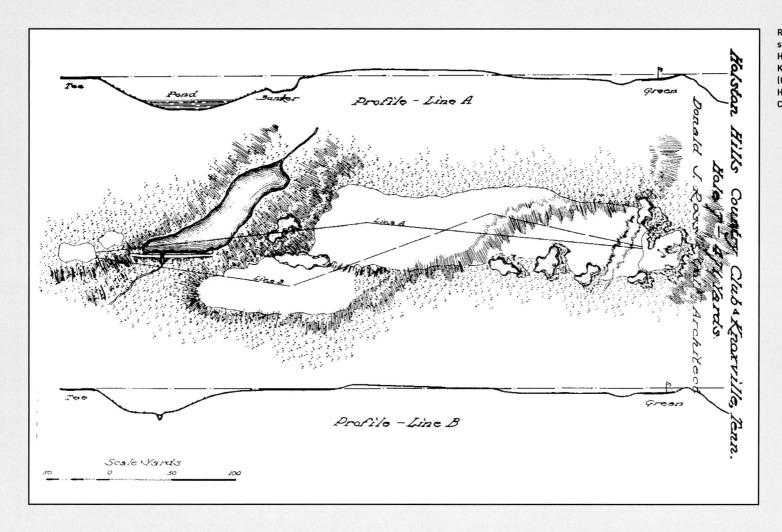

Holston Hills Country Club & Knoxville, Tenn.
Hole 7 — 478 Yards.
Donald J. Ross & Son, Architect

Tee   Pond   Bunker   Profile – Line A   Green

Line A

Line B

Tee   Profile – Line B   Green

Scale Yards
50   0   50   100

Ross's plans for the
seventh hole at Holston
Hills Country Club,
Knoxville, Tennessee, USA.
(Course layout courtesy of
Holston Hills Country
Club.)

measuring them against a single stroke-play standard.

Ross had a genius for sound routings, with very little walking required from one green to the next tee. If there was any real estate to consider, it would frame the entire golf course, not block the path between holes. Nor did he have the convenience of cart paths to rely upon to solve thorny routing sequences linking point A to point B. He also, it must be said, enjoyed a certain latitude of land use in two regards that modern architects don't have. If a parcel in question proved inadequate for golf, he could move down the road to another readily available lot and adapt it. And if swamps (there were no wetlands designated as such in those days) needed to be filled or drained, there were no environmental agencies telling him he couldn't.

His routings were efficient, with no wasted ground. At Detroit Golf Club in Michigan, he routed thirty-six holes on a tight, triangular site. Perhaps his greatest use of land came at Seminole, where he used a modest sand ridge in a corner of the property to locate four teeing grounds and five putting surfaces, creating along the way a comfortable sense of departure and return, and a layout which feels more elevated than it really is.

He would commonly route his short par-4s on uphill ground. Outstanding examples of this genre include the 298-yard thirteenth hole at Franklin Hills, Michigan, the 308-yard second hole at Brae Burn, Massachusetts and the 331-yard fourth hole at Plainfield, New Jersey. Other trademarks included greens that invited run-up shots, but with deep trouble over the green—usually in the form of fall away slopes—to punish the overly bold golfer. Ross was also not averse to placing cross-bunkers in play to punish the topped shot— off the tee, or some fifty yards short of the green. Sadly, a great number of these hazards have been taken out of play over the years in the misguided pursuit of 'ease of maintenance' or 'making the course more playable.'

Ross was a founding member and first president of the American Society of Golf Course Architects, a group that formed at Pinehurst in December 1946. A manuscript he first drafted in 1914 called *Golf Has Never Failed Me* (1996) contains useful glimpses into his craft. Not that he was an elegant writer. Indeed, the loose collection of little essays is more a practitioner's guide than an overall view of the game. Yet a modern student of architecture will learn from these words, especially when assessed alongside Ross's design work.

Contrary to modern designers (and tournament chairmen) obsessed with 'Tiger-proofing' courses and making them hard, Ross felt that golf should be a pleasure not a penance. Courses located smack in the middle of heavily trafficked real estate or commercial areas were, he thought, anathema to the spirit of the game as retreat and refuge. 'Unless absolutely necessary, don't for a minute consider a property divided by either a street or a railroad', he would advise. 'The very intent of a golf course is to get away from just such things.'[11]

As for the demand that all golf be somehow fair, and that all hazards should be visible, Ross argued instead that 'there is no such thing as misplaced bunker.'[12] For those who have tried over the years to beautify their courses with aggressive tree planting, Ross was keen to preserve wide angles of play. He also knew that hardwoods and evergreens would rob turf-grass of what it needed most: sun, air, water and nutrients. 'As beautiful as trees are, and as fond as you and I are of them,' says Ross, 'we still must not lose sight of the fact that there is a limited place for them in golf.'[13]

Back to the past

In recent years, dozens of Ross courses have undertaken dramatic restoration programs designed to reverse years of decay—and in most cases, successive generations of so called modernisation that had altered Ross's work. Among the many layouts engaged in such retro-fitting are Skokie Country Club, Illinois, Holston Hills Country Club, Tennessee, Charlotte Country Club, North Carolina, Minikahda Club, Minnesota, Belleview Biltmore Golf Course, Florida, Augusta Country Club, Georgia, Metacomet Country Club, Rhode Island, Charles River Country Club, Massachusetts and Lake Sunapee Country Club, New Hampshire. The work, largely taken up by a dissident group of architects focused on reclaiming golf's ground game traditions, involves tree removal, recapturing of green surfaces, closer integration of putting surfaces with green surrounds, taking out the flashed sand look of bunkers, and restoring sodded vertical walls, reintroduction of cross bunkers, cultivation of native rough grasses, squaring off tees, and firming up the course to facilitate short-game and shot-making options.

The revival of interest in Donald Ross parallels a general move towards restoring the game's traditional design heritage. A century after he began his design work and a half-century after his death, Ross continues to influence and impress.

OPPOSITE: **Ross playing golf. (Photo by E.C. Eddy, courtesy of Tufts Archive.)**

The rhythm of layout at Lahinch

Dr Martin Hawtree

One aspect of the layout of a golf course seldom discussed is the rhythm and dynamic of hole combinations. There is certainly a lot of theory, plenty of first principles laid down by old masters such as H.S Colt, Alister Mackenzie, and Tom Simpson, and not much improved upon in recent times. Yet there is no sustained analysis of the combined impact of holes in their various contexts: historical; golfing; landscape; estate development; planning; and stylistic. We may read of a links or parkland layout, two loops of nine holes, a Colt layout, good use of natural terrain and features, or a challenging test, but not a great deal more.

We are schooled to think in terms of having balanced nines, with a variety of hole orientation in respect of wind-direction, hole lengths, and shot-making requirements. The testing of every club in the bag is deemed important, as is the arrangement of pars. Where possible, there should be judicious punctuation of the layout with short holes, avoidance of parallelism, skilful concealment of steep gradients, and distribution of the highlights or viewing points of the site through the round. Steering the finishing holes away from the setting sun is mandatory, and throughout the layout, the architect makes provision for sensible safety margins between holes.

The vast majority of players will single out holes for discussion or criticism, but not often a sequence of holes. This concept of sequence, and the rhythm attached to it, is not simply the logical first step of any golfer's appreciation of layout as opposed to individual holes, but fundamental to the enjoyment of the course, even if the effects of the enjoyment are not immediately apparent. A person may enter a building, feel comfortable, and want to explore further without knowing why—that is the skill of the architect—but it will certainly have something to do with the sequence of spaces through which the visitor moves. Likewise, the way in which a golf course moves through a site is something to be evaluated, whether celebrated or reproached.

Take a well-known golf course, Lahinch, a links on the west coast of Ireland. The course is often referred to as a Mackenzie layout. It was certainly he who reorganised the golf course to lie entirely on the coastal side of the Liscannor road. Yet only six or seven of his green sites are played today, and only three or four retain his style. All great golf courses evolve, and Lahinch has been inscribed by more than a few architects, including, Old Tom Morris, Charles Gibson of Westward Ho fame, and Mackenzie. But in Lahinch's case there has been some loss of unity because of this multiple authorship. And the club's recent resolve to extend or reintroduce the Mackenzie style as the dominant influence is understandable.

The golf course starts out with a magnificent ascent from the clubhouse, which is set low down, to a high, broad dune, setting the grand stage for the Lahinch drama. It is a green position which surveys much of the golf course and surrounding landscape. The undulating fairway sets the pattern for the rest of the golf course, and the axis of the hole establishes the tone of the layout, north-west/south-east. Mackenzie's green was well to the left of the present position, but both positions are good, reaching into the heart of the site. The second hole is a disappointment—not as a hole in itself—but as a weak link in the sequence of opening holes; simply, almost banally, returning back down the same hill, sliding past the club house from where the golfer has only just set off. The hole feels like a displaced ninth. The third and fourth holes, in effect, restart the layout. The blind drive at the fourth suggests 'where now?' and excitement only returns at the summit of the hill, revealing a magnificent green site and coastal backdrop beyond. This entire sequence was in place in Gibson's layout of 1907. Mackenzie shifted them seawards and John Burke added the short hole and recontoured the greens.

The reason for the false start becomes clear at the fifth, Klondyke, an Old Tom Morris creation of 1897. This hole suddenly sets off at right angles in what is to be the second key axis of the course, north-east/south-west, repeated in the sixth and seventh holes, and then recapitulated at the eleventh, twelfth, and thirteenth. The hole lies in a deep, narrow valley boarded for much of its length by high, impassable dunes. The hole effectively blocks any possibility of returning to the clubhouse other than at the far North Eastern end, where the hole leaps up out of the valley over the Klondyke dune into open ground. With the green pushed to the limit of the road boundary wall, a crossing hole to return to the clubhouse for the eighteenth is inevitable. The second, third and fourth holes have to be played before Klondyke for these physical reasons. However, the dramatic change of direction for the Klondyke hole bottles up and ensures a far from ideal start to the round.

The fourth hole introduces a weakness in theory, namely blindness: the drive at the fourth, the second shot at the Klondyke, the tee-shot at the sixth hole (the famous Tom Morris Dell Hole), plus both tee-shots at the seventh and eighth holes—all being entirely blind to the golfer. Now Lahinch is an historic course. The blindness perhaps imparts that spirit of holiday golf but by the eighth hole the elements of fun and surprise have become threadbare and indeed, physically quite wearisome. With blind shots still to come on the tenth, fourteenth, and seventeenth holes, the club has now taken steps to reduce the dangers and perhaps tedium of some of these with the aid of equipment not available to

Gibson or Mackenzie. The early layouts paid some price for a more than usually dramatic and undulating site. The blindness of the Klondyke and Dell, however, engraving the spirit and personality of a bygone era of golf, are regarded as sacrosanct.

The sequence of the holes from the sixth through to the eighth, nevertheless, represents a fine series of steadily rising green sites in stepping-stone fashion on the way to the highest point of the course, the ninth tee—a very fine, mid-round climax introduced by Mackenzie. Recent alterations will return the sequence to Mackenzie's original format of a doglegged seventh hole out to sea, and a par-3 as the eighth. This will further strengthen the majesty of 'onwards and upwards' to the ninth tee position, now approached from behind rather than walking back up to it as previously.

The remainder of the layout is a fine piece of Mackenzie design, reworking some older Morris and Gibson green sites, and introducing four new holes to produce the full eighteen-hole course on the one side of the road. The sequence breaks the tonic axis with the eleventh, twelfth, thirteenth, and again at the sixteenth hole, so that the apparently rather repetitive, and crammed tenth, fourteenth, fifteenth and seventeenth holes do not pall from their parallelism. The eleventh, and the turn at the twelfth—entirely new holes—are a stroke of genius, a final refreshing push out to sea with the eleventh hole quietly transformed by the 180 degree turn, and the serene view back up the river estuary towards the old Liscannor bridge and castle ruins beyond. The layout turns at the thirteenth hole and again at right angles for the fourteenth from where the drama of the site is left behind. What remains is a most solid sequence of tough-looking holes to focus the attention on winning the match.

The only blemish to this series has been the sharing of the fourteenth and fifteenth holes

The par-5 second hole at Lahinch demonstrates how golf has interwoven itself into the fabric of everyday township life. (Photo by Paul Daley.)

of a semi-blind fairway, which is quite hard to credit to Mackenzie. These two holes have been recently prised apart on simple safety grounds and to improve visibility. But that vital element of fun and surprise is still the secret of Lahinch. The exhilaration of a true seaside course does not allow the rather aggressive urban scenery of the town of Lahinch itself, and the housing development creeping steadily the length of the Liscannor road—all too evidently confronting the homeward-bound golfer—to interfere with the enjoyment of the course.

Lahinch is as fine a piece of golfing terrain as anyone is likely to find. Its very drama produces most of the constraints on the layout; even the sea has devoured two of Mackenzie's greens. This comprehensive subject of the sequence, rhythm, interest and variety of movement in a golf course, only summarily sketched here, is more than an academic exercise to be undertaken behind the closed doors of architectural practices.

There is a value to identifying the reasons for greatness or weakness in a sequence of holes. It is the sequence rather than the single hole that influences the player's enjoyment or displeasure of a course, and which can go on to underpin reform and improvement. Curiously, the most-often talked about weakness of Lahinch—crossing the eighteenth hole over the fifth and sixth holes—is the one that players and members would least like to change. The club has adopted the safety formula of the London Underground: in refusing to dig up all of the curved platforms, they announce 'mind the gap' before every train enters the station. Likewise, Lahinch posts a heroic gentleman on top of the Klondyke to conduct play when it is safe to do so.

Splendour in the grass
Mike Keiser

And I have felt a presence that disturbs me with the joy
Of elevated thoughts; a sense sublime
Of something far more deeply interfused,
Whose dwelling is the light of setting suns,
And the round ocean and the living air,
And the blue sky, and in the mind of man:
A motion and a spirit, that impels
All thinking things, all objects of all thought,
And rolls through all things. Therefore am I still
A lover of the meadows and the woods,
And mountains; and of all that we behold
From this green earth; of all the mighty world
Of eye, and ear,—both what they half create,
And what perceive; well pleased to recognise
In nature and the language of the sense
The anchor of my purest thoughts, the nurse,
The guide, the guardian of my heart, and soul
Of all my moral being.

William Wordsworth,
from *Tintern Abbey* (1798)

First hole, Pacific Dunes, Oregon, USA. (Photo by Wood Sabold © Bandon Dunes Resort.)

Let us be serious about the poetry of a well-wrought golf course. Like a heart-stopping Wordsworth poem, it will be with us for all time, and his verse inspires us to look through his eyes at golf courses when the beauty of nature is crafted by human intervention.

A great golf course is 'nature perfected'. It is neither wholly natural nor can it be wholly unnatural or manufactured. A gifted golf architect, like an inspired poet, desires a creation that transforms nature by tricking the human eye into a perception of transcendent nature. Wordsworth called this 'the pleasure which the mind derives from the perception of similitude in dissimilitude'. A walk in the barren and vast sand hills of Nebraska is not nearly as compelling as a round of golf at Sand Hills Golf Club, and that conclusion will be likely shared by the non-golfer as well. As visually appealing as the purely natural can be, the sublime splendour of a carefully wrought string of fairways at daybreak is even more visually compelling.

The site of Bandon Dunes and Pacific Dunes 'disturbs me still with the joy of elevated thought'. And like the poet, both David Kidd and Tom Doak were similarly moved even though their two sites, adjoining 350 acres of sand dunes, could not have been more dissimilar.

David Kidd had the first opportunity to perfect nature. His goal was to build a links such as that which reared him—Machrihanish, in Scotland. To do so he had to convince me to remove all the shore pine trees and gorse that grew in great profusion, so much so that it was impossible to walk the site. With each new wave of tree cutting, more of the natural sandscapes and sea views were revealed. I readily admitted that each cutting made the site many, many times better. Perfecting nature, in Kidd's case, meant restoring the site to the condition it had enjoyed for hundreds of years when the Coquille and Coos tribes 'managed the estate'. Indeed, the modern-day Coquille and Coos tribe members are grateful to the resort and Kidd in particular for returning their centuries-old site to its prior state of natural grace.

David Kidd was a restorationist, while Tom Doak was a preservationist who sought to preserve the much more irregular, vertical, wind-blown, heaving peaks and valleys of his site as he created Pacific Dunes. He gambled on natural drainage rather than make even the smallest cuts in the site. And it worked. No heavy equipment was allowed on future playing areas for fear of unnatural compaction. Natural blowouts for bunkers, and flat tops for greens complexes were sought and preserved. Natural vegetation, grasses and even gorse were left untouched to preserve the wild, natural look. It is no surprise that so many of Tom's best golf holes were those that he and his splendid team first discovered and then preserved in all their natural glory.

Unbeknown to all but the two young architects, there was a quite remarkable beneficence involved in the completion of both golf routings, without which neither course would have been as successful. Kidd's final first routing included four interior holes that suffered from uninspired flatness. We were morose, but stuck. At that very moment the owner of the contiguous and wholly fenced 400 acres declared personal bankruptcy, enabling me to quickly purchase it. Kidd peered covetously over the fence and in time secured the gift of

ever happened before? David Kidd's Bandon Dunes championship eighth tee, facing due west, was recognised as the perfect championship tee location for Tom Doak's Pacific Dunes north-facing eighth hole—after construction of Pacific Dunes was completed.

The south-facing fourteenth hole, Pacific Dunes. (Photo by Wood Sabold © Bandon Dunes Resort.)

forty of those 400 acres which quickly became the fifth, sixth, seventh, and eighth holes at Bandon Dunes. Similarly, Doak's first routings for Pacific Dunes had two too many flat interior holes. The solution: a 'gift' of 500 yards of ocean frontage from the adjoining parcel to the north, which became the thirteenth and fourteenth holes. As Doak said in

gratitude: 'the hole [thirteenth] was just waiting for us in its natural state. All we had to do was grass it.'

Also unknown to both architects until a perspicacious observer noticed, was the odds-defying coincidence that both golf courses shared a tee. And it was for the same hole—the eighth—on both courses. When has that

Does it tempt?

Geoff Shackelford

When discussing the strategic merits of any design element, a simple question can settle the matter: does the placement, size, shape and character of the feature in question tempt a player into a bold shot that is out of character for the golfer? Should the answer be that the hazard does not tempt or tease, then the strategy will ultimately fail.

During course construction, architects and their associates often debate the size, location, angles and purpose of a hazard. The strategic designer only has to ask: is this hazard situated in such a way to tempt the player into flirting with or carrying this obstacle to gain some sort of advantage? Again, if the answer is no, the feature in question is of the penalising type and will fail to provide interesting golfing options.

Consider any of the world's most admired and copied hole designs. They are usually beautiful to look at and provide a difficult challenge for most players. However, their lasting beauty lies not in the number of azaleas running the length of the hole, or in the roads running near their greens. Instead, their enduring character relies on their ability to beguile, captivate, lure, woo, cause doubt, and in general, tempt the golfer into bold, sometimes unwise, play.

The first and best reference to the notion of temptation in course design came from the brilliant John Low in his *Concerning Golf* (1903): 'The true hazard should draw the player towards it, should invite the golfer to come as near as he dare to the fire without burning his fingers. The man who can afford to take risks is the man who should gain the advantage'.[14]

Temptation defines the Redan (North Berwick), the Road hole (Old Course, St. Andrews), a Cape (Royal North Devon), any interesting short par-4, the back nine at Augusta National (prior to 1998), and even the difficult sixteenth hole at Cypress Point. These are all difficult holes, but their challenge can be overcome. Each remains timeless because of its ability to seduce and lure the greatest players of every generation into unwise plays, while providing enough of a safe route that could avoid disaster if the player would swallow their pride. Each of their options for play seems attractive.

Alister Mackenzie noted in discussing Cypress Point's sixteenth green, that 'water

holes should tempt, not torture'. The successful architecture of this beautiful par-3 is not simply the grandeur of the shot over the clear blue sea. In fact, the hole would be considered too difficult and not particularly interesting if it were not for the space provided to play safe. Also, the closer the golfer places his shot to the green, the riskier the shot becomes. The experienced golfer knows this. Over time he becomes more aware that the safe play is the percentage play, rarely leading to worse than a tolerable four.

The prospect of this lay-up sanctuary only makes the temptation to shoot at the green even greater. Weighing on his mind, he desperately wants to experience the accompanying rush of excitement when the ball lands safely on the large, forgiving putting surface. And yet, he knows he can break eighty-five for the first time with three bogies coming in; meaning, he really doesn't need to be overly reckless. What to do?

Temptation explains the overwhelming popularity of the Redan hole at North Berwick in Scotland, and why golfers never grow tired of seeing yet another rendition of

this classic par-3 model. However, some clumsy attempts at replication lack tempting character when they pose only one option for the golfer: to play to the green opening and hope their ball funnels near the hole. Such a one-dimensional Redan lacks the option to make a direct assault on the hole. Though not a bad thing, different options make each possibility that much more tempting, assuming each alternative presents potential benefits. If one option is too simple or too obvious not to try, then the architect has not created lasting strategic charm. Clearly, there is no temptation when the solution is too obvious.

The 'Redan' second at Somerset Hills, though a fascinating one-shotter on one of the world's most original designs, fails as a tempting hole. The raised face atop the green's fronting bunker combines with the slope of the putting surface to render the direct shot at the hole impossible. The only route is to the right-hand opening, with the player hoping to use the slope to gain a twenty-foot birdie putt.

The emergence of advanced equipment and longer flying golf balls threatens the character

Having safely laid up from Cypress Point's sixteenth tee, this is what remains to be negotiated. Most likely a safe bogey will result. (Photo by Neil Crafter.)

OPPOSITE: Meanwhile, the brave, the bold, or the foolish, may submit to the temptation and try to reach the green. For most golfers, it will require your 'Sunday best'. (Photo by Neil Crafter.)

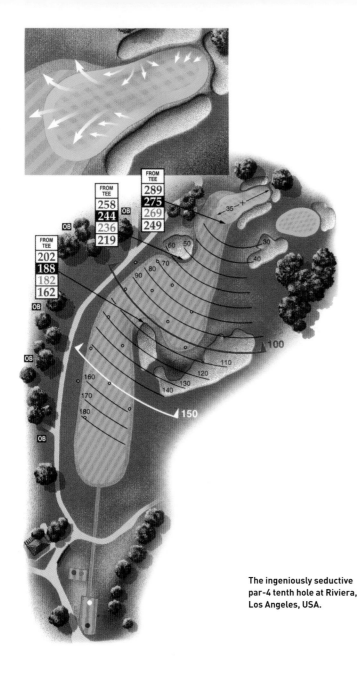

The ingeniously seductive par-4 tenth hole at Riviera, Los Angeles, USA.

of the game because it puts a dent in the tempting qualities of many great holes, or in some cases, eliminates temptation altogether.

Consider that just six years ago during the 1996 Masters, we watched Greg Norman and Nick Faldo dissect the approach to Augusta National's par-5 thirteenth green for almost ten minutes. As viewers, we thought Faldo was debating whether to go for the green in two. It transpired he had no concerns about reaching the green, but instead was trying to select the proper club and the wisest line of play. He was also considering his opponent's plight and waiting for Norman, who was 'away' with the honour.

Norman's predicament was even more exciting to observe. His ball sat on pine needles, the green within reach, and the lie acceptable enough for a player of his calibre to feel he could strike the shot solidly. He wanted to go for the green. His lead was gone; he wanted an eagle three to reinvigorate his game, even though a birdie four would have been sufficient. Norman grabbed the club needed to reach the green, but his caddie, Tony Navarro, openly disagreed and ulti-

mately convinced Norman that a lay-up would still provide a good chance at four.

When it was all over, both players made birdie, but not until after they were teased, tortured and tempted by all the options the hole presented. The architecture combined with the pressure of the tournament to provide the ultimate strategic battle. Meanwhile, defending champion Ben Crenshaw was in Butler Cabin commentating for CBS television. After the compelling battle between Faldo, Norman and Augusta's thirteenth had concluded, Crenshaw said: 'I just can't get over the brilliance of this hole. Every year it just absolutely wrings you out with the decisions it forces.'

During the 2001 Masters final round, Tiger Woods and Phil Mickelson were battling for the lead. Both hit an 8-iron into the thirteenth green. Though their talent to hit such bold and long tee shots under pressure was impressive, the hole's ability to tempt was gone—a victim of technology. There was no question that the green was within reach for both players, relegating the pin location to an afterthought. From each player's perspective, their opponents' predicament and lie, the trickling creek, the shape of shot required and the number of holes remaining in the round—once vital considerations—were no longer factors. Technology helped eliminate the best attributes of the most tempting hole in the world.

However, as discouraging as the technology trend appears to be, the architect must still consider the majority of players. He must ask himself questions when considering the role of every contour he creates, every bunker he places, every water feature he locates, every green he designs, and every decoy he puts in front of the player. Is the creation of this feature producing tempting scenarios? Is it presenting equally inviting options? Is the hazard angled in such a way that the player considers biting off more than he can chew? Is it providing enough width for the safe play, while keeping the risky play within reach to give the player enticing options?

Whether it is a corner hole location, an alternate fairway, or the most basic dogleg par-4 imaginable, the element of temptation should drive every feature the strategy-minded architect creates. The architect should ask

himself whether the location and size of the hazard conspires with the overall width of the hole to lure the player into the daring play, while also dangling an equally tempting safe play at him. He should analyse whether the green is designed to pose the same questions with regard to provocative hole positions versus safer locations.

Posing these tempting quandaries not only creates timeless championship golf, but also fosters memorable situations for golfers of all abilities. They are the types of unforgettable decision-making thrills that we all enjoy, and the kind of compelling golf that we hope golf architecture will tempt us with.

Another view of the seemingly innocent tenth hole at Riviera. The preferred approach angle is from the left-hand side of the fairway. Aggressive right-handed golfers with a powerful fade often attempt to drive the green. (Photo by Neil Crafter.)

Democratic strategic design

Tim Liddy and Tom Climo

Today's game of golf is relatively simple: drive 300 yards, select a pitching wedge, then fly the ball at the pin. Golf is becoming a game of non-choice. It is no longer the person who knows the value of each of his clubs, and who can work out when it is proper to lay one and when to play another that succeeds at the game. Rather, it is the power hitter getting so far down the fairway that he has a privileged ease for the remainder of the hole. Against this unfortunate development, we recommend a new approach for golf course architecture that will neutralise the power hitter's privilege. We call it 'democratic strategic' design.

The ills of capitalism: golf course technology

'What the market will bear' is a commercial principle referring to the price a manufacturer can get for his product, as distinct from the actual cost of its manufacture. Driven by supply and demand, the demand-side of the market is influenced by the prospect of influencing consumers through advertising. In golf, we have a gullible set of consumers. Possessing a perfectly sound set of clubs, our golfer will gladly trade-up to gain an additional two yards off the tee, or land two yards closer to the pin. The effects of advertising are heightened when professional players on tour display their skill while adorning a cap, ball, or bag with a golf company logo. This practice has been going on for years, and is part of the lure of being attracted to the game. In just the last two years, tee shots alone have increased over twenty yards on the PGA tour. At the 2000 Millennium Open Championship at St. Andrews, the winner never visited a bunker in four rounds of tournament golf. Fly the ball at the pin, seventy-two times! The extra distance off the tee now part of the new technology accompanying golf has made the St. Andrews Old Course, and the philosophy behind its design redundant.

Architects need to be better

St. Andrews and strategic design in golf are synonymous. We've all learned the wisdom of golf course design, courtesy of Tom Simpson. He wrote: 'St. Andrews is the ideal to aim at in all golf course construction [it] is difficult, not because bunkers are placed to catch inaccurate shots, but because the results of misadventure is to make the next shot infinitely more difficult than it would otherwise have been.'[15]

We can no longer expect long hitters to drive into short bunkers. A simple prescription for deterring the long hitters is to extend the yardage from tee to green. However, where could this response end: 500-yard par-4s and 700-yard par-5s? Taking golf design into the direction of length only is a disservice to the ideal of strategic design inherited from the founders of golf course architecture. We are against such an approach, finding it an undemocratic disservice to the non-expert player, and unsatisfactory because it requires no imagination.

Curing the ills with democracy

In a world where the expert golfer gains an extra twenty yards off the tee, his adulation of golf course technology is understandable. Where the non-expert is still spraying 180-yard drives, we have to look at the consequences of extending yardage on him. Make no mistake, despite lack of swing strength, swing pattern, swing finish, or whatever, it is our daily hacker, the average golfer, who drives the sales numbers enabling the golf technology industry to be an industry. It is his purchasing power that builds private and public clubs, keeps them in existence, not the dilet-

tantes on tour. Yet the very industry the average player supports does not focus its efforts on him, but upon those who least need it. Political revolutions have been founded on more equitable arrangements. It is time to think about introducing the world of golf to a wonderful concept called democracy: allowing the majority to dictate the manner in which golf is played instead of depending on the kings and princes of the game. As the formidable nineteenth century US political and military figure, General Schenck, has instructed: 'Put not your trust in kings and princes. Three of a kind will take them both.'[16]

Rather than making a golf course harder for the average player in the likely unsuccessful attempt to also make it harder for the touring pro, let's take our philosophy in a different direction. Let's make golf courses more manageable for the non-expert, and subject the expert player to severe penalties for their style of play. Fly the ball at the pin; take this! Drive 320 yards; take that! Here, a dramatic set of options become available at a variety of locations on the golf course that will cause concern for the expert, while at the same time, owing to

lack of skill, have very little effect on the non-expert. At the heart of democracy in golf course design is the urgency to re-examine the manner in which golf is played by experts and non-experts, keeping in mind the disproportionate advantage golf course technology gives the expert. Compensation must be made in favour of the average golfer so that design ingredients are applied that work directly against the expert player while neutralised because of lack of skill in the average player.

In this way, golf returns to the tradition of providing an equitable level of play for all skill levels. Just because you hit the ball a ton, you shouldn't be spared the same second shot challenge facing the short hitter.

Democratic strategic design

Democratic strategic design is in contrast to conventional strategic design. Figures 1 and 2 provide a quick sketch of the basic concept. Figure 1 depicts the manner in which hazards and angles are currently used, and includes the usual narrowing approach to the green, all of which goes to penalise the average player. The expert flies the bunker then has the

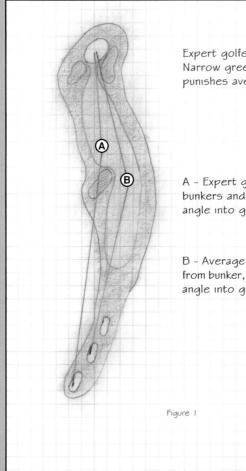

Expert golfer flies shot to cup. Narrow green approach only punishes average golfer.

A - Expert golfer carries fairway bunkers and receives preferred angle into green.

B - Average player must play away from bunker, which leaves a tougher angle into green over bunker.

Figure 1

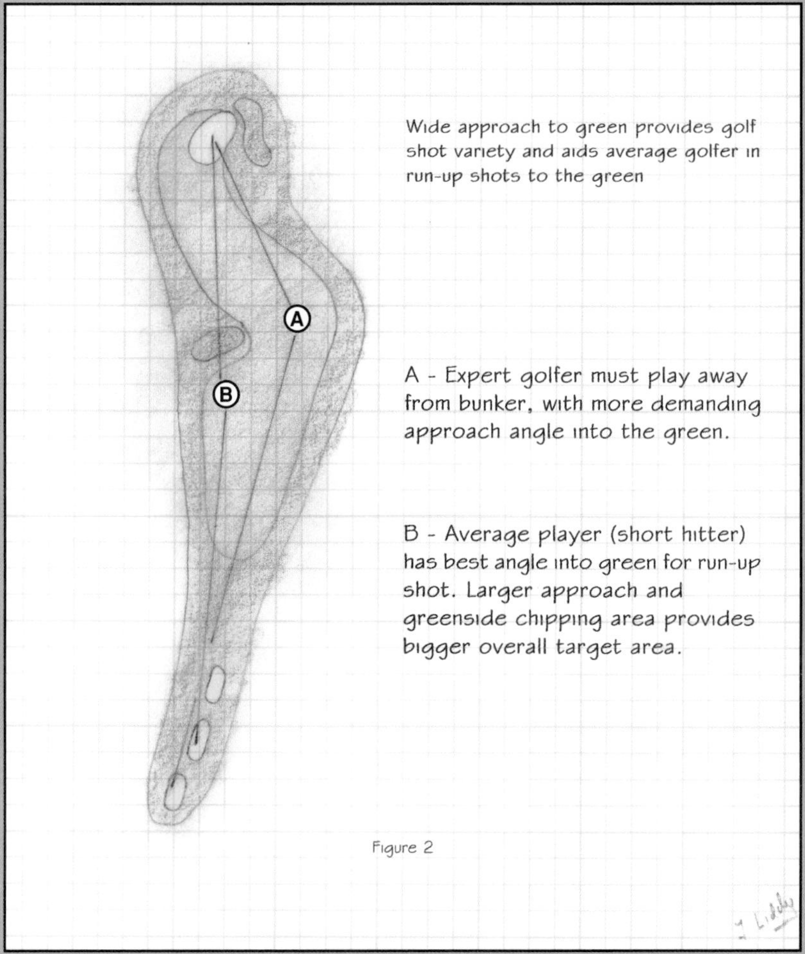

Wide approach to green provides golf shot variety and aids average golfer in run-up shots to the green

A - Expert golfer must play away from bunker, with more demanding approach angle into the green.

B - Average player (short hitter) has best angle into green for run-up shot. Larger approach and greenside chipping area provides bigger overall target area.

Figure 2

preferred angle into the green. Figure 2 remedies this abuse of power by setting a bunker where the expert is likely to land, forcing him to an in-fairway drive, and harder approach to the green. The average golfer drives short of the bunker to win the preferred angle. Although still left with a long iron shot, the average golfer now has the better approach, while the expert, although still left with a short iron shot, now has the more severe one. Then, for final good measure, a widening into the green is provided to add variety and aid to the average golfer.

To the untrained eye, Figures 1 and 2 appear virtually identical, yet the effects of a slight difference can be revolutionary. Just as inserting 'for the people' instead of 'for the King' dramatises the events in America of 1776, the insertion of holes designed around majority play will lead to fairer, more playable golf courses. That such an approach will also nullify the power weapons of the touring professional, rendering him unable to any longer humble a golf course, is not an inconsiderable side benefit.

Earlier we had occasion to use Tom Simpson's observation about golf course construction and St. Andrews. Simpson also made another salient observation even if he was seventy years ahead of the problem facing golf course design from recent technological advancements. He said: 'It is necessary to point out certain mischievous tendencies that can influence the progress and spirit of the game, tendencies which in the long run, reduce the imaginative element of our courses to a lower level than they should rightly possess, and have the effect of diverting the poetry of golf into less desirable channels.'

Isn't it bad enough with residential housing and single row irrigation, that fairways have been narrowed and straightened to resemble bowling alleys? Now, owing to the predominance of the power hitter on tour, we are facing the proposition that the solution to this dilemma is length. We can think of no worse solution. Instead, we propose a return to the roots of the game, to the very player that has always made golf possible and great, the average player. We propose design techniques made to facilitate and improve the average golfer's chance of par while at the same time generating untold challenges to those that drive the ball too far. We are in polar opposition to the long-standing and accepted hypothesis of Dr Alister Mackenzie: 'Long drivers should be rewarded, and as a general rule have greater latitude, and not less than short drivers.'[17] Mackenzie's hypothesis is undemocratic and indicates to golf course architects that we should favour those already favored. It would be like giving the fastest professional sprinter in the world a head start in a 100-metre event against a geriatric. It is wrong, and we wish no part in this elitism.

Democratic strategic design can meet present and anticipated challenges from tour and average player alike through imagination not length. Ultimately, the profession of golf course architecture rises or falls on our ability to be innovative and creative. Disagree as we do with Mackenzie on the earlier point, he is nonetheless absolutely right when he said: 'The ideal golf hole is one that is pleasurable to all classes of golfers.'[18]

OPPOSITE: **Eighth hole, Chisholm Trail Golf Course, Kansas, USA. (Photo courtesy of Ronald Whitten.)**

Restoration at Bethpage Black

Rees Jones

When the governing body of golf in America, the United States Golf Association (USGA), begins to look for sites for its national championship, it often seeks out tried and true, classic courses with a rich history and tradition. And because these courses have been played for decades, chances are they will need to be brought up to standard for the United States Open Golf Championship.

It is my good fortune and challenge to have worked on six of these tournament courses in recent years. In fact, the golf press refers to me as the 'Open Doctor', a nickname that I seem to have inherited because my father Robert Trent Jones did quite a bit of upgrading of Open courses himself.

Each of my six US Open renovations has had its own issues, history and goals: The Country Club in Massachusetts (1988); Hazeltine in Minnesota (1991); Baltusrol in New Jersey (1993); Congressional Blue near Washington, D.C. (1997); Pinehurst No. 2 in North Carolina (1999); and Bethpage Black in New York (2002). Four of them had hosted the Open in years past. Some of the courses needed extensive work; some required only a modest amount of refinement. All of them were great jobs, but Bethpage Black was a special case. It was history in the making.

Bethpage is a publicly owned golf course, the first ever people's course to host a US Open. When the USGA offered me the job of overseeing the restoration, I quickly accepted, just as I accepted their suggestion that I donate my services. I considered working on this project more of an honour than a job. Golf history was being made there in June 2002, and I wanted to be a part of it.

Designed by A. W. Tillinghast in 1936, the Black is a long, tough, demanding layout intended by its designer to be of championship calibre. However, through the years, many of its distinctive features had been lost due to storms, natural deterioration, and limited maintenance budgets. When the USGA first looked at Bethpage as a potential site for the Open, Tillinghast's fundamental design was still intact. But it was clear to everyone that if it were to withstand the onslaught of the modern pro with his arsenal of new equipment, it needed to be lengthened, updated, and restored.

My task was to bring the Black Course—the most difficult of five courses in this park complex owned and operated by the State of New York—to tournament conditions without destroying its essential character as a public course.

OPPOSITE: **The climactic par-4 eighteenth hole at Bethpage Black, New York, USA. (Photo by Brian Morgan ©)**

Every restoration for a major championship is different. At Congressional, much of the work we did for the 1997 Open involved fairway regrading. We kept most of the original routing and redid all the greens, tees, and bunkers. At Pinehurst, we rebuilt the greens, expanded the surfaces to their original size and enlarged the closely-mowed areas surrounding Donald Ross's famous crowned greens. Players in the 1999 Open had several shot options to recover when their shot missed the green. Before the 1988 Open at The Country Club, we studied the changes made since Willie Campbell designed it in 1893. We eliminated features that were out of character and restored others, particularly the greens, to their former size and style. At Hazeltine, we rebunkered the entire golf course and added length. Baltusrol was restored by adding length and bunkers to provide the challenge for modern equipment. It is near my home in New Jersey; I make numerous visits every year, refining every little detail.

So how did we decide what to do at Bethpage Black? It was invaluable in this case to be a life-long student of Tillinghast's architectural style. Having read all the available material, played many of his designs under tournament conditions (such as Winged Foot and Baltusrol), and restored five of his courses for tournament play, I felt a kindred spirit with this giant of American golf architecture. I was familiar with his personality, his design characteristics, and his philosophy of giving the golfer shot options. I felt instinctively what to do and what not to do with this brilliant layout.

The superb original routing of the holes had remained unchanged, as had most of the green surfaces. (In this respect, Bethpage, as a public course, was unique: there had been no overreaching green committees through the years constantly fiddling with the course). What had changed were Tillinghast's trademark bunkers. Years of wear and tear, low maintenance budgets, storms, and hundreds of thousands of rounds of golf had taken their toll. Once we had identified the issues, we went to work.

We carefully studied photographs from the archives including an aerial shot of Bethpage Black taken in 1938. The beautifully sculpted bunkers created with grassy tongues and rounded noses with sharp edges had lost their form and elegance. They lacked definition. Some of the bunkers had been abandoned or had caved in during heavy rains and were left to become grassy slopes. In other cases, as to the right of the second green, one large bunker had become three or four small shapeless bunkers. (One 'old timer' that we talked to still wistfully remembers how these bunkers once looked.) Behind the fourteenth green, we discovered a puzzling bunker clearly not in the Tillinghast style. Investigation revealed it had been added a decade or so ago, to catch errant shots to the green and therefore speed up play.

We rebuilt every fairway bunker on the course except the large one on the seventh hole. In every case, we painstakingly restored the characteristic Tillinghast features of noses, fingers, and bays. We also moved several of the fairway bunkers forward to better serve their original intent of penalising errant shots, especially in light of the huge distances professionals are hitting their drivers these days.

In the case of the greenside bunkers, we wanted to restore the penal character that Tillinghast intended. To do this, we moved

most of them closer to the putting surfaces and swept them up to the green at an angle steep enough to be a real challenge for even the best sand players. We actually sent the construction crew to nearby Winged Foot to study the authentically maintained Tillinghast 'flashed' bunker style there. The sand in the bunkers will probably be soft during the tournament, making recovery shots more difficult if the ball hangs on the steep slope of the bunker face. If this sounds too severe, bear in mind that the modern professional will be hitting into the greens with a much shorter club than his 1930s counterpart. And when the tournament is over, the sand can be packed and therefore be less treacherous for the public player.

When we assessed the greens, we decided that less modification was preferable. We did very little other than to slightly expand some (holes three, eight, fifteen and seventeen) to give the USGA more hole locations. To create a tougher finish, we shrank the size of the putting surface of the eighteenth to half the original size. We left Tillinghast's contours alone, realising that the greens would be enough of a challenge with stimpmeter readings of a fast twelve or thirteen. Even the best putters will have to come to grips with putting surfaces that have subtle, sometimes indiscernible, dips and rolls.

In general, we added 350 yards to the course, a luxury afforded by the generous acreage in Bethpage State Park. Bethpage is now the longest course in US Open history—another step taken to address the issue of advances in equipment technology. By changing the par-5 seventh hole to a par-4, we lowered par from seventy-one to seventy, therefore diminishing the par-5 advantage for the longer hitters.

We maintained the Tillinghast concept, typical of golf course architecture and construction during the Depression, of utilising the rolling topography of Bethpage State Park to site greens and tees on elevations and letting the valleys become fairways. This creates a number of interesting stances even for the accomplished golfer, which we did not change.

There is still virtually no water on Bethpage Black. With its massive, bold, masterfully sculpted bunkers, the Black is all about sand.

Our overall philosophy is in tune with that of the original designer, which is to make the player plan their strategy on the tee. Like Pine Valley, which Tillinghast knew well and almost surely was competing with at Bethpage, it is a penal, thinking person's course. I like to think that we enhanced that style and intent. I believe we have met the challenge of creating a true test of championship golf.

Once the Open is over, can the average public golfer manage a decent score on the renovated Black? Probably not. Actually, they rarely could! For many years the Black has a huge sign by the first tee that reads

WARNING: THE BLACK COURSE IS AN EXTEMEMLY DIFFICULT COURSE WHICH WE RECOMMEND ONLY FOR HIGHLY SKILLED GOLFERS.

Tillinghast was able to get away with creating this 'monster' because Bethpage State Park boasts four other courses, giving plenty of options for all levels of public golfers. Interestingly, the Black is the only one of the five that requires walking—no carts allowed.

So any passionate golfer who has the patience to sleep in his car, or line up at 3 a.m., and has thirty-one dollars in his pocket, can play one of the world's greatest courses.

The USGA paid for the renovation and it is truly a gift to the public player. I also consider my work there a gift to the game that I have loved all my life.

OPPOSITE: **The second green and its surrounds at Bethpage Black. (Photo by Bruce Strober.)**

Creating the strategic tee-shot

Jeff Brauer

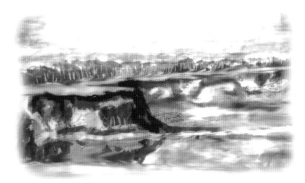

One historic golfing constant is the desire for lower scores. To most, this means buying a better game. For serious players, this also means playing strategically, which has obvious cost advantages over high tech equipment, and probably better odds of success. My firm incorporates strategic design features for this perhaps small and appreciative audience.

Hole strategies should usually be quickly obvious, and provide at least two tee shot choices—to force decisions about obtaining the most advantageous fairway position for the approach shot, and selecting the best shot pattern to get there. Par-4s dominate because we can establish this architectural relationship in the highly efficient minimum of two shots.

Serious golfers use all available tools to maximise success and minimise failure. They incorporate wind, ground slope, and, if capable, shot pattern, to gain distance, find fairways and avoid hazards. If target areas angle to the right then fades find them more easily. The fortunate golfer who can shape shots is able to utilise the axis of the fairway. As is often the case, playing good defence wins championships in all sports.

Generally, we provide wide fairways for more and better play options. We locate hazards considering natural features, inherent difficulty, and temptation. Hazards should be in play, but allow recovery to encourage bold shots over safer ones away from key hazards.

The strongest strategic hazards encroach upon the fairway slightly, requiring a combination of distance, carry, and shot pattern to avoid. Generally, we place hazards where they occur naturally or, if artificial, in order to provide a basic tee shot challenge. Hazards that provide a strategic challenge include: a carry hazard, just short of the landing area; a flanking hazard in the normal landing area; or a pinching hazard, in the longest portion of the landing area.

Ideally, fairway and hazard design work together to create premium landing areas that present a clear advantage to the thinking golfer. This occurs by creating a shorter approach (always an advantage), a better angle (usually a frontal opening without hazards in between green contours assisting the

OPPOSITE: Sixth hole, Colbert Hills, Kansas, USA. When downwind, the bunker fronting the left-hand edge of the green produces the dilemma of how far to carry over the fairway bunker. The elongated fairway bunker effectively asks the same question of all golfers, regardless of their length capacity. Given the widening disparity of tee-shot lengths in today's golfing population, it is becoming increasingly necessary to elongate fairway hazards. (Photo by Mike Klemme/Golffoto ©)

approach), an upslope facing one side of the fairway to help stop their shot, preferred stance and lie (usually a level or uphill lie to make the shot easier), better vision to the green (not as important given yardage books, but still providing psychological comfort), and taking major hazards out of play on either shot.

We ensure that most holes are strategically based, with an emphasis on reward rather than penalty, as these play well for all golfers. We mix in old-fashioned penal holes and dramatic heroic holes for variety. All players like the occasional challenge of a difficult shot, provided it's not a steady diet.

We create these strategic tee shot relationships with just a few basic concepts. Even if using natural features and a variety of hazards, there are infinite possibilities for the final, unique designs. Most tee shots fall into the following basic categories.

The position paradox tee shot
A 'damned if you do and damned if you don't' situation, where you really want to hit a portion of the fairway, but that position is elusive and guarded by an equally difficult hazard that you don't want to be in.

Like the bully, an architect tells his victim, 'Do what I command, or face the consequences'. The architect can spell out this scenario visually, or conceal it perhaps by dictating the best angle through varying receptivity of green contours.

Often these holes require a heroic tee shot, with a strategic carry hazard. While they are strong holes conceptually, they disproportionately reward length, so most balanced courses shouldn't overdo these. They work well in a prevailing downwind, tempting the golfer to carry the hazards more, increasing the value of an open front green, and typically reducing backspin on the approach.

The variable strategy tee shot
Here, strategies vary daily according to wind and/or pin locations by dictating play left off the tee one day, and right the next for maximum advantage. The design usually requires wide double fairways with staggered bunkering, intruding on both sides of the fairway at different distances, and large greens to create a variety of pin locations.

While not particularly difficult, they form the backbone of the course, and their strength is that they play slightly differently every day. These holes work well over a variety of wind directions and lengths, and staggered bunkering works especially well on par-5s, where play among differently skilled golfers tends to spread out.

The democratic tee shot

These offer approximately equal choices, allowing players a way to play based on their relative strengths of power, finesse, accuracy, or on their preferred shot pattern. Like choosing between a light comedy or a drama, your choice depends on your mood. Often, the fairway must have no hazards, or hazards on both sides to make it democratic.

The diminishing returns tee shot

With gradually diminishing fairway width, the golfer must judge between the advantages of a shorter approach against the possibility of missing the fairway and play accordingly. On long holes, the advantage of length is usually too strong, and on short holes many players prefer to be farther back for a full shot with maximum backspin, so these often work best on medium-length par-4s and reachable

OPPOSITE: **Seventh hole, Colbert Hills. The staggered sand hazards, combined with the fairway angling left encourages a soft draw (right-handed golfers) to reach the fairway, while providing hazards for golfers of varying hitting strength. The bunker pattern and required shot-pattern are completely opposite from the previous Colbert Hills hole, balancing shot requirements. The holes run in the same direction.**

ABOVE LEFT: **Fourth hole, Cowboys Golf Club, Grapevine, Texas, USA. At this short par-4, two fairway bunkers pinch in just behind the normal landing area. One obvious option is to lay-up. Another is to get close to the green, which ensures a better approach angle for some pin locations.**

LEFT: **Fourth hole, Ridgeview Ranch, Planco, Texas. The staggered 'hazards' on this fairway include a natural rock shelf short left, and a clump of trees beyond the landing area on the right. Both must be avoided to gain a clear shot to the green. Any carry bunker on the outside of a dogleg, like this one, usually needs a strong hazard on the inside to make it come into play. (Photos by Mike Klemme/Golffoto ©)**

At Trails of Frisco, Texas, the seventh hole is a reachable par-5 with a double fairway. The adventurous can opt for the 'challenge' fairway, thereby avoiding the dogleg and reducing the hole's length by forty yards. The prevailing wind is into the player's face, making the choice of tee-shot line far from straight forward. (Photo by Phil Arnold/ Golfscape photography ©)

par-5s. The spin question comes into play more for downwind holes than holes into the wind.

The dictator tee shot

These penalising tee shots come in three varieties: The 'cut em off at the pass' tee shot. Occasionally, and more frequently with current restrictions on stream use, a creek crosses the fairway just past the landing area, usually about 300 yards from the tee, so that it prevents a full tee shot. The tease and difficulty arises when the hole plays downwind, or is severely downhill. This complicates club selection, for it is necessary to get as close to the stream as possible without actually going in.

The forced carry tee shot

A creek or man-made hazard may require a forced carry to attain the fairway, without any openings or angles to provide strategic interest, if crossing between the tee and landing area. Most golfers dislike forced 'lay-ups' and

carries, making each of these sometimes necessary, but rarely intentional in design.

The 'we're surrounded' tee shot

These offer no choice other than placing the tee shot in a restricted area between a narrow line of trees in the landing area, a narrow line of trees just off the tee, with a wide landing area, a 'bottleneck' of bunkers pinching the landing area, or an 'island fairway' virtually surrounded by sand or water.

Strategic considerations include picking shot patterns to avoid difficulty through hook or fade, height and roll control, and so on. A less difficult approach shot may compensate for tee shot difficulty.

The heroic tee shot

This shot gives the option of driving well over a daring hazard, and is the true 'action thriller' of golf design. Most courses should have at least one. These occur as: 'Cape' holes, with a diagonal carry over lake or similar hazard, or as challenge fairways, where an alternate fairway straightens and/or shortens the hole significantly, yielding a distance advantage as reward.

The open field tee shot

Seemingly little strategy is required, but sometimes creates a delayed penalty by virtue of design of the green. These holes work well early in the round, or on holes with a difficult approach shot.

The 'fairway is its own hazard' tee shot

This is an open field fairway with a catch. Fairway grades, like cross-slope dictating play to the high side, or moguls in selected areas, can dictate play to limited areas.

The battlefield tee shot

A battlefield inspired fairway of randomly strewn craters provides a change of pace if used sparingly. Golfers can find these a bit unnerving as distances are often deceptive, and fairways partially concealed.

The forced curve tee shot

Ground features suggest a curved shot without it being forced. Well-placed trees can dictate a flight pattern. Golf shots reach maximum curvature, both horizontally and vertically, at about two-thirds through its flight

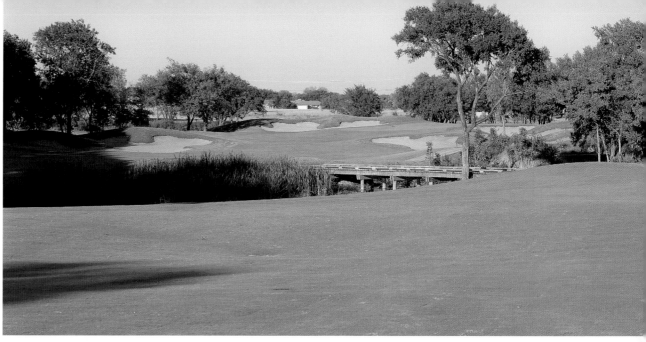

path. A fairway encroaching tree 180-200 yards from the tee allows players to create shots around it to premium areas. These holes should have especially wide fairways to allow all players a chance to hit some part of the fairway regardless of shot pattern.

Of course, there are other considerations in designing holes for strategic tee shot variety: interest, and challenge. Certainly aesthetics plays a role, as do environmental issues, tree protection, safety, speed of play, and the superintendent's maintenance concerns. The latter often leads to narrower fairways.

Many golf courses call for fourteen long tee shots. There are many more distinct concepts and sub-concepts than there are tee shots on any one course. With other concepts both broad and site specific, and an infinite number of subtle variations, it seems a shame that so many courses have so many blandly repetitive tee shots. A course can easily be designed to eliminate repetition, except perhaps mirror concepts to balance shot patterns requirements. It will prove to be a more interesting course than most, if it does.

ABOVE: The opening hole at Whitestone, Benbrook, Texas gets the round off to an attractive start. The creek and two fairway bunkers form an effective 'bottleneck' for the second shot to this par-5. (Photo courtesy of Jeff Brauer.)

LEFT: Ninth hole at Wild Wing (Avocet Course) Myrtle Beach, South Carolina, USA. This is an example of a 'variable' strategy hole with a double fairway, where your tee-shot should be aimed towards the fairway opposite the pin location to enable the best approach angle to the green. (Photo by Mike Klemme/Golffoto ©)

Putting the terrain to work at Maple Country Club

Takeaki Kaneda

In contrast to other parts of the world blessed with abundant open spaces, more than eighty per cent of Japan's terrain is hilly or mountainous. In fact, the infinitely varied work of golf course designing has to be conducted in Japan in an environment that differs greatly from that of other countries, not only in the geographical but also in the legal sense.

While it is commonly accepted that golf course architecture largely depends on the available terrain, we also apply our knowledge and enthusiasm to the task, and are fortunate to have the valuable backing of our country's highly developed civil engineering sector.

Using as our model a course that has been described as 'a work of God', we first try to understand the potential of the site. Then during the design stage, we do our best to ensure that the completed course will reflect our technical capability and overall judgment based on our golfing proficiency, experience, and aesthetic sense.

The 357 yards eleventh hole at Maple County Club was given the name Warlock-Knowe, which in Gaelic means 'hill where magicians meet'. However, in Japanese it is known as 'Majo-no-oka' [witch's hill]. On top of the hill on the right, 180 yards beyond the teeing ground, is a rock just over one yard in diameter—the only rock on the property. When I first saw it, I felt it could be the tomb of the witch of this so named 'witch's hill', as it reminded me of a similar-looking stone in Dornoch, Scotland, called the 'tomb of the last witch'.

The areas marked as A and B on the left along the boundary previously consisted of marshland covered with a thick growth of kumazasa bamboo. I felt strongly that these areas should be made into hazards, and for this purpose, I tried a number of different routings before deciding upon the final layout. A bonus was the view from the tee that includes wild cherry trees to the right, and Mt. Iwate directly behind them.

The tee shot must carry the valley up ahead. For players unable to manage this, an option is to fall short of the bunker on the right. My initial intention was to turn areas A and B into difficult hazards by having them covered with indigenous bamboo. Area A, which forms a valley about eight yards deep, would be a 'sea of bamboo', and area B, about three yards deep, would also have a thick covering of bamboo. This hole obliges the player to decide whether to be ambitious or to play safe with both tee and second shot. Currently, both areas are covered with grass and do not present a hazard, but in the future when members' technical levels have improved, it would be an interesting idea to reintroduce the bamboo.

Members call area A the 'Big Witch' and area B, the 'Small Witch'. This is fine with me, because it's more or less what I intended. As there is unused space of about fifty-five yards behind the tee, in future it might be possible to move the tee backward and thus enhance the hole. Following the Scottish custom, all holes (this is a nineteen-hole course) have nicknames.

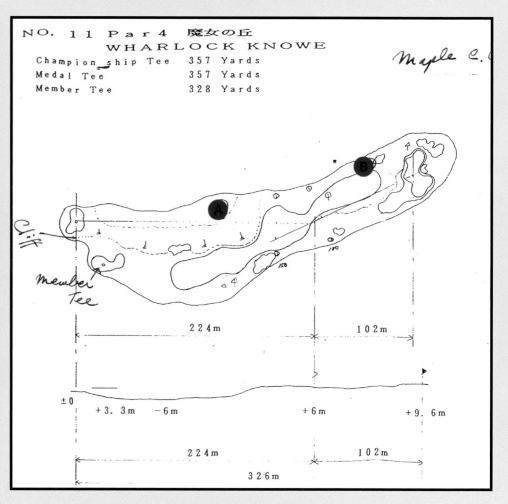

The most beautiful course in the World

Michael Wolveridge

There can be few more pleasurable moments in golf than those opening minutes of anticipation and camaraderie which accompany the walk down the opening hole of a fine links, especially after a good tee shot. The feel of springy seaside turf underfoot, a whiff of bracing air on a fresh breezy morning, early banter between friends, and the prospect of an optimistic assault on a layout not yet given the opportunity to intimidate or draw blood are fine things to experience. Charles Dickens's genial Mr Pickwick might have said, 'Here is a golf course, let's have a game'.

While links golf has been my primordial golf experience, over the past forty years I have come to experience the sensory delights of a wholly other type of terrain and climate becoming deeply involved in the design and building of some fifty golf courses in tropical locations. Having in golf, I fancy, 'seen it all twice', I firmly believe that a game of golf taken early on a tropical morning, especially with a favourite local caddy alongside, can make even the company of a playing partner a distraction. The exotic pleasure of being part of the sights and sounds of the local village waking to a moist, warm morning, has to be experienced to be believed. It is likely the only time one might allow Mark Twain to get away with his wicked suggestion that golf is a good walk spoiled.

My introduction to the game in Indonesia came unexpectedly in 1968 with an invitation from the office of the Director of Tourism to attend the opening ceremony of the new Bali International Airport, and to look for sites which might be suitable for a golf resort or two. General Suharto had come to power in 1966, and had appointed a trusted friend General Subroto as his new tourist director. Subroto was possibly Indonesia's best golfer on a four handicap, and it is significant that Peter Thomson, a five-time winner of the Open championship and a pioneer of the Far East circuit, had played his part in introducing Subroto to our firm, following a memorable series of exhibitions he and the General had recently played throughout the archipelago. They played on makeshift layouts at military bases, freshly mowed nine-hole layouts, and over the three or four established eighteen-hole

OPPOSITE: **Proud village people turn up for caddie training at Bali Handara, Indonesia. (Photo courtesy of Michael Wolveridge.)**

OPPOSITE: **Lake 'A' while under construction. (Photo courtesy of Michael Wolveridge.)**

clubs in a country of some 190 million people. The rounds re-kindled considerable enthusiasm for golf in Indonesia in those fledgling years of the Suharto regime.

With the opening ceremony out of the way, the next few days were spent exploring Bali with local officials and visiting sites which might become available, though my guides were horrified when they learned at the amount of land a golf course can require. Leaving the beaten track, I saw first hand the stunning effects of a golden sun on brilliantly engineered rice fields, which impossibly followed the hillsides they adorned. Our leisurely journey round the island looking for suitable sites was punctuated by small villages, pockets of rainforest, banana and coconut plantations, wonderful beaches, and views of spectacular mountain peaks. There was laughter and bright, smiling faces everywhere. It was so splendid and I loved it all.

Almost reluctantly, I left for Jakarta to report to Subroto, in high praise of all I had been shown. I recommended that a series of beautiful sites be found for golf courses to be established beside suitable hotel accommodation and not too far from a decent airport. In those days, Bali was it, just!

Although silence followed for a couple of years after this visit, the call eventually came, announcing that land had been found for their first project. In true Indonesian style, the site was at none of the places I had reported on but instead turned out to be a dairy farm, high among the craters of two enormous volcanoes, mercifully extinct at 4000 feet in the mountains of central Bali. What a place! There were two magnificent lakes flanking the site, it was cooler up there, which meant that we might have bent grass greens eight degrees from the equator. The volcanic soil would grow anything, and we were surrounded by towering walls of pristine tropical rainforest. Numerous forest trees, streams and temples were scattered across the site. It was the perfect setting to create the most beautiful golf course in the world.

In 1970 there were precious few hotels in Bali, and looking for somewhere to stay, I stumbled upon the Tanjung Sari Hotel at Sanur. Thirty years on and 100 visits to Indonesia later, it remains my favourite hotel.

I had found a good base. The next two years were blissful. Money was no object, and our instructions were to do what was necessary to put this golf course on the international map and to spare nothing. Those were the days, and no surprise as our client was General Ibnu Sutowo, recently appointed as president of Pertamina, Indonesia's oil and gas company. He was to become chairman of the Indonesian Golf Association. The golf course was to be named Bali Handara, after his daughter. General Subroto was a director of the project, and a man I came to know very well, Bob Hasan, President Suharto's golfing partner for thirty years, called the shots. With these people and this site, we surely could not miss. It was an exciting moment as we assembled our own team to do justice to this most promising scenario.

However, all was not presented on a plate. There was no survey undertaken in the traditional manner and aerial photography was forbidden. Another drawback; there was no earthmoving equipment on Bali except a clapped out, wartime Russian bulldozer which wouldn't cut butter. We gave it a try for a while,

Bunkering at Bali Handara, fourth hole. (Photo courtesy of Michael Wolveridge.)

I carried out a survey of sorts from the rooftop of the old farmhouse, the only building that occupied a commanding view. Not surprisingly, it subsequently became the clubhouse site. Bali's 'Mr. Fixit', Made Sumantra was to become indispensable in the next two years as my trusty assistant, and he and his pals would stake out the course according to my instructions. Talk about shouting from the rooftops! It was one of those projects which was right from the beginning. After about a week, we were ready to clear site lines and make a start.

We had in those days an office in California, and our American partner, Ronald Fream, took charge of the agronomics and construction specifications and all those innumerable details with patience and great skill. The irrigation system needed to be designed from site, and with so little information available, it required a great deal of ingenuity and prowess. We were lucky to have Paul Jones take on the task in his first big assignment. Thirty years and at least 100 jobs henceforth, Paul still designs our irrigation systems. Fream introduced an American construction supervisor to

the project who set valuable guidelines for our growing manual workforce. It must have seemed strange to an American used to dealing with machines to have to do everything by hand. He is probably still shaking his head. Yet I believe that the essence of this project's success is that it was hand-built by the people who lived there.

We needed some help, and it arrived in the form of great friend and tour golfer, Guy Wolstenholme. The amusing Englishman and golfing companion of many years to Peter Thomson and myself expressed a desire to join us in our enterprise at a time when there was a niche for someone who understood the game perfectly to take an overview by putting the 'golf' into the course design. And that he did.

With Made Sumantra, and a young Balinese landscaper named Tunas, who had become our course superintendent, all was proceeding nicely with the workforce. It was a great opportunity to introduce Guy to the golf course construction business. Also, our manual workers had never heard of golf and needed an explanation. Wolstenholme gathered them round, hitting balls over the makeshift fairways at

but when it inevitably broke down, we buried it to the cheers of our workforce now grown to 1250 strong. These people were a mixture of Javanese, recommended as good workers who became the main earthmovers, and local Balinese villagers, from grandma to the grandchildren, who comprised the planters and landscapers.

distant flagsticks, as only he could do. His grand clinics were conducted before more people than he had possibly ever played before, all cheering, all wanting to try for themselves, and keen to learn. Made and Tunas had both acquired sets of clubs, and were becoming quite good. The local chief wanted special lessons, though when Guy asked him to take the gun off his belt so he could free up his backswing, he refused. He said there might be a coup if he dropped his guard.

Work went on every day from first light until just before dark, unless there was a ceremonial occasion when without warning the workers would just disappear. After a year the course was taking shape. As everything was done by hand including the lake building, it took a long time, but the work was exquisite. Lake A was to be our irrigation lake, and with such porous soil, a huge liner had been ordered from Singapore. Finally completed with the liner ready to install, they all stood around the edge whilst the first wide strip was ceremoniously rolled down into the bottom. About that time it started to rain, as it always

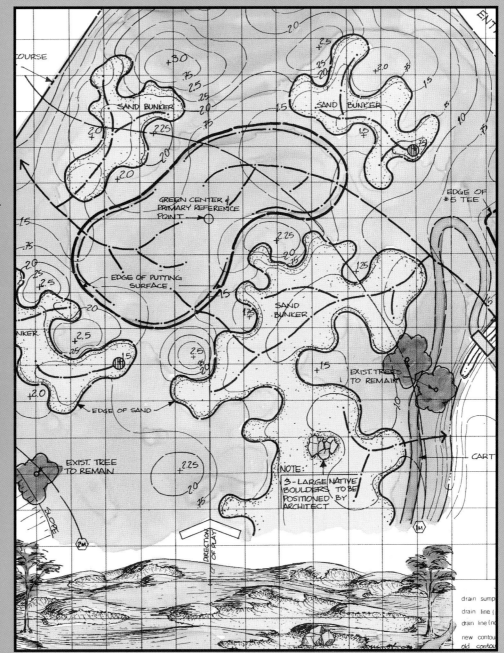

A map of the fourth green at Bali Handara. (Illustration at a scale 1:300 courtesy of Michael Wolveridge.)

did in the late afternoon. As the rain hit the liner and ran down, it became too much for the children and some of the bold ones were sliding down, shrieking with laughter until Guy and I were pushed. The laughter stopped until we reached the bottom. Soaking wet and covered in red mud, we looked up and grinned—what else could we do? That was the signal for one of the funniest times we ever had, even the chief slid down, his gun firmly attached. It was also the end of the lake liner strip, so we ordered another.

With occasional helicopter visits from the generals, including President Suharto, to view work in progress, Bali Handara was getting to be news in Indonesia. Cottages began to appear in Indonesia's first golf community development, and for good measure, General Ibnu proudly ordered the largest gates in Indonesia to be erected at the entrance close to where the bulldozer lay buried. When the shaping had been completed, the Javanese dismantled their camp and left for home, leaving the local Balinese villagers to plant the grasses and continue with their splendid land-scaping. Flowers and ferns, trees from the forest, waterfalls, local sculptures and carvings, all magically appeared under the watchful eye of Tunas whose natural instinct and flair for this work was blossoming. Wayan Tunas is now a legendary figure in Indonesia as a golf course superintendent and golf course builder of note.

After two years it was done. The grasses had established swiftly in the perfect conditions, and the golf course was being mowed daily. We had all played it, and the course was ready at last to be handed over. Made was chosen as general manager, recruiting his staff from among the most suitable villagers of the workforce, and training the young women and children as caddies. Tunas became the golf course superintendent, his staff already picked and proficient in their tasks, and the gardeners, just kept doing what they do best. What joy it was that at least 250 local Balinese were employed to look after their handiwork in an assortment of positions best suited to them. Between us, 1250 Indonesians and a handful of foreigners, we had created a masterpiece high in the mountains in a blissful climate, on the most beautiful tropical island you could imagine.

Many hands make light work. (Photo courtesy of Michael Wolveridge.)

OPPOSITE: The Bali Handara clubhouse under construction. (Photo courtesy of Michael Wolveridge.)

President Suharto, General Ibnu, General Subroto and Bob Hasan came to play at weekends and brought their golfing pals, President Marcos, Lee Kuan Yew, Tunku Abdul Rahman, General Ne Win and the Sultan of Brunei with them. Inevitably it became the favourite place for the annual Association of South East Asian Nations (ASEAN) conference, in being exclusive, safe, and offering plenty of golf. Word soon got around and golfers from all over the world came to play and stay, declaring it paradise on earth. And so it was. Bali Handara was swiftly acclaimed by *Golf Digest* and *Golf World* as one of the top fifty courses in the world, an award it managed to hold on to for many years.

An innovation in links style bunkering

Phil Jacobs

The concept of a bunker as a hazard on a golf course originated on the early golf courses in Scotland and Ireland in the face of dunes where sheep often huddled for protection from the wind. In trampling these areas the native sands were exposed to develop naturally into bunkers. Golf course designers later started incorporating bunkers in new golf courses for strategic, penalising, plus aesthetic and directional purposes. Over the years, the harsh links bunkers were softened into a variety of styles, which are found on golf courses all over the world. In most instances, bunkering has become highly formalised, and on modern golf courses, it seldom penalises the good golfer.

The early bunkers were extremely punishing for the player, and not being raked at all, were treated as natural hazards. The formalisation process of bunker design evolved over the years to the point where today bunkers often look artificial within the context of their environment. This cannot be avoided on golf courses within housing developments or parkland. In such instances, bunkers would always look artificial, which is not to say that golf course designers should do without bunkers on these types of courses. On the contrary, bunkering is often the single most dynamic tool in the arsenal of the designer, adding interest and challenge for the golfer. All the great golf courses in the world have one thing in common: dramatic looking and challenging bunkers. Although the style and look of the bunkers on these courses vary considerably, they are similar in that they are all relatively deep. Even though bunkers can be placed perfectly from a playability point of view, it is the dimensions of depth and height of face that truly differentiate the great from the mediocre bunker.

Not only is the depth of the bunker important in giving it character and reasonable challenge, the steepness of its face is equally so. Creating relatively steep faces on a golf course, be it with sand, grass or railway ties, greatly assists the golfer in judging depth and distance, and allows the designer to define the challenge to the golfer.

OPPOSITE: **A new way of constructing links-style bunkers (Sketch by Phil Jacobs.)**

During the last sixty years or so, thousands of golf courses have been constructed where the bunker design has lost steepness in the face, by either being very shallow or, alternatively, by bringing the grass down to the sand on a slope soft enough to accept a mower. Such bunkers were designed to reduce maintenance whereby all areas on the course could be mowed by motorised mowers, thus eliminating mowing by hand.

In recent years, many designers have reverted back to some of the classic concepts in golf whereby bunkers have become deeper with relatively steep grass faces.

There is a strong school of thought that promotes a bunkering style that would in the majority of instances not enable the good golfer to reach the green from a fairway bunker. Such a design asks the golfer to gamble with the lip of the bunker. The golfer would select the lowest loft of club possible to try to get the ball as close as possible to the green. In some instances the golfer would be challenged strategically, such that the best option is not necessarily to get the ball as close to the green as possible, but rather leaving a full shot to the green. Such bunkering adds significantly to the psychological challenge this will pose to the golfer. Even the best golfer in the world knows that he cannot hit the ball onto the green from certain fairway bunkers. This certainly applies to all the fairway bunkers on a golf course like the Old Course at St. Andrews. Under these circumstances, you also offer a significant advantage to the golfer who hits the ball straight, or who plays strategically to avoid such fairway bunkers. One of the most amazing feats of Tiger Woods's victory in the 2000 Open at St. Andrews was his ability to avoid all bunkers during the course of the championship. This is a classic example of strategic play.

Often golf course designers have tried to imitate links style bunkering. Sometimes this follows the traditional style of predominantly small roundish bunkers, and other times combining small with larger, free flowing bunkers. Mostly in these instances, the bunker face would consist of a relatively steep grass slope, which requires intensive manual maintenance. In the northern hemisphere or cool season climates, the sod-revetted, bunker-face construction method is used on only a few golf courses, mainly in Scotland and Ireland. This method calls for the placement and compaction of a layer of turf placed one upon the other until a new near vertical wall is constructed. It is obviously relatively successful having been in use for so many years on the traditional links. However, such bunker faces have to be re-built every seven or eight years; a process that is time and labour intensive.

For the golf course designer who wants to create the look, challenge and psychological value of the traditional links bunkers, a modern alternative could be considered. The proposed new method, as detailed in the sketch, uses the same principle as sod layering or revetting but the material is different. In this instance, a man-made synthetic material called geo-textile, which is commonly used in the engineering industry, is used to build the face of what could be called a typical links style bunker. Historically, such bunker faces have not been built successfully in warm season or high rainfall areas. However, the new construction method allows the golf course designer to use this style anywhere.

Once a decision has been made to use such a bunker design style, constructing the bunker in this way offers significant benefits. The bunker face lasts for a very long period of time, it requires very little or no maintenance, and motorised mowing can easily be completed around the perimeter of the bunker.

Typically the geo-textile should be ordered or painted in a natural earthy colour. Seed should be placed on the inside of the geo-textile within each roll and to germinate as conditions allow. The finished look will be pleasingly informal. Some turf growth may occur on those sides of the bunker that receive less sun, creating a highly natural looking bunker.

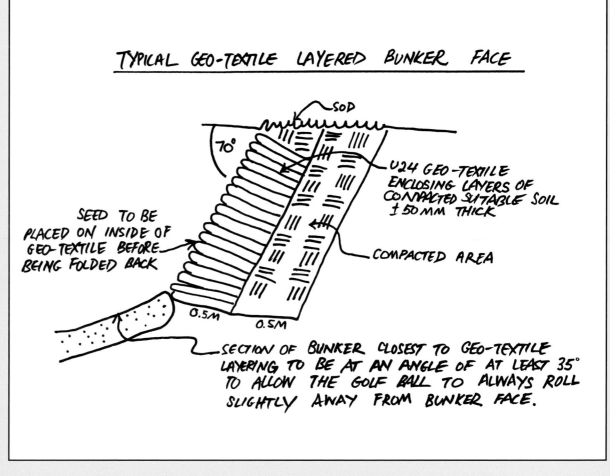

TYPICAL GEO-TEXTILE LAYERED BUNKER FACE

SOD

70°

U24 GEO-TEXTILE ENCLOSING LAYERS OF COMPACTED SUITABLE SOIL ± 50 MM THICK

SEED TO BE PLACED ON INSIDE OF GEO-TEXTILE BEFORE BEING FOLDED BACK

COMPACTED AREA

0.5M   0.5M

SECTION OF BUNKER CLOSEST TO GEO-TEXTILE LAYERING TO BE AT AN ANGLE OF AT LEAST 35° TO ALLOW THE GOLF BALL TO ALWAYS ROLL SLIGHTLY AWAY FROM BUNKER FACE.

Institutionalised fraud: prostituting the Royal and Ancient game

Tony Ristola

Since its inception centuries ago, golf has been historically rooted in honesty and integrity. Fraud can be described as a person (or thing) that is not what (it) seems or pretends to be. This would generally be the last word associated with our great game.

Through featherie balls, and hickory shafts, to multi-layer rocket balls, and graphite shafts, values of honesty and integrity in golf have been revered, and bequeathed to succeeding generations like a sacred torch. These values are truly the core of the Royal and Ancient game, the constant and the foundation for fair play. Accidentally move your ball in the rough, even without witness, no matter how costly the additional stroke, and you undoubtedly call a penalty upon yourself. This inflexible reliance to individual honour is the *sine que non* of golf, and alone separates it from other sports, where cheating is condoned, encouraged, and perfected to a high art. It is the spirit of competing honestly versus winning at any cost, illustrated clearly by the role of the referee. Our referees are for rule interpretations as opposed to catching cheaters.

Sadly, golf course architecture no longer represents the standards of honour, and integrity that distinguish the Royal and Ancient game. Scores of courses bear names of individuals who have contributed little or nothing to their creation beyond signing a contract, showing up for photo opportunities, and offering suggestions punctuated by dramatic arm waving. The 'signature architect', with the emphasis on signature, is the bar they trip over in becoming an architect of record.

Had Picasso, Renoir or Rembrandt rubber-stamped their names onto others' work would it have been considered fraudulent? Most certainly. Yet in golf course architecture such deliberate misrepresentation has reached pandemic proportions.

During the past two decades, the brunt of offenders has emerged from a profession that should know better, tournament golf professionals. They hold a unique responsibility to protect the integrity of the game by acting in a manner consistent with it. By accepting credit for architecture they have had little or no meaningful involvement in realising, they distort historical record and trivialise the efforts of legitimate architects. Could you imagine if the same liberal methods employed to distort the architectural record were used to write their professional history? What level of ear-shattering protest would erupt if celebrity instructors Ballard, Leadbetter, Pelz, or Harmon had their names inscribed on trophies indicating they were the champions of record? Would tour professionals stand idly by to allow the obvious distortion? Absolutely not, and justifiably so. Why then should it be acceptable for the architectural record?

In company with prominent golf professionals abandoning their responsibility to the game, culpability should be directed to golf journalists, their publications and broadcasts for perpetuating the celebrity architect myth.

Mainstream golf journalists and broadcasters don't hesitate to question or criticise an entire generation of tournament players, breaches of etiquette, or decisions like Chip Beck laying-up on the fifteenth hole at the US Masters. Yet unbelievably, there is little analysis regarding the mockery inflicted upon modern golf architecture by celebrity architects. It appears the only candid discussions can be found on Internet forums such as www.GolfClubAtlas.com or publishing houses that explore golf course architecture's past, present, and future.

Preceding the rash of celebrity tainted architecture, golf historian Herbert Warren Wind, analysed the business of golf architecture and soundly criticised professional architects for their limited involvement during construction in his essay, 'The Imperishable Genius of the Master Architects'. He notes:

How, during the affluent post-war period, when a good number of American architects were given the financial backing, time, land, and support (not to mention all the rest of the advances in knowledge and technique) to build courses of championship standard, more often than not they flunked it, chiefly because of their preoccupation with making as much money as possible. Consequently, what should have been a Golden Age of Golf Architecture yielded little beyond that rhinestone jewel of a thought.[19]

Eleven years later, in his foreword to the 1987 reprint of Dr Alister Mackenzie's *Golf Architecture* (1920), at a time when signature architecture was 'losing its training wheels', he repeated the theme in a reprint of one of golf architecture's most treasured tomes. Wind asserts:

During the last twenty-five years or so the (professional) architects had so many scattered projects on their agenda that they could not find the time to stay put at any one course during the critical weeks and sometimes months, when rough ideas are translated into holes that really play.[20]

Wind unequivocally challenged modern golf course architects to elevate standards, to provide more and better service, and to reduce their workloads in order to spend more time focusing, communicating, and crafting details in the field during construction when it matters most. This is the Wind standard.

Rather than elevate standards, the 'McSignature' standard has emerged. Its hallmark being untrained, unqualified and uninvolved individuals accepting credit for work they have not accomplished. Since nobody challenged this lower standard, it has been accepted and promoted to the incredible threshold of being desirable, and even thought of as necessary! This perversion has been fostered with the complicity of the press, golf professionals, and most curious of all, individual architects and architects' associations.

The following excerpts are from the Code of Professional Ethics and Guidelines for Professional Conduct of a golf architects' association. These unambiguously outline when credit is due and when it is not.

Code of Professional Ethics

- The golf course architect furthers the welfare and advancement of his profession by constantly striving to provide the highest level of professional services.
- The golf course architect shall . . . respond morally and ethically.
- The golf course architect shall avoid unprofessional conduct and shall conform to the Guidelines for Professional Conduct.

Guidelines for Professional Conduct

- A golf course architect shall not engage in conduct involving dishonesty, fraud, deceit, or misrepresentation.
- A golf course architect shall not indulge in exaggerated, misleading or false publicity.
- A golf course architect shall recognise the contributions of others . . . and shall not knowingly make false statements about their professional work.[21]

It is unmistakably obvious these codes and guidelines have been fully ignored, as the epidemic of celebrity prostitution doesn't even raise an eyebrow in golf's professional ranks let alone in the press. Regardless of compensation, or the number of tournaments a celebrity has won, taking credit for work they haven't accomplished is dishonest and fraudulent. Accepting false credit, even if nobody really sees or understands the process, is akin to moving the ball in the rough and not calling the penalty on yourself, or accepting the championship trophy even though you weren't in the field.

Through decades, and even centuries, of written and unwritten common sence charters to prevent such deceptions, this seedy practice continues. Along with it, grows the divide between the hallowed traditions of golf and the reputation of professional golf course architecture.

During our generation's brief time managing this portion of the Royal and Ancient game, we have smothered the sacred torch by allowing fraud to have the same currency as fact. By allowing such dealings to become commonplace, we have publicly divorced golf course architecture from the game's centuries-old values.

Rekindling the torch mandates remarrying golf course architecture with historical integrity. Those in positions of responsibility should do the right thing as stipulated in the time-honoured codes they agreed to uphold. Simply assign credit to the individuals who are responsible for and accomplish the work. Nothing more, nothing less!

An overview of the reverse Old Course, St. Andrews

Jeremy Glenn

The Old Course, St. Andrews—the home of golf—is without doubt one of the oldest, most famous and greatest golf courses in the world. This golfing treasure has been the site of over two dozen Open Championships, going back nearly 150 years. And is the lair to some of the most infamous features in the game: the Road Hole, Hell, Strath, the Swilcan Burn, each of which have ruined the hopes of countless golfers, whether for the Claret Jug or in a Saturday best-ball. Yet with the eyes of the world turned towards it, few realise that the course is in reality two different layouts. The first is the famous Old Course as we know it today, which is played in a generally counter-clockwise fashion, going out on the right side and back in on the left. The second is the long-forgotten Reverse Course, which as the name suggests, is played backwards, which is to say clockwise.

From the first tee, play is directed towards the seventeenth green, then on to the sixteenth, and so forth, until finishing the round, from the second tee to the eighteenth green. In fact, up until the middle of the nineteenth century, the Reverse Course was the standard layout. Gradually, however, players began to alternate between the two, doing so on a weekly basis for a number of years. It is perhaps when Old Tom Morris built the existing eighteenth green that the current Old Course circuit finally gained favour to become the accepted design.

While the greatness of the Old Course is well known, many of those familiar with the Reverse Course are of the opinion that this lost course is at least as good as the former, the 'Grand Old Lady', and perhaps better. Studying the characteristics of the Reverse Course may help us understand why it is no longer used, and convince us that it needs to be restored perhaps even for an Open Championship.

The goal of this study of the Reverse course is two-fold: first, to ascertain whether the Reverse Course is useable. In other words, is it possible to play it without feeling as if one is playing a second-rate, backwards contrivance? Indeed, some would query how is it possible to play a golf course backwards and not feel as if you're doing just that? Second, is the course interesting and enjoyable? If the Reverse Course is a genuine layout, then just how good a layout is it? And, if need be, could it be improved without affecting the Old Course?

This essay does not purport to be an historical study. We are not attempting to understand how the course once was, but rather how it could be. Rather than limiting ourselves to a factual account of the Reverse Course, I will illustrate the course the way it could be played today.

For a golf course to be played in opposite directions, its features cannot be designed in a manner that favours one playing orientation. Yet this is precisely the manner in which all golf courses are designed today: they face the direction of play. Tees are gradually stepped down from the back tee to forward tee to promote enhanced visibility and to cater for a range of golfers' abilities. Sand in the bunkers is often flashed up the lip, and the bunker itself is moulded to be low on the tee-side and have a high lip on the green side. But most importantly, greens are nearly always sloped from back-to-front, both for visibility and playability. Incidentally, this is done under the false pretence that a golf green is supposed to hold a shot, as if doing so should be the

responsibility of the architect rather than that of the golfer.

St. Andrews, on the other hand, is a different beast altogether from this design theory. Tees are often positioned directly at ground level. Fearsome bunkers are rarely seen; instead, they lay hidden among the countless undulations. Significantly, greens don't slope towards the front, they are merely an indistinguishable extension of the surrounding area. Consequently, the golfer's view is often little more than a flag in a sea of tightly turfed waves.

An obvious charm of the Old Course is how it doesn't just face one direction. It never was designed in a formulaic, 'join-the-dots' manner. The huge greens are not framed by white-faced bunkers, and containment mounds won't kick your ball back into play. Yet being able to play individual holes in an opposite direction is only half the story. It is equally important that these holes are strung together in a cohesive manner. The relationship and safety between one hole and its neighbours, must also be considered and resolved. This applies equally to both courses.

The routing of the Old Course is one of its most controversial features. Nevertheless, some praise its functional simplicity and its quirks. Others denounce those same quirks as a monotonous linearity with dubious safety considerations. Yet it is largely due to its simplicity and linearity that allows the course to be negotiated either clockwise or counter-clockwise. Most greens serve a double function, with two flags being each approached from opposite sides. Furthermore, the treeless landscape, combined with the close proximity of greens and tees, allows the golf course to be seen as one core entity rather than eighteen separate compartments. This aspect is often missing on modern courses, where walks from one hole to the next can extend to several hundred yards, and annoyingly feel like commercials breaking apart the flow of a memorable movie into short-lived sound bytes.

The two-sided way of playing St. Andrews works with delicious simplicity for most holes, only requiring a more careful study in certain specific areas. In fact, there are five holes that are especially worth delineating, as they illustrate some important themes at St. Andrews.

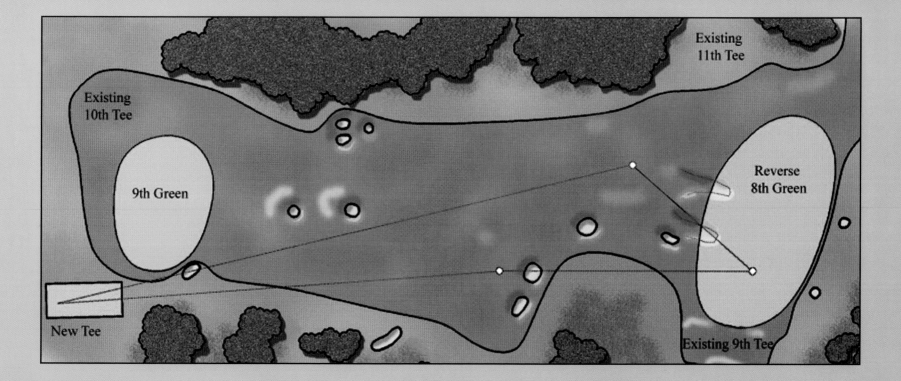

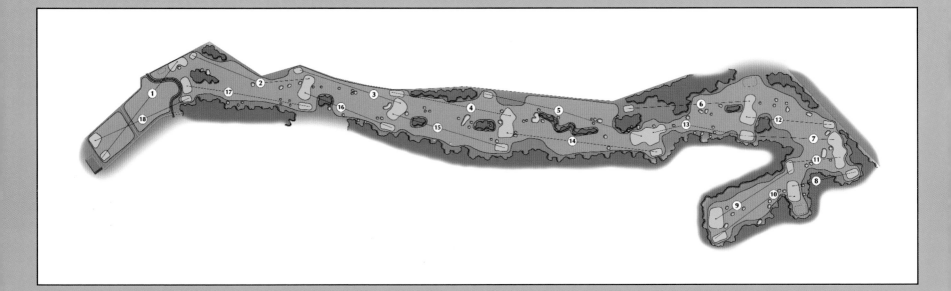

The first hole on the Reverse Course exemplifies the quirks and charms of the Old Course, and the importance of well-placed bunkers. The second hole demonstrates just how readily the Old Course can be reversed—playing the infamous Road Hole backwards. The fifth hole is a fine example of the versatility conferred by double greens, while the tenth illustrates how we should re-route some holes altogether to counter the difficulties of 'The Loop'. And finally, the fifteenth hole on the Reverse Course is a wonderful example of true strategic design—after all these years, still the hallmark of St. Andrews.

Beginning our round, the first hole cuts right across the Reverse eighteenth—unacceptable on any other golf course, but this is St. Andrews! In a short study such as this, it is impossible to fully outline the manner in which this course has become so great, not least because it impudently breaks all the so-called rules of design. Incidentally, don't the seventh and eleventh holes on the Old Course crossover today? So one would not be surprised if this new crossover would become yet another quirky charm of St. Andrews, as it perhaps once was.

The first hole on the Reverse Course is a very strong, strategically sound introduction to the round. Players still face the widest, hazard-free fairway in golf, yet similarly, can be lulled into a false sense of security. There is a definite preferred line to be taken for the tee shot: the green being severely guarded by the daunting Road Hole bunker.

Due to the angle of the green and the bunker, approaches coming in from the left side of the fairway are much easier, as shots can be run up the throat of the green. For the tee shot, however, this route not only brings the Swilcan Burn into play, but the out-of-bounds left looms ever larger as you seek a more favourable angle from which to attack the green. The safest play from the tee is to hit towards the fattest part of the fairway. Although holding the green from there becomes quite a challenge with the target being pinched between the bunker and the road directly behind it.

Speaking of the Road Hole, the tee shot on the 460-yard second hole amplifies the general strategy at St. Andrews: driving towards the middle for safety, while flirting with the property lines for a better angle in.

Staying well away from the Old Course hotel is the safest play when driving off. However, this will leave an approach of well over 200 yards, with a trio of bunkers protecting the flag. One either aggressively runs the ball up the length of the double green with a low draw, or more cautiously rolls it onto the Reverse sixteenth green hoping for a good lag-putt.

On the other hand, attacking the hole from the tee would mean aiming for the gap between Cheape's bunker and the corner of the wall, and staying short of both. Indeed, the further the drive, the more the out-of-bounds creeps into play. A good drive will leave a mid-iron to the green, from where getting a four is a much easier task.

Continuing to the green of the fifth and thirteenth holes, this is another area where the flow of the Reverse Course doesn't run as smoothly as hoped. On that double green, the flags are one behind the other, rather than side-by-side, and players would thus be required to hit over one flag in order to reach their own. Obviously the simplest solution to this safety concern is to keep the green numbering as they are now. The fifth green will be the fifth for both the Old and Reverse courses, and the thirteenth green will remain the thirteenth. Players will continue to shoot for the front flags rather than over each other's heads.

In these situations we must forgo what we'd like to do—celebrate the romantic appeal of a pure Reverse Course—and follow what the land and situation dictates. Being alert to alternative solutions is a cornerstone principle of golf course design, and the famous 'Loop' at the far end of the property is another such area that routing-wise would benefit from the attempt. This is preferable to restricting ourselves to the true Reverse Course. Actually, all the greens in 'The Loop' will be used in the proper order for the Reverse Course, with only the tees being re-numbered or relocated to clear the congestion and address safety concerns that would otherwise be present. This will create entirely new holes that are both interesting in themselves and maintain cordial relations with their neighbours, as we had set out to do in the beginning.

The tenth hole is a good example of these changes. This 325-yard hole still plays towards the existing eighth green. However, rather than starting from the existing tenth tee, a new tee-ing ground will simply be built to the left of the existing ninth green, thus avoiding crossing the line of the Reverse ninth. The result is an intriguing golf hole that, incidentally, reinforces my belief that length should not automatically be equated with quality. Many golfers will be attempting to conquer this hole in three shots, and might be disappointed if they fail. Yet, it is no easy task, due to pronounced swales at the front of the green.

This green really has two entrances: one guarded by heather, the second dealing with those swales. Staying back short of Kruger bunkers, albeit a conservative play, can be a smart one. The approach shot would then be hit with enough spin to stop the ball quickly, thus taking most of the hazards out of play.

Many golfers, while tapping into their natural inclination, will aggressively drive to the left of the fairway bunkers, leaving a short bump and run towards the flag. However, if the hole is towards the right of the green, as it invariably is, this second shot becomes a more delicate task, rewarding only those with imagination and touch. Players must now either bump their ball across those swales, or flop a wedge over them.

Finally, we come to the marvellous fifteenth hole, perhaps one of the best and most strategically laid out holes on the Reverse Course. An omnipresent feature of many of the world's finest courses is how the hazards are often placed precisely where the golfer would otherwise wish to place their shot. In other words, most think of golf like a game of archery, where points are progressively awarded the closer you get to the bull's-eye. However, what if rather than being awarded the most points for hitting the centre of the target, one is penalised? The game would no longer be one of pure execution, but also one of inherent strategy. How close do you dare flirt with the bull's eye? Or how close do you dare flirt with the bunker? The result is certainly an entirely different game than the appropriately named target golf that most modern courses favour. Indeed, it makes for a much more interesting game.

Measuring 440 yards, the fifteenth hole features a sharp fall-off about 275 yards from the back tee, precisely where you'd wish to drive and splitting the landing area into two separate tiers: a narrow, lower section to the left, and a generous, inviting area above.

Staying on that higher plateau to the right certainly seems to be the most prudent choice off the tee, and overall the safest way to play the hole. The landing area is seventy-five yards wide, and thankfully for once, hazard free.

The catch, however, is that the further right you drive, the longer and tougher becomes your approach. Indeed, a menacing pot bunker guards the front right of the green, making the approach quite tricky. Remember, the greens don't hold at St. Andrews. To ease your predicament, be advised to keep left. And driving down the twenty-yard wide lower chute to the left, while a risky play, offers a much better view of the green.

The fifteenth hole is a fitting example of one of Alister Mackenzie's key thoughts on golf architecture. He said it so well: 'most golfers have an entirely erroneous view of the real object of hazards. The majority of them simply look upon hazards as a means of punishing a bad shot, when their real object is to make the game interesting'.[22]

And so, having studied the routing and individual holes, one can confidently conclude that the Reverse Course is, at the very least, a perfectly playable and legitimate golf course. Moreover, it is clearly deserving of a less humble label. We've already highlighted a number of fascinating golf holes, while the flow and feel of the overall course is as balanced and fluid as the Old Course itself. In keeping with the Old Course, it is not without certain distinctive quirks, yet offers great variety both in the length of the individual holes as well as the undeniable challenge of surmounting its features.

Furthermore, apart from the construction of new Reverse tees, shaving back some of the rough in front of some of the greens, and a few other minor or optional touch-ups, everything is already in place, waiting to be discovered, or more to the point re-discovered.

The question remains: why has the Reverse Course disappeared? Just what are we waiting for to revive it? After all, it is a true diamond in the heather, the greatest lost links of all. It lies in waiting for us like an old musical instrument yearning to be dusted off and played again.

Never mind the quality, feel the length

Paul Daley

It is well acknowledged that things are getting out of hand technology wise, but many suspect it will take a really eye-catching round figure—a prominent 8000-yard golf course—for us to finally say 'No more!' Amazingly, the mark had already been hit nearly forty years ago in Massachusetts, and an even longer course exists in China—the Jade Dragon Snow Golf Club—an 8400-yard Nelson and Haworth monster several thousand yards above sea-level and set against a snow-capped backdrop. Even when allowing for the fifteen to twenty per cent distance-enhancing effect of altitude on the ball, that is an awfully long stretch!

Currently, the search for golfing perfection by professionals is forcing them beyond the benefits of modern technology. They acknowledge the improved application of weight training, diet, mental skills coaching, and overall fitness preparation. When this concentrated human element is combined with the best that modern technology can offer, the golf produced is an awesome sight. Unfortunately, it perpetuates the push towards longer courses.

Operating under the spotlight of this assault, architects naturally try to stay one step ahead. But such a cat and mouse strategy is not sustainable. Properties have finite boundaries, housing encroachment is rearing its ugly head worldwide, and golf course budgets will soon be more widely considered repugnant. At the club level, a growing disquiet is gathering against raised club levies. A change of focus from 'length, more length' is urgently required.

The first step is to acknowledge that unduly incorporating length is a bandaid remedy. Why be bullied by technology and the myriad other issues that are clearly out of one's control when course design is controllable? Some architects have forgotten that subtlety and ingenuity lies within their minds and at the tips of their fingers—on the drawing board and in the field. Intuition alone should enable the following design elements to flourish: pinching in the rough at certain distances; reintroducing 'risk and reward' golf situations; placing intrigue above 'slather and wack'; and opting for cleverly designed green complexes over back-breaking hole lengths. To illustrate

OPPOSITE: **The 115-metre par-3 sixteenth hole at Thirteenth Beach, Victoria, Australia. When the wind is quartering hard from right-to-left, the starting line is out over the coastal tea-tree. (Photo by Peter Turrell ©)**

this last point, much could be learned from studying the greens and near surrounds at Commonwealth Golf Club, Melbourne. Of particular note, are its second, fourth, fifth, eighth, ninth, eleventh, fourteenth, fifteenth, and seventeenth greens. They serve as a vital compensatory factor in a layout considered short by modern standards.

Too many in the golf industry equate the word 'championship' with a golf course that measures in the vicinity of 6300-6400 metres. It's like a watershed mark that must be attained. The figure is marketable. But why should this be? Once, the word championship referred primarily to the quality of the course, not its length. One high-profile club to have suffered under the weight of this expectation has been Merion Golf Club in Ardmore, Pennsylvania. For years this celebrated layout was considered an icon of subtle, imaginative, and strategic design. It produced historic scenes as easily as it collected accolades: Bobby Jones's debut at fourteen in the 1916 US Amateur; his victories in the 1924 and 1930 US Amateur championships; Ben Hogan's triumph in 1950; and that famous two-iron to the last green—curiously reported as a one-iron; Lee Trevino's outgunning of Jack Nicklaus in 1971 on a course that was around twenty yards shorter than in 1930; and David Graham's victory and near flawless final round in 1981. And yes, this was the same venue that Jack Nicklaus mauled in the 1960 World Amateur Championship. It is reprehensible that a course steeped in such tradition and glory can be deemed unsuitable for championship play. Merion shouldn't need to keep pace with the game; surely, it is incumbent upon the game to keep pace with it.

As golf course distances creep up, almost imperceptibly at times, the folly of building onerous courses is easily overlooked. The demise of the short but great par-4 is partly responsible. Simple arithmetic will show how the re-inclusion of this feature will keep a lid on yardage, and without compromising the overall challenge of the layout. I can think of no finer examples than the tenth holes at the Riviera Country Club, Los Angeles, at 315 yards and The Royal Melbourne Golf Club (West Course) at 279 metres. Occasionally some downplay the wonderment of Royal Melbourne's tenth hole as one arising from superlative terrain. There is an element of truth in this perspective, but nevertheless, the hole was still the result of visionary golf architecture, and construction. While declaring a bias towards classic short par-4s, moderation is still the key. Were all short par-4s driveable, golfers would soon tire of them. Actually, one of the challenges of the tenth hole at Royal Melbourne West is not so much to reach the green when the wind is favourable, but in stopping your ball from careering down the steep embankment behind the green where an assortment of lies and stances are to be found. You take your chances, or lay up off the tee. When playing in a southerly bluster, the hole can be downright brutish.

Pleasingly in Australia, many beguiling short par-4s are found at courses such as Commonwealth, Kingston Heath, New South Wales, Huntingdale, Royal Melbourne (East and West), Royal Adelaide, Yarra Yarra, Royal Sydney, Metropolitan, Victoria, and numerous others. Soon enough, there will be similar acclamation for this feature at The Peninsula Country Golf Club's North course

in Frankston. Perhaps a closer inspection of these examples, by a wider audience, would serve to demote length and restore a sense of balance in course design.

Some months ago, I had the occasion along with several others to play Ranfurlie Golf Course, an addition to the Melbourne golf scene, with its designer Michael Clayton. After he detailed to group members the intricacies of the 272 metre par-4, sixteenth hole, Clayton nonchalently drove his ball to within eight metres of the flagstick. My attempt at emulation veered off to the right, some twenty metres short and nearly pin-high. Upon reaching the ball, I was greeted by a downhill lie in the rough to a green sloping away from me, with intervening bunkers. Suffice to say, it was the easiest bogey I pencilled in all day. Cricketers will be familiar with the tactic of the bowler 'laying the bait' outside the off-stump—attempting to induce a 'false' shot, leading to the batsman's dismissal. It struck me that Clayton's design had indeed induced a false shot.

Many lovers of inspired golf architecture view the short par-4 with reverence and

ABOVE: **A view of the sixteenth hole at Thirteenth Beach from behind the green.**

LEFT: **The sixteenth hole captured from the thirteenth tee. (Photos by Peter Turrell ©)**

romanticism—the main course among available treats. But to fully ensure that a golf course is fun, playable and memorable, why can't we sample more often the tasty entrée of the tiny par-3? At Thirteenth Beach Golf Links, on the Bellarine Peninsula, Australia, its sixteenth hole is being heralded by all who play this fine golf course. Situated on high ground and subject to ferocious crosswinds, double-bogies are proving to be as prevalent as threes. Befitting a hole of its length, the target is appropriately elusive. Wouldn't golf be more enjoyable if similar holes to the seventh at Pebble Beach—barely 106 yards—were built today? Sure, the Pacific Ocean won't always be at hand, but substitution of other picturesque hazards can stand in. Among people who take an interest in golf course architecture, the same chorus resonates: 'more of these shorter holes please!'

A disturbing trend has emerged with the mechanical designing of long par-3s. Yes, there is a place for such holes, but should a golfer be made to 'walk the plank' more than once per round? Site dependant, what can be simpler than at least considering plans for one short,

one medium, one medium-long, and one long par-3? And by long, I do not mean Carnoustie's sixteenth hole, verging as it does on 250 yards. With the agency of a gale it is easily reachable for many golfers with irons, but when presenting with the contrary wind direction experienced during the 1968 Open championship,

that type of par-3 length is absurd.

Every golfer harbours their own notion of optimum hole length. My reasonable upper-limit par-3 length is around 205 metres, providing that half the time, the various winds encountered won't make the hole an embarrassment to the club, or architect. An

Fifteenth hole, Paraparaumu, New Zealand. (Photo by Justin Walker ©)

OPPOSITE: Second hole at Paraparaumu. (Photo by Justin Walker ©)

interesting exercise to ponder on these lengthy par 3s, is at which point does shot-making end, and bludgeoning begin?

When assessing ways to address the 'technology' problem, I wholeheartedly support the opposite, albeit radical, approach of reducing the length of courses. An obsession with length covers up a multitude of designing sins, and worse, encourages laziness on the part of the architect. Shorter, more interesting, and better designs would see the return of an element that has all but vanished: golf played like a game of chess. Just as Nick Faldo exploited his chess-player's aptitude during a golden ten-year playing stretch, architects, too, will find themselves winning more contracts by adopting a similar modus operandi in their designs.

For most architects, reducing the length of golf courses is counter-intuitive, and so is the staging of golf tournaments on diminutive courses like Paraparaumu Beach in New Zealand. But when analysing the results of the 2002 New Zealand Golf Open, it demonstrates how exciting and unpredictable results can follow. The tournament winner over this 6052-metre, par-71 links, established in 1929 and completed by Alex Russell in 1949, was Australian Craig Parry—one of the shorter hitters among the professionals. These days, whenever Tiger Woods plays and doesn't win: that is news! He played moderately well at Paraparaumu, finishing at five under par and six shots behind Parry. Only two days prior to the first round, the links was running fast and furious, and bouncy. But thereafter, the country was awash, and there was plenty of rain in the months leading up to the event. The vagaries of links golf, combined with fairways and rough that placed a premium upon driving accuracy, and an unusually short tournament course, produced a refreshing spectre. Of note, other relatively short-hitters apart from Parry featured in the top ten. It is a privilege to be living in this era: watching and reading about Tiger Woods cutting a swathe through talented fields, almost at will. But Woods must surely break out into a knowing smile each time he learns of an established course being lengthened, or a new and excessively long tournament course that plays directly into his hands.

While some architects rely on length as a crutch to an appalling degree, let us make an important distinction between those architects encumbered by instructions from a developer, club, or organisation to custom build a course against their better judgement that is boorishly long. Let's instead praise those architects who, with a free reign and clear canvas, choose to make an architectural statement without resorting to length, more length.

Meaningful selection and placement of hazards

Richard Mandell

History has shown there are too many hazards in the world of golf architecture. Albert Tillinghast and Alister Mackenzie made separate careers by consulting clubs to remove extraneous bunkers. Operators, owners, and players alike bemoan the proliferation of hazards, particularly sand bunkers. Why? Because most hazards originate less from a need to challenge and more as means of penalty and aesthetic. These trends damage golf architecture as design to appear as a 'paint by numbers' ideal supposedly appealing to the masses.

The irony is that the masses are not the true golfing masses, but industry experts who have turned a humble sport into big business, expanding the game's appeal to a golfing public at an increasing cost. Returning to the strategic roots of the game through meaningful selection and placement of hazards may rescue golf from the masses and return it to the golfers in a more affordable and enjoyable way.

In order to discuss selection and placement, let us first define a hazard as it relates to golf architecture. A hazard is any device challenging the golfer in the attempt to overcome an opponent, par or otherwise. The biggest mistake today's designers make is to incorporate hazards to punish the golfer. In practice, I utilise hazards primarily to challenge the golfer, not to penalise. One should never introduce a one-dimensional hazard with the duty of penalty.

What constitutes meaningful selection of a hazard? People first associate sand and water when discussing the virtue of a hazard. Yet there are other devices which summon the role of hazard. Hazards vary in degree of penalty, with water and out-of-bounds being the most damaging, and grass rough being the most benign.

Sand bunkers are the most popular and excessive hazard. They effect more penalty and aesthetic than challenge, and come in many shapes and sizes from the small pot Walter Travis favoured, to the large waste bunkers fashioned by Pete Dye. Dye often balances waste bunkers with pots typically to challenge the stronger golfer more so than the less skilled.

Moguls, mounds, or hillocks are relatively modern hazards utilised by many an architect.

Often they are utilised to accentuate aesthetics, yet create many difficult lies and stances for the golfer. Today, architects utilise mounding less for strategy and more for framing or screening outside views, creating shadows, or in attempts to keep stray shots in play. Nonetheless, efforts to corral missed hits can backfire. Wayward golf shots can just as easily be deflected further into the woods, water, or out of bounds.

Conversely, mounds can be more effective hazards in challenging golfers to attempt a more daring shot. Mounds can conceal specific parts of a fairway or green, requiring a golfer to place a shot more precisely so as to gain advantage for the next. George Thomas used intervening mounds to differentiate alternative strategic routes for a golf hole. These features would help define the bolder approach.

Similar to hillocks are grass hollows and swales. Grass hollows and swales define a plateau fairway or green. They can also make targets appear more elevated or further away than the lay of the land would dictate. Donald Ross often utilised hollows and swales as the more challenging hazard around greens. A golfer may shy away from a sand bunker as a defence mechanism, only to realise that playing closer to that hazard would result in an easier recovery than from the grass hollow. Hollows and swales incorporated into a green approach can create exciting shotmaking opportunities, especially on long par-4s and par-5s. Not only is accuracy and length important, but also the ability to control trajectory, bounce, and roll to negotiate these approaches.

Mounds and hollows are great strategic features that should be created as a single element. Both hollows and hillocks help define

each other in nature. As landforms are created, the material from a hollow migrates to an adjacent area creating a mound. In nature, erosion creates an inherent balance of cut and fill, replicating the natural wave patterns of broader, sweeping hollows balanced by more acute high points.

Rock outcroppings are natural hazards that create much heartache from unfriendly bounces. Rock should only be utilised where naturally found. Any attempt at artificial creation for strategy's sake should be avoided. Rock is part of the natural framework of golf courses in the north-eastern United States, and deserts of the west. One would scarcely find outcroppings in the sand hills of North Carolina or the marshes of Florida.

Hazards also come in vertical form. Structures are rarely considered legitimate hazards, yet architects have been known to leave old chimneys in sand or make an occasional windmill a focal point. Who can deny the Old Course Hotel at St. Andrews is not a formidable hazard for someone standing on the seventeenth tee? Trees are certainly hazardous, whether left in the middle of a fairway, or as woods defining a penal runway strategy for a golf course such as Sahalee in Washington State, home of the 1998 US Professional Golfers Association (USPGA) Championship.

Unfortunately, trees today render many other hazards ineffective strategic elements. Many sand bunkers are left between trees and targets. Hazards that were once focal points are now grown over by oaks and viewed as simple annoyances. As more trees are unwittingly planted on golf courses, it results in holes absent of strategic value. This tendency does not challenge the majority of golfers, yet is favoured by the typical professional who views challenge as simply keeping the ball down the chute each time.

One hazard not to be ignored, but often undervalued, is simple undulation or slope. Undulation is a wonderful design tool, which can dictate many strategic options and create shotmaking opportunities, though not unduly penalise the less skilled golfer. Shotmaking is the ability of a golfer to be creative in the face

ABOVE AND OPPOSITE: Twelfth hole at Creekside Golf and Country Club in Atlanta, Georgia. A sand bunker placed at the base of a rise can work in concert with undulation, providing an open view to the target (opposite) or playing safe from the tee, with a less desired angle into the green (above). (Photos by Richard Mandell.)

of architectural challenge and to control the flight of the golf ball. The best way an architect promotes shotmaking is in the shaping of the land, challenging golfers to shape shots—draws, fades, low runners, high, soft shots—in response.

Undulations can isolate a specific part of a fairway providing golfers a better angle for the next shot, an unobstructed path to the target, or a shorter route to the green. Golfers may gain an elevation advantage providing better views. Undulations as hazards can call upon challenging placement of shots to avoid other more penal hazards. The essence of a Redan hole is to utilise the undulation of the land in front of the green to avoid sand on both sides of the approach and properly control the correct bounce and roll to the target. As a challenging hazard, undulation can be a great equaliser when designing a golf course playable for all, unlike sand or water, which penalise the less skilled golfers to excess.

Meaningful selection of hazards depends primarily upon the lay of the land. The ground always determines what hazard I introduce, and often creates the strategy of any given golf hole. Ridges, saddles, plateaux, hollows, water, and wetlands are among the primary natural features to be utilised when designing a hole, whether strategic, penal, or heroic. These features help develop a golf course routing, ensuring naturally appearing strategic character. They act as hazards themselves, or become the framework for introducing sand bunkers, grass hollows, or undulation. Natural rises in the land may accommodate a well-placed sand bunker. This is an ideal that Donald Ross and others utilised often, creating plateau greens and setting sand bunkers naturally within the slopes. Using the land as a starting point for strategy and placement of hazards will always ensure variety in design from hole to hole and course to course. As course designer, Charles B. MacDonald noted: 'Variety is not only the spice of life, but is the very foundation of golfing architecture. Diversity in nature is universal'.[23]

In practice, if the lay of the land does not lend itself to natural hazards, or requires such manipulation to fit a hazard into the hole, then it is best left out of the equation. One should redefine a particular strategy before forcing that strategy onto the ground. Another relevant point is the need to avoid blind hazards. Blind targets are sometimes acceptable, yet blind hazards do not naturally fit a golf hole. If we obey the lay of the land in selecting the type and placement of hazards, we can avoid inappropriate design.

Golf architect George Thomas wrote: 'strategy of the golf course is the soul of the game'.[24] Meaningful placement of hazards certainly reflects this observation. From a strategic standpoint, I incorporate hazards as motivators for thought and choice, rewarding smart play. The best location for a hazard is where the golfer would normally place a shot. A client once remarked as we were discussing renovation that everywhere I proposed a sand bunker is where he always plays. Exactly. When a hazard is located in such a way, it forces the golfer to ponder avoiding the hazard or risk bringing it into play to gain reward.

All great golf strategists place the majority of hazards along the most direct flight line, as that is where hazards intuitively fit. Early American course architect, Max Behr, sum-

Fourth hole, Bethpage Black, New York, USA. The line of instinct becomes the line of charm. (Photo by Richard Mandell.)

marizes this ideal best: 'The direct line is the line of instinct, and if we wish to make a hole interesting we must break up that line and create the line of charm'.[25]

One sand bunker off-centre from the middle of the fairway can be more effective than many bordering the same hole, challenging those so inclined with many options. This strategy provides open, less penal areas to complement this hazard, and allows the less skilled golfer a chance for recovery if needed.

Unfortunately, architects do place multiple hazards away from the direct line of flight in an attempt either to toughen up the golf hole, or for aesthetic notions forgetting the simple challenge in executing a golf shot. This scenario provides only one choice for the golfer. When golfers hit a shot off target and find these hazards, problems compound the playing situation. Sand bunkers bordering both sides of a fairway are much more troublesome for the less skilled, much less challenging for the more skilled, and quite costly to build and maintain.

In the end, a hazard should not penalise, it should challenge. Strategy helps determine the virtue of a hazard, yet nature will always act as a point of balance. If a hazard does not naturally fit onto the land, then it should not be forced into the layout for strategy's sake. In this instance, an alternative hazard may be considered, or no hazard at all. With these philosophies constantly in the forefront of architects' minds, golf can recapture its roots and ensure long-term success.

Great design: getting the balance right

Chuck Ermisch

Golf is at an elevated level in terms of popularity. Despite this increased popularity, the number of rounds being played continues to decrease annually as attested to by several industry publications and organisations. What then is the key negative force that is driving players away from the course instead of down its manicured fairways?

Of all of the theories that are being presented for the decline in rounds, there is one particular factor that needs to be discussed in order to reverse this negative trend. Could it be that the facilities being opened are so caught up in providing and maintaining an image that the playability of the course is an afterthought, if not completely forgotten? If so, who is the responsible party that allows for

this oversight to occur? In most cases, one would speculate it is the owner. But, let's not totally discard the role of the design professional and their obligation to assuring the success of the final product.

The design of a successful golf course is a detailed, complicated, scientific and creative undertaking. The final product is truly unique because it is a living entity that has evolved from and is subject to many factors that are typically unforeseen and unimagined by the user and owner. Wind, water, sun, elevation, circulation, science, and imagination all are key ingredients to a competent design. But the most important characteristic of a quality design is the playability factor and the resulting user perception.

Therefore, the first item that the golf course designer should address when providing services for a client is to identify the predominant user. In comparison, when a structural architect is contracted to design a building, what is the first question posed to the client? The inquiry typically has something to do with the user and what function needs to be fulfilled by the structure. Shouldn't this also be the first subject that is addressed by the golf course design professional?

As an example of positive architectural response to owner desire, let's evaluate the following scenario. If the client is trying to make a large dollar value per round, it must be understood that he has inadvertently stated that he wants to provide a facility more conducive to supporting corporate tournaments, business people who are networking, high-end clientele and destination players. Identifying the specific user groups is the means by which design can promote repeat playability of the facility. The beginner level player, youth, senior citizens, high handicappers, and most women have been alienated from enjoyment of most courses on a regular basis. In response to the owner's intentions, if the design of the facility is dedicated to providing a tournament style design, then steeper slopes, penal bunkers, smaller greens, more hazard areas become the defining characteristics. As a result, the course will have a distinct look or flavour that promotes this perception. In contrast, if the owner is trying to promote as many rounds as possible, the design of the facility should reflect this and be accessible to beginners, women, seniors, youth, and high-handicappers. The fairways should be wider, the greens larger, fewer hazards and penal bunkering, and most importantly, larger teeing spaces positioned correctly and fairly on each golf hole. In turn, a forgiving and undiscriminating course should evolve. It is in these

scenarios that functionality and playability are successfully addressed and incorporated into the final product. The designer has responded to the owner's wishes and has translated those qualities into a product that truly invites and promotes proper user participation.

Reverting back to the example of the role of the structural designer, one must also realise that a successfully designed building is typically depicted by the positive response to the economical and physical requirements of the clientele and the function of the primary user. Yet the facility is ultimately open to all. In comparison, it is my opinion that golf courses, not unlike buildings, should be designed with these same segregating factors in place. All levels of player should feel welcome and invited to participate at any facility. Depending on the product image, however, this participation may be limited or constricted. That said, if a beginner golfer chooses occasionally to play a course built for high-end events, they should see the experience in a light different to playing such a course on a daily basis. The player should approach this experience as a nostalgic event for the brag-

ging rights of having played there. The experience should be viewed as a destination or special event. As an everyday facility, the beginner would probably become frustrated with the game because the playing field would be too difficult and therefore not enjoyable. It would fail to cater to the player's needs.

There must be a facility made available to the beginning player so that he does feel comfortable in learning and participating in the game. This niche in the development industry, unfortunately, is being forgotten. It is in this instance that designers and owners need to work together in determining just who is the targeted user. Not every course needs to be designed as tournament golf. The architect must understand what the owner is requiring and his design must emulate this perception to the user. Image is a creation of design, but it should never overpower the functionality. Recent trends however are redefining architects' services and forcing them to become more budget focused. As a result, designers are reducing the functionality and are gearing more towards providing a marketable image. It is my philosophy that design should not

Tenth hole at
Thunderbirds Golf Club,
Arizona, USA. (Photo
courtesy of Ronald
Whitten.)

solely be predicated upon a dollar value, but should respond to these predetermined playability values as guidelines for success in creating a functional facility. Owners many times confine themselves to a certain product or solution based on a pre-established image, without realising what they are sacrificing. The key role of the designer should be in assisting the owner in the establishment of a budget that realistically depicts the final desired product. A poor scenario is when the architect responds and adjusts services to meet a pre-determined dollar value. If the designer is put in a position of response, then they ultimately are put into the mindset that they have "X" amount to spend and they need to justify this value even if the functionality of the product suffers.

It is my observation that the relationship between owner and architect needs to be revived from its present deteriorating and neglected state. There are too many facilities that make a great attempt to be inviting and marketable, but badly miss the mark of creating a repeat user base. In these instances, the golf courses do not respond to, promote, and incorporate the true values of the game that all players require from this experience. As a result, the expected player base does not return on a regular basis. In order to repair this situation, owners need to be realistic in their goals, and they must also discuss those goals with the designer. Then and only then, can the true product be showcased and presented to the user.

The most noted and accepted courses designed today and in the past have one element in common. This shared characteristic is the balance between the proprietor's hopes for their project and the users' perceptions. The only one who can successfully provide this service of balance and integrity is the golf course design professional. In response to this realisation, diligence, faith and trust must be used in forming the professional relationship between the owner and the designer of the facility. The best and most under-appreciated service an architect can provide is to allow for functionality. The associated beauty of the facility and positive user perception is the true benefit for all.

Mackenzie's thirteen point prescription and its relevance today

Neil Crafter

Why is it that Dr Alister Mackenzie's list of the essential features of an ideal golf course is so often quoted, even today? Although not the first writer on the subject to encapsulate his thoughts in such a list, nor the last, there is something special about Mackenzie's principles that drew other architects and students of golf course architecture towards him. And perhaps that is because the Thirteen Points, as they have become known, are relatively timeless in their nature.

The origins of the Thirteen Points can be traced back to a series of lectures given by Mackenzie in 1912 to the Golf Greenkeepers' Association in Leeds, which were developed into book form later and published as *Golf Architecture* (1920). This little book, not even fifty pages long, was well used by Mackenzie as a promotional tool for his services, and given away to clients both current and prospective. It is believed that many of the copies of this work that are in collections in Australia today were among those brought here by Mackenzie himself in 1926.

Mackenzie's predecessors such as Horace Hutchinson, and his contemporaries like Robert Hunter and Tom Simpson, all prepared their own lists. Mackenzie's essential features of golf course architecture contain many common elements with other architects' lists, but with some notable exceptions that contribute significantly to the timelessness of the Thirteen Points. Mackenzie introduced his list early in on the first chapter and spent the remainder of the chapter elaborating upon these features. What are these points and their relevance to us today?

1   The course, where possible, should be arranged in two loops of nine holes.

Mackenzie himself did not religiously pursue this feature at all costs, as he realised that to arbitrarily return the nines to the clubhouse on all courses could be to the detriment of the course layout. A number of his courses, such as Cypress Point and Alwoodley, do not have returning nines, while the nines at Royal Melbourne (West) and Crystal Downs do return. There is obviously a strong, logistical rationale behind the modern preference for returning nines. However, it must be said that in a number of cases, this appears to be done as an automatic design reflex without perhaps the exploration of whether non-returning alternatives might yield a better course as a result.

2   There should be a large proportion of good two-shot holes, two or three drive-and-pitch holes, and at least four one-shot holes.

Interestingly, Mackenzie does not refer to the par of these holes, but talks in terms of the number and type of shots needed to reach in regulation. No mention is made of a recommended number of par-5s. Mackenzie's own courses yield the evidence that he was not arithmetically constrained in how he laid them out, and today's standard of four par-3s, four par-5s, and the balance of par-4s, with a par of $36 + 36 = 72$ contrived to fit each and every property regardless of the individual situation, would be anathema to him.

Fortunately there are positive signs that this standard is being ignored today by enlightened architects and owners who have learnt from the works of Mackenzie and others. Courses with an imbalance in the par of the nines, and with pars lower or even higher than seventy-two are becoming more common. As such, architects are tailoring their courses specifically for each property, and the par-72 mindset is diminishing. The result is better site-suited routings and more interesting golf. No doubt the Doctor would approve of this.

A recent case in point is Pacific Dunes in Bandon, Oregon, designed by Tom Doak. Here Doak smashes the standard by delivering a par $36 + 35 = 71$ course, that has only one par-5 on the front nine, starts the second nine with consecutive par-3s, and then delivers three subsequent par-5s. To be sure, Doak could have designed a more conventional layout that more evenly distributed the one-shotters and three-shotters through the course, and even achieved a par of seventy-two had he felt the need. However, the best routing and flow of holes was his goal, and it is to his credit that he has achieved this without resorting to complying with an arbitrary standard that has no place in modern golf design, especially considering the contradictory pressures of minimising site area and catering for a golf ball that is travelling further than ever.

3   There should be little walking between the greens and tees, and the course should be arranged so that in the first instance there is always a slight walk forwards from the green to the next tee; then the holes are sufficiently elastic to be lengthened in the future where necessary.

The Doctor's courses do tend to have that sense of proximity about them, with the next tee a short walk forward from the previous green. Further, his courses generally have stood the test of time rather well as very little evidence of lengthening over the years is apparent at courses such as Royal Melbourne, Cypress Point and Pasatiempo.

Such courses were laid out well before the scourge of the golf cart, and so architects were less willing to develop routings that might involve a considerable walk from one green to the next tee. Today, this is less apparent, especially when the golf course is part of a real estate development, and large distances

between a green and the next tee are disturbingly common. This disrupts the flow of play if the golfer is walking a course that has been designed primarily for carts.

Mackenzie's allowance for future lengthening is one of those timeless provisions proven to be quite prophetic. Since his time, and well before, golf club and ball technology improvement has been marked by some cataclysmic advances due to events such as the introduction of the guttie, the rubber-cored ball, the steel shaft, the graphite shaft, two-piece balls, and metal woods. The evidence of the past suggests that today's architects should take heed of the Doctor's prescription and build in an allowance for future lengthening in their courses.

4   The greens and fairways should be sufficiently undulating, but there should be no hill climbing.

In Mackenzie's day, undulating greens were introduced as a design feature that was sustainable given the greenkeeping skills of the time. However, as turf grasses have been bred ever finer and maintenance practices improved,

green speeds have advanced to the point where some of the undulations on many of the classic greens of this period are indeed now marginal from the perspective of fairness. The view that these should be retained unmodified at all costs is quite appealing, but the pressure to increase green speed rather than perhaps lowering it to better suit these character-filled greens is proving difficult to withstand.

Mackenzie's view was that playing every approach shot from a dead flat fairway was monotonous, and modern architects do try to incorporate interesting undulations within fairways not only as a playing feature, but also to assist in positive course drainage.

5   Every hole should have a different character.

Mackenzie's explanation of this principle was 'to ensure variety and make everything look natural'. The variety of hole types and character that he and his partners were able to introduce in courses such as Cypress Point and Royal Melbourne was exemplary, but precious few architects are lucky enough to be blessed by sites like these. However, more attention to

the variety of hole character on today's courses would be most beneficial to the game.

6   There should be a minimum of 'blindness' for the approach shots.

There was a strong distinction drawn by Mackenzie, and indeed other authors, between blind tee shots and blind approaches. The former was occasionally acceptable while the latter never. Given the plethora of heavy equipment at their disposal, modern architects should never have to settle for a blind shot unless very special circumstances are involved.

7   The course should have beautiful surroundings, and all the artificial features should have so natural an appearance that a stranger is unable to distinguish them from nature itself.

This is one of the principles that separated Mackenzie's list from all others. Surprisingly for a man without formal training as a designer or artist, he could see the total value of a particular landscape setting rather than just the immediate area of a golf hole.

Further, he prided himself and his associate constructors like Australian Mick Morcom, on being able to build undulations indistinguishable from those of the British linksland which was their model.

8   There should be a sufficient number of heroic carries from the tee, but the course should be arranged so that the weaker player with the loss of a stroke or portion of a stroke shall always have an alternative route open to him.

Heroic carries appealed to the Doctor and he wasn't afraid to use them, not only to give the course his desired variety, but to introduce an element of risk and reward that also gave the weaker player an alternate way round. At Royal Adelaide, Mackenzie took the existing Gardiner and Rymill routing and shook it up, so as to make far better use of Seaton's renowned sand craters, of which he was very much enamoured, using, in his own words, 'all four, three of them being utilised twice'. The carry over the sand crater at the fourth hole became the defining characteristic of this two-shotter, even though there is no way round it, except over.

No better example of his eighth point exists than his wonderful sixteenth hole at Cypress Point. The Doctor's phrase 'pleasurable excitement' defines this hole perfectly.

9   There should be infinite variety in the strokes required to play the various holes— viz., interesting brassy shots, iron shots, pitch and run-up shots.

It is certainly debatable whether this point has been impressed upon too many modern architects. Maintenance conditions conspire to prevent run-up shots being a feasible alternative on many shots and a return to more dry and bouncy conditions is unlikely. Architects must be prepared to use their imagination, while carefully studying the principles and examples from the past, so that such variety can be reintroduced today.

10   There should be a complete absence of the annoyance and irritation caused by the necessity of searching for lost balls.

No golfer likes hunting for a lost ball, except perhaps if it belongs to one's opponent!

Mackenzie espoused this tenth point through the use of wider than average fairways, one side or the other of which gave the canny player a preferred line into the green. At Royal Melbourne and Cypress Point, for example, the rough off the fairways in some places is now horrendous, and it is true to say that this is certainly far thicker than Mackenzie ever envisaged. Early photographs of the ninth hole at Cypress Point show the fairway as a green sliver in a sea of white sand. Since that time, this sand has been progressively overwhelmed by dune-grasses, which has made the 'lost ball' scenario far more likely than in the early days.

11   The course should be so interesting that even the plus man is constantly stimulated to improve his game in attempting shots he has hitherto been unable to play.

Again, this is another of the points that set Mackenzie's list of design principles above all others. The notion of playing interest and challenging better players to create shots was most illuminating for the time. The ability to create such interest is not handed around

AN AUSTRALIAN COURSE.

Our picture gives a fine idea of the country on which the Royal Adelaide Golf Club's course is constructed.

Photo of the carry at Royal Adelaide's fourth hole taken during Mackenzie's Australian visit in November, 1926. (Photos courtesy of SAGCA's journal, *Golf Architecture*.)

The spot where the man is standing marks the site of the third green on the course of the Royal Adelaide Golf Club, reference to which was made in an earlier instalment of Dr. Mackenzie's article.

Fourth hole at Royal
Adelaide. (Photo by
Neil Crafter.)

lightly, and there are few modern architects endowed with this gift.

12 The course should be so arranged that the long handicap player, or even the absolute beginner, should be able to enjoy his round in spite of the fact that he is piling up a big score.

For most golfers the chance to play at Cypress Point, Crystal Downs or Royal Adelaide is rare indeed, and to be savoured regardless of the score. But in the courses we play every week, the principle of this twelfth point is rarely in evidence, especially on those with tree-lined, narrow fairways and flanking hazards.

More architects are learning from the past and from masterpieces like the Old Course, St. Andrews, where alternative routes for all levels of players abound and with infinite variety present in abundance. Hopefully this trend will continue, and we will see more courses designed that give alternate routes of play. Mackenzie espoused the notion that holes should look more difficult to play than they really are, and that players get great pleasure from conquering a hole that looks hard and yet plays easy. However, the theme of variety should be a prime consideration. This type of hole should be kept to a minimum.

13 The course should be equally good during winter and summer. The texture of the greens and fairways should be perfect, and the approaches should have the same consistency as the greens.

Perhaps golf has gone too far in achieving this ideal. Many courses, especially a number here in Australia, seem to have lost the seasonal differences in the way they play. Dry, crispy and bouncy conditions in summer are now viewed as maintenance failure and, as a result, courses are groomed to play the same way all year round. This is a shame, and the ability to conjure up interesting and imaginative shots is increasingly impaired.

Alister Mackenzie's list of Thirteen Points has proven to be of great value for architects, golf club committees and superintendents to consider. The Doctor may be long gone, but his clarity of vision remains for those with the willingness to embrace it.

Protecting the old and inspiring the new on-line

Ran Morrissett

Remember as a youth drawing your ideal golf holes, or trying to best British writer Pat Ward-Thomas by creating the perfect eclectic course? Probably not too many of your friends did the same, but that never stopped you. Bitten by the golf architecture bug, there wasn't much you could do about it. Sadly, you had few ways to vent your passion. In the past, the only outlets were confined to those within the trade, that is, an association for architects or superintendents, or to a society focused on a particular architect.

However, with the advent of the Internet and its rapid acceptance, another option became available to unite people who share a similar passion. For instance, a person in Far Hills, New Jersey, could easily communicate with a person in Bondi Beach, New South Wales, and that's exactly why my brother John and I decided to start GolfClubAtlas.com in 1998.

For two years prior, John and I had mailed booklets that profiled a dozen favourite courses to a small circle of friends. However, with no pictures and with no exchange of meaningful dialogue, the booklets were more passive entertainment than we preferred.

In Australia's summer of 1998, two friends approached me in Sydney regarding their newly formed company called SiteSuite, where they design, build and maintain web sites. They needed people to provide them with content so that they could show businesses how well their package performed. In part, they told me that our potential web site could house several thousand photographs of great golf holes, and that we could have a discussion group as well.

The notion of creating a golf architecture web site was intriguing. I decided to wear the moderate cost of site maintenance myself so that GolfClubAtlas would run as a non-commercial venture. Rather than pay a telephone company several hundred dollars a month talking to my friends in the States about golf, why not create this web site and continue such discussions on-line?

The first half of 1999 was spent assembling our golf course photographs and course profiles into a meaningful presentation. Three years after starting this venture, we are approaching 2000 photographs contained within 140 course profiles. From Herbert

Fowler's use of the rolling topography at Eastward Ho on Cape Cod, to Harry Colt's heathland masterpiece at Swinley Forest outside London, exposing people to the different forms of great architecture vividly highlights that a course doesn't need to be 7200 yards long to be inspiring to play.

Apart from the course profiles, we knew that we wanted to conduct a monthly feature interview with a known insider in golf architecture circles, in large part because there exists few outlets for them. Eighty per cent of the space within most golf magazines seems dedicated to gaining more length and improving your game via new swing thoughts or better equipment. Little is reserved for the analysis of golf course architecture. Doesn't someone like Bill Coore deserve the opportunity to share his thoughts on the subject?

We got lucky when Tom Doak agreed to be our first interviewee and Brad Klein our second. We have done subsequent interviews with some of our favourite architects like Gil Hanse and Pete Dye and some of our favourite writers like Geoff Shackelford and Daniel Wexler. In addition, the feature interviews have been a great outlet for people to share their passion with the world, like George Bahto and Khris Januzik, who have devoted so much time and energy to the study of Charles Blair Macdonald and Donald Ross respectively.

However, for the site to be successful, we were keenly aware it needed to be interactive. People needed the opportunity to contribute their own writings to the site. Thus, we created a section where people can profile what makes their home course special to play on a regular basis.

Perhaps more importantly, we created an opinion section whereby participants can go into as much depth as they choose, having virtually no space constraints, on any subject related to golf course architecture. Dunlop White did so with his wonderful piece entitled 'Anatomy of a Restoration', which should be required reading for any club board member.

Likewise, someone can contribute a scholarly piece on a specific subject, a subject so particular as to have too small an audience base for a magazine to consider, given the demise of *Country Life*. Tom MacWood in Columbus, Ohio, did that very thing when he submitted a fifty-page document with thirty photographs entitled 'Arts and Crafts.' He traced how the Arts and Crafts movement in England influenced the development of golf course architecture around the turn of the twentieth century and in turn, how and why golf course architecture came across the pond in the manner that it did. This is powerful reading and we are proud to host such a well-researched piece of literature.

Even with the 140 course profiles, feature interviews, home course profiles and opinion articles, what drives sixty-five per cent of the page views of the site is our active discussion group. A former tour player in Melbourne might be readily conversing with an electrician in Los Angeles who might be conversing with a doctor in New York city who might be conversing with a retired person in London who might be conversing with a writer in Canada, who might be conversing with a design consultant in Pittsburgh, who might be conversing with someone in New Zealand whom no one knows!

As one would hope, the subject matter on the discussion threads varies greatly, and

Seventh hole at Sand Hills Golf Club, not found on the British coastline as the uninitiated may assume, but in Nebraska, USA. (Photo courtesy of Ronald Whitten.)

Shinnecock Hills Golf Course, Southhampton, USA, has proved itself as a worthy US Open venue. This photo shows the fifteenth hole. (Photo courtesy of Ronald Whitten.)

architecture of golf and the old classic clubs is what has always drawn me to the sport. I've gotten away from it over the last couple of years but stumbling on this site draws me (very thankfully) back in. When I read the dedication to your father of why you put the site together, it lights a fire under me to get back into this wonderful game and teach my three boys about it.

How about that for the power of the Internet and of golf course architecture!

Another participant once wrote to us from Clementon, New Jersey, 'All in all I think you really brought forward the concept of protecting the old and inspiring the new'. Whether GolfClubAtlas.com could ever live up to such a lofty purpose remains to be seen but hopefully, we will have fun trying.

ranges from such topics as restorations of old classics to new modern courses to the design benefits of central hazards to greens that slope from front to back. Sometimes, the action gets heated, which is wonderful to see. Like many forms of art, golf course architecture inspires passion and debate. Through this on-line exchange of ideas, many people have learned a

great deal, and friendships have been formed.

Since inception, hundreds of emails have been received from people expressing their gratitude regarding the web site. None kinder than this one:

I want to say a heartfelt thank you for taking the time to do this. The

Changes to the Melbourne sandbelt courses

Michael Clayton

Inevitably, golf courses change over time, and a study of the famed Melbourne sandbelt reveals a myriad of reasons why courses alter. In some cases they change to a point where the original designers would struggle to recognise many parts of them. Three things can change a course—nature, a committee, and an architect—and all three have had a hand in the evolution of the sandbelt golf courses.

Clearly the outstanding design in Melbourne is Royal Melbourne where there are two wonderful courses. The West Course is the superior one, and the masterpiece of Alister Mackenzie and unsung hero, Mick Morcom, the local greenkeeper who Mackenzie deputised to construct his plan.

A member of Royal Melbourne, and partner of Mackenzie, Alex Russell, designed the much-underrated East Course and again the dramatic influence of Morcom and his unique style of bunkering can be clearly seen.

Nature has altered the two courses over time as trees have grown and raised the profile in places, but fortunately they have never been planted in places where they could influence the play. The strategy of Royal Melbourne has always been based on hazards on the ground and not in the air.

Never has there been a call to alter the basis of the work of Mackenzie or Russell, but one of the most striking features of the courses are the heathland plants and at many holes, the stretch from tee to fairway necessitating a

carry of up to ninety metres. They are an integral part of the feel and atmosphere of the courses. However, one can imagine the curses of the duffers as they search for their whiffs. Other courses have replaced this feature with perfect turf, and they have lost much. Claude Crockford, the long time greenkeeper who replaced Morcom, nonetheless managed these plants perfectly for decades.

Royal Melbourne, then, can be seen as the course that has changed the least on the sandbelt, while others have seen the hand of architect and committee to a much greater extent.

Some changes have been forced on clubs because of the suburban environment in which they operate. The most dramatic alteration was inflicted upon The Metropolitan

In 1923 Kingston Heath's fifteenth hole (pre Mackenzie's visit) was a 225-yard blind par-4. Two club gentlemen are standing on the proposed green. (Photo courtesy of Kingston Heath Golf Club, Melbourne.)

People marvel at the great par-3, fifteenth hole built by Mackenzie and Morcom.

A study of that hole over time shows how some incredible bunkering was lost for years before being restored by Graeme Grant, who counts Morcom amongst his heroes. Grant also rebuilt several greens, adding significant undulation, and both restored lost bunkers as well as adding several new ones that are largely indistinguishable in style from the ones Morcom had done half a century earlier.

The other significant change revolved around the removal of trees and the push for local indigenous trees and plants. Until recently, clubs of the sandbelt placed little emphasis on the strict use of local plants, and imported trees did much to alter the feeling of the land and the profile of the courses.

Yarra Yarra is a terrific course designed by Alex Russell, and the changes undertaken over the years have in some cases been forced, and in others, self-inflicted. Surrounded by housing and built on a small piece of land, almost inevitably meant the two holes down the sides of the course, the third and the twelfth, had to be altered with the sole criterion being the

Golf Club when in the late 1950s the state government decided it wanted to build a school on the back nine. Almost unbelievably they were able to force the club to surrender some of their best holes and relocate them onto an adjoining market garden.

American architect, Dick Wilson, did an admirable job at integrating the two nines. However, the near impossibility of seamlessly melding the two is still evident. The fairway bunkering was largely redone for the 1997

Australian Open in an effort to make the course more difficult, and it certainly did that as did the lengthening of the course when new tees were added at three holes.

Kingston Heath, generally recognised as the second best course in both Melbourne and Australia, is also a course that has undergone much change over its history. Arguably, the alterations have been the most successful of all sandbelt clubs, where much of the work came under the heading of restoration.

Another photo (1928) of the fifteenth hole at Kingston Heath, by then a par-3 upon its new plateau site, and shortened by some seventy yards. (Photo courtesy of Kingston Heath Golf Club, Melbourne.)

Kingston Heath's fifteenth hole in 1970 from behind the green looking towards the tee. (Photo courtesy of Kingston Heath Golf Club, Melbourne.)

OPPOSITE: A contemporary view (2001) of the fifteenth hole, Kingston Heath. Many golfers consider his hole to be the premier par-3 in Australia. (Photo by David Scaletti.)

necessity of keeping balls out of the houses. To the detriment of both holes, trees were planted far out from the boundaries, tees were altered and pushed into corners, and bunkers added in an attempt to alter the line of play.

Two other changes are stories of alteration that, no doubt, can be told at courses all over the world.

Perhaps the two most dramatic Russell greens—aside from the incredible green at the par-3 eleventh—came at the tiny par-3, fourth hole and at the short par-5, eighth. Ferociously difficult to putt upon, especially from above the hole, they were the only defence these two holes had. However, it was deemed the greens didn't afford sufficient pin positions, and they were subsequently flattened so that the two holes became relatively simple propositions.

Commonwealth, aside from Metropolitan, is the club that has most significantly altered its original routing and the reasons were many and varied. One is forced to question whether it became a better golf course.

The beautiful par-3, seventh hole was rebuilt on an adjoining piece of land the club didn't own when it was originally laid out.

One justification was that the original architect would have built the hole there if Commonwealth had owned the land. The question is would he have built a hole exactly the same as was built, or one more like the new one, which is almost twenty-seven metres longer, and strongly suggests a low draw, as opposed to the original hole, which demanded a high fade.

This change allowed the lengthening of the par-5, sixth hole, and the par-4 twelfth, which unquestionably, made the course more difficult, but like Metropolitan, it has been almost impossible to seamlessly integrate the new holes.

Victoria is another of Melbourne's historic clubs that in 1954 had the extraordinary honour of two of its members, Peter Thomson and Doug Bachli, winning both the Open and Amateur Championships of Britain.

An aerial photo hanging in Victoria's clubhouse shows the unmistakable influence of Mackenzie in the dramatic bunkering. Subsequent aerial studies taken every decade or so show a course altering as the bunkering was rounded off or filled in, and one can only imagine why. Reasoning includes poorer players complaining about the difficulty, the cost of maintenance after World War II when club resources were not as plentiful as they subsequently became, and a lack of understanding of how important such great work was to the quality of the course. As with every sandbelt course, great bunkering is at the heart of it, and the club has spent much time restoring as much as is practical of the original.

I have been involved in that work, and members constantly question the wisdom of 'changing' the course. It is interesting to point out how much the course had altered over time, and the changes are in most cases simply the restoration of lost features.

Modernisation is a word used by many to justify change, but these wonderful courses were products of the imagination and skill of extraordinary and passionate men. We alter them at our peril. Some of the changes have been forced on clubs and some haven't. Altering them is a dangerous path to go down.

Disorientating the golfer: providing a constantly changing vista

Pat Ruddy

It could be argued that the old-time golf architects like Donald Ross and Alister Mackenzie had the best of things, and people have been known to bemoan the passing of the golden age of opportunity in course design. Moan one: the old chaps had the pick of the best sites for the game. Moan two: they didn't suffer restrictions from the environmental lobbyists. Moan three: they worked at a time when the best players could be made to use every club in the bag. Moan four: they practised their art against a populace which judged shots by the eye and didn't even dream of laser beams, sprinkler heads giving exact distances to the green, and sophisticated yardage books!

The first two moans can be disposed of very quickly. There are still good sites about, and it was never easier, thanks to modern technology, to make up features where none were bestowed by nature. And working with nature was never that bad a thing, in any case, so the environmental problems can be surmounted with thought and careful site selection.

The third moan is more soundly based. How does one make the best players of today use every club in the bag during a round? Even during an entire four round tournament?

The modern ball and club are so technologically advanced, and the best players are so much fitter and stronger as they are motivated by huge rewards, that the underlying

mathematics of course architecture have changed irrevocably.

As recently as 1980 the 'longest drive' category on the US Tour was dominated by Dan Pohl with an average tee-shot of 274.3 yards. By 2001, the entire US Tour field averaged 279.4 yards and the 300-yard plus drive had become widespread, with thirteen players averaging the metric equivalent of 290-yards from the tee.

For those who would argue that this is an American phenomenon thanks to wide fairways, light desert, and Florida air, it will come as a shock that on the European tour in 2001 no fewer than twenty-three players averaged more than 290 yards from the tee.

The shot over water is one of the most glorious situations in the modern game. Nobody is ever so conscious of the flight time of the golf ball until it is aloft and travelling over a body of water.

The late British golfing great Sir Henry Cotton, had an exercise drill in the early 1950s which, quite accidentally, gave one an understanding of the flight time of the ball. The old master would have a pupil line-up five balls in a row, maybe four or five inches apart, and swing at them in quick succession so that all five were in the air before the first one touched the ground. It proved that a player could 'find the ball' with his swing without having too much worry about the niceties of grip and stance. The key to the exercise was to get a clean hit on the first ball so that it would stay aloft long enough for the other four to be swiped into the air.

There wasn't much time for hanging about, mind you. But it could be done, and it was quite amazing how the ball could be sent away with a good flight even when the hands had moved around on the grip.

But it was only when the shot across the water came into vogue that the awareness of flight time became a major factor in the designer's thoughts. With the ball out over water, the eye looks up to the ball, down to the target, and up to the ball again trying to judge: 'will it make it?'

There is time for doubt, glorious and agonising doubt, to eat into the soul before the ignoble splash or the glorious landing on the far side. Even the best players worry in this situation because failure brings with it an absolute penalty with no chance of a brilliant recovery shot.

The combination of the fear of a penalty, the strength and direction of the wind, allied to expected flight time, and the fitness level of the player, work in the designer's favour. These factors become all the more important towards the end of a competitive round when the tension is highest.

Longer courses will demand greater fitness. The creation of a requirement for greater fitness by arranging rising ground in front of the positions from which shots are to be made, whether from teeing-grounds or from slightly raised fairways, will serve to tax a player's strength and open the possibility of lapses in concentration.

Of course, all of this talk of warfare, physical and mental, is aimed at the superior player and how those courses which aspire to greatness must be set-up to combat them. The champions have technology, their fitness trainers, their sports psychologists, their dieticians, and huge monetary awards awaiting them should they learn to destroy courses.

The best courses must be set-up to make players stretch nerve and sinew for the goal ahead, while at the same time, keeping the game's excitement intact by not overtly discouraging them to use the driver and any other club they choose.

Moreover, 'wind instruments' are created by the use of varied elevations of tees and greens to further demand variation in shot trajectory, each with its own implications regarding ball behaviour. A prime example of this is to be found at the seventeenth hole at The European, where a movement of the tournament tee in 2001 just twenty yards back, but fifteen feet higher, has had huge implications for the shot which now fairly sails out high over the sunken fairway. Any impurity of strike, which could be induced by the awesome aspect of the shot, will allow the wind to play havoc with the ball.

The wind is ever present along the Irish Sea and is a most dependable ally for the player. However, there can be few inland sites that do not enjoy vigorous winds on occasion, and the careful placement of golf elements to openings in trees can produce

much of the same golfing aerodynamics.

Optical illusions are the designer's next best friend. A knowledge of landscape art or photography will prove useful in setting-up traps in this area of design. To know how a telephoto lens can foreshorten and lengthen the perspective of a scene, and to understand the workings of depth-of-field, is to learn how to position mounds or other visual masses so as to challenge the player's judgement of distance.

The easiest example of this, is a shot that has to be played out between two hills to a distant green. By moving those hills closer to or further from each other, or by adjusting the angle of approach to the gap between the hills in order to narrow the gap visually and avoid the need to move either of them, will lengthen or shorten the perspective. Add to this, the variable of a hill behind the flag, and the green will seem somewhat closer but tiny, or place the green against a seascape or skyline, and it will seem much further away than it is.

To complete the cocktail of confusion, throw in a few hidden swales with the near and the far high spots matching at eye-level and thus hiding the extent of the valley floor. When constructed skilfully, only the most astute players will reach for the correct club, and it is amazing how often excellent golfers over-ride all the solid yardage information to hand and make a wrong move.

Varied landscape situations will help to disorientate the player, too. Give him a variety of enclosed settings in valleys or avenues of trees followed quickly by panoramic vistas over the miles of countryside or sea, and the eye will fairly quiver sending wrong information back to the command post. Just as the auto focus lens on the camera whirs when the hand shakes and moves the point of focus, so too does the eye. This phenomenon is exaggerated when light and shadow play across the scene and the eye quivers even more.

Happily, just as David found a way to deal with Goliath, golf architects have a range of tools they can enlist in order to defend the citadel of par.

Golf is an outdoor sport, and so it is that the elements from wind and rain to light and heat, must be used to best advantage. The terrain must be utilised to test stamina in the hope of affecting concentration. And the devil's own potions of doubt and fear must be induced in varying degrees in order to play a symphony on the nerves.

Today's best designer must be even better than the best designers of previous ages at employing elements from the crafts of the optician, the neurologist, the artist, the illusionist, the psychologist and the athletics coach if they are to have any hope against the power game of the next fifty years.

The next fifty years? Yes, surely when such investment is involved in golf course establishment it is important that the outcome will stand the test for at least fifty years without major reconstruction requirements. The designer must not battle merely today's best players, but also anticipate the future.

Science has made no huge inroads into turning humans into super humans. Everyone is still prey to lust, greed, hunger, fear and tiredness. So the course designer must seek out these weak spots in the players who seek out the weak spots in his courses in order to overcome them.

The first weapon that the modern designer

must utilise to the fullest possible extent is the wind. A shot of 160 yards with a strong wind behind is a different 160 yards to that which runs into or across the same wind. The laser and the yardage book are reduced to mere guides in these circumstances and human judgement becomes paramount once more.

At The European Club, Brittas Bay, Ireland, I have had fifteen years to work on the project up to 2002, and hope to continue evolving the links all without intrusions from committees or other parties. Care has been taken to direct six holes broadly south and seven holes broadly north as these are the dominant winds. An intrinsic balance is brought to the round along with varied club selections for holes of similar length running in opposite directions.

The fact that the dunes system is wide as well as long, unlike the narrow links such as the Old Course, St. Andrews, allowed two holes to be oriented due east and the remaining three almost due-west.

No matter what the wind direction of the day, the player at The European will be entertained to a variety of shot-making demands, and this is complicated further by the arrangement of openings in the dunes and sweeping valleys to accentuate wind currents into swirls and updraughts.

How do you get a player to work through all the clubs in their bag? Indeed, how do you hope to fool and disorientate the player, when they get so close to the green from the tee every time? Worse, how do you hope to fight golfers who have at their disposal laser technology, pin placement sheets, a highly trained and diligent caddy, and sprinkler measurements augmented by yardage information painted on the edges of the fairways by tour staff? Alister Mackenzie's worst nightmare has arrived.

Just as the art of camouflage—which served Mackenzie and his colleagues so well during the Boer War, and which he transferred to golf course design—would not stand-up against today's scientific weaponry of war, so the warscape has changed on the golf course.

The club golfer, and even the lazy tournament player, will still fall victim to the guiles of the course architect who seeks to trade in visual deception. More is needed to protect a course against the best players.

If it is these players' mission to seek out and destroy, they must, however, be prepared for a counter-offensive, and this is as it should be always. Deception and disorientation must be mingled with the fact of a good mathematical base and the available elements to provide that test which will distinguish the great from the merely good players.

That is the true test of a course's merit, and lesser mortals too will relish the test, albeit, from modest starting points. That said: there is still scope for everyone to enjoy a day out on a true classic links or inland course.

Reversing the reward

Pete Dye

As modern equipment has increased the length of stronger players, and the watered fairways decreased the roll for those of lesser strength, my wife, Alice, and I have reversed the reward for long carries. We now do not reward the player capable of a long carry shot with the easy shot to the green, and leave the shorter hitter with a difficult second shot. While this strategy was a favourite of the old-time architects, we now design so the long hitter has a challenging second shot, and the shorter hitter with the longer second shot will have an easier opening to at least part of the green. This variation can be achieved by skilful positioning of tees and fairways hazards. We are diligent in placing the forward tees so that women get a good start on the hole and their second shot will put them on or close to the green. We always leave an opening to some portion of the green. Forced carries are difficult for less skilled players, so our hazards are placed to the side of the targets. Our courses remain challenging from the back tees, but highly manageable from middle, front and forward positions.

OPPOSITE: **Sixth hole, The Architects Golf Club, New Jersey, USA, is known as 'Colt and Alison'. (Photo courtesy of Ronald Whitten.)**

Endnotes

1   Martin F. Sutton, *The Book of the Links: A Symposium on Golf* (London: W.H. Smith, 1912) 85.

2   David Owen, *The Making of the Masters* (New York: Simon and Schuster, 1999) 63-64.

3   Bernard Darwin, *The Golf Courses of the British Isles* (London: Duckworth and Co., 1910) 46.

4   E. O. Wilson, *Consilience: the Unity of Knowledge* (New York: Alfred A. Knopf, 1998) 58.

5   E. O. Wilson, *Consilience: the Unity of Knowledge* (New York: Alfred A. Knopf, 1998) 63.

6   Charles B. MacDonald, *Scotland's Gift, Golf: Reminiscences 1872-1927* (New York: Charles Scribners and Sons, 1928) 278.

7   www.usga.org/about/perspective/march _april_2002.html

8   Donald Ross, *Letter to Leonard Tufts*, November 3, 1923. (Courtesy Tufts Archives, Pinehurst, NC.)

9   Robert Hunter, *The Links* (New York: Charles Scribners and Sons, 1926) 76.

10 Donald J. Ross, *Golf Has Never Failed Me* (Chelsea: Sleeping Bear Press, 1996) 75.

11 Ross (1996) 23.

12 Ross (1996) 75.

13 Ross (1996) 110.

14 J. L. Low, *Concerning Golf*, (London: Hodder and Stoughton, 1903) 172.

15 H. N. Wethered and T. Simpson, *The Architectural Side of Golf* (London: Longmans, 1929) 25.

16 P. J. O'Rourke, *Parliament of Whores* (New York: Atlantic Monthly Press, 1991) 235.

17 Geoff Shackelford, *Alister Mackenzie's Cypress Point Club* (Chelsea: Sleeping Bear Press, 2000) 64.

18 Alister Mackenzie, *Golf Architecture* (London: Kent and Co., 1920) 96.

19 Herbert W. Wind: 'The Imperishable Genius of the Master Architects', *The World Atlas of Golf* (London: Mitchell Beazley Publishers Ltd, 1976) 33-34.

20 Alister Mackenzie, *Golf Architecture*. Reprint. (London: Grants, 1987).

21 Code of Professional Ethics: 3; 4; and 5 Guidelines for Professional Conduct: 1; 2; and 7 (American Society of Golf Course Architects.)

22 Alister Mackenzie, *The Spirit of St. Andrews* (Chelsea: Sleeping Bear Press, 1995) 53.

23 Charles B. MacDonald, *Scotland's Gift, Golf: Reminiscences 1872-1927* (New York: Charles Scribners Sons, 1928) 299.

24 George C. Thomas Jr., *Golf Architecture in America, Its Strategy and Construction* (Los Angeles: The Times Mirror Press, 1927) 37.

25 Alister Mackenzie, *The Spirit of St. Andrews* (Chelsea: Sleeping Bear Press, 1995) 122.

Picture Credits

Phil Arnold: 152
Steve Burns: 28; 29
Jeff Brauer: 153
Courtesy of St. Andrews University Library: 6; 10
Courtesy of Geoff Shackelford: 134
Courtesy of Holston Hills Country Club: 119
Courtesy of Kingston Heath Golf Club: 11; 212; 213; 214; 240; 241
Courtesy of Marnoch and Gaunt: 81
Courtesy of Pasatiempo Golf Club: 86
Courtesy of Rex Johns: 67
Courtesy of Royal Liverpool Golf Club: 31; 32; 35
Courtesy of the Brooks Collection: 88
Courtesy of the Fairchild aerial photography collection at Whittier College: 89
Courtesy of The Valley Club: 90; 91
Courtesy of Justin Trott: 47
Courtesy of SAGCA *Golf Architecture*, 5 (2002): 204
Courtesy of Tufts Archive: 116; 120
Neil Crafter: 132; 133; 135; 201; 205
Paul Daley: 68; 98; 122; 125
Ronald W. Fream: 105; 106; 107; 109; 110
Simon Gidman: 113; 114

Jeremy Glenn: 117; 178
Graeme Grant: 9
Gil Hanse: 97; 99
Phil Jacobs: 169
John R. Johnson: 136
Peter Johnson: 94
Takeaki Kaneda: 154; 156; 157
Mike Klemme: 148; 150; 151; 153
Alex Kramel: 39; 41
Bob Labbance: 23
Larry Lambrecht: x
Grant Leversha: 166
Tim Liddy: 139
Iain Lowe: 17; 18; 20
Thomas McBroom: 101; 102; 103
Richard Mandell: 190; 191; 193; 194
Kelly Blake Moran: 49; 51
Brian Morgan: 15; 42; 45; 142; 145
Shannon Morris: 93
Jeremy Pern: 36; 37; 38; 41
Gary Prendergast: 68; 174
Forrest Richardson: 71; 73
Tony Ristola: 170

Pat Ruddy: 219
Wood Sabold: Cover pic; ii; xiv; 2; 4; 5; 127; 129; 130
David Scaletti: 215
Christoph Stadler: 54; 57; 58
Bruce Strober: 146
Peter Turrell: 182; 185
Justin Walker: 186; 187
Ronald Whitten: iv; vi; xiii; 53; 60; 63; 64; 65; 77; 85; 140; 197; 209; 210; 222
Michael Wolveridge: 158; 161; 162; 163; 164; 165

Glossary

Amen corner
Pertaining to Augusta National Golf Club, and a section of its course: the eleventh, twelfth, and thirteenth holes.

Agronomy
The science of soil management and crop production.

Arborist
An expert who has made a dedicated study of trees.

Barranca
A term frequently used in Southwestern US to describe a deep ravine or gorge, initially caused by heavy rains or a watercourse.

Bedrock
Solid rock underlying alluvial deposits.

Bite off design
By attempting a bold or audacious line (generally from the tee) the golfer may be rewarded with (a) reducing the length of the hole or (b) a better approach angle, (c) both of these outcomes.

Bottleneck
To ensure that long-hitters are subject to penalties for aimlessly 'blazing away' from the tee, a portion of fairway may narrow down to a bottleneck framed by rough. Bottlenecks are usually utilised for tee-shots, and often on par-5s to encourage thoughtful player strategy for the second shot.

Burn
The word is derived from Old Teutonic – *burna*, *burne*, *bournon* and latter from the Old English words meaning spring, fountain, or river. More recently, it refers to a brook in the north of Britain and the name for a water hazard on many links. Some famous ones include: Swilcan, St. Andrews; Barry, Carnoustie; Wilson's, Turnberry; Bluidy, Cruden Bay; and Pow burn at Prestwick.

CAD
Computer assisted design

Cape
Can relate to a 'cape' within a bunker, a finger-like projection, a bay, or a famous British golf hole known as 'Cape'.

Caroming
Striking and rebounding; ricocheting and glancing.

Cayman ball
Devised to reduce the potential distance that golfers can attain with this lightweight golf ball, and reduces the need for large properties on Cayman courses.

Chocolate drops
On some of the older-style courses debris from construction was kept on-site and bundled into small mounds. These rough-covered mounds became known as chocolate drops, but eventually lost favour due to their artificial and jarring appearance.

Civil engineer
An engineer who designs or maintains roads, bridges, and dams. Also a person used in establishing property

boundaries as well as coordinating and designing infrastructure systems used by developments, for example, sanitary systems and major storm water drainage systems.

Cookie-cutter syndrome
A derogatory term relating to the practice of mass-producing designs, applying them like a stamp, and superimposing pre-conceived design concepts onto the landscape regardless of suitability of terrain and other design issues.

Cross-bunkers
As opposed to flanking the fairway laterally, cross-bunkers lie across the fairway. Formations vary between horizontal and diagonal placement.

Dell
Hollow or valley that is sometimes wooded, but rarely on a links. The name is given to the famous blind par-3 sixth hole at Lahinch in Ireland.

Featherie
This type of golf ball was used between 1618 and 1848. Bird feathers were crammed into a leather casing and stitched. In spite of a tendency to become waterlogged in heavy conditions and being prohibitively expensive, the featherie was an advance over the hard wooden balls used previously.

Fescue
Any grass of the genus *Festuca*. The fine-leafed variety is an especially important links grass species, while tall fescue is commonly used in the rough on American courses, and has a coarse leaf.

Firth
An arm of the sea, an estuary. Some famous Scottish firths in golfing circles include the firth of Fourth, Tay, and Moray.

Flashed bunker style
Bunkers constructed with sand flashed up the bunker-face, for example, the 'white faces' of Merion.

Floater
A ball devised to limit the distance-attaining ability of the power-hitter, but not adversely affecting the short-hitting golfer's capacity. At one time, architect Donald Ross campaigned for the floater to become the standard golf ball.

Geomorphology
The study of the physical features of the surface of the earth and their relation to its geological structures.

Geo-textile
A synthetic material commonly used in engineering. For golfing purposes, the material provides an alternative method of stabilising a bunker-face from the traditional British sod-revetment method, which requires frequent attention and re-facing on rotation.

Golden Age of golf design
Many of the finest courses in the world were built during the first third of the twentieth century, but activity ground to a halt with the onset of the stock market crash, bank foreclosures, and the Great Depression. Some of the most admired architects of this era were Alister Mackenzie, Donald Ross, H.S. Colt, A.W. Tillinghast, Stanley Thompson, Tom Simpson, J.F. Abercromby, Herbert Fowler, William S. Flynn, C.B. Macdonald, C.H. Alison, George Thomas Jr., and Seth Raynor.

Gorse
Any spiny, yellow-flowered shrub of the genus *Ulex*. Also known as furze.

Gutta-percha golf ball
The ball that replaced the featherie around 1848 was made from a sap-like, gummy substance extracted from indigenous Malayan trees. The substance was malleable when boiled, but hardened upon cooling. Previously, the material had been used for underground cable. Golfers affectionately referred to their gutta-percha ball as a 'guttie'.

Great Triumvirate
Between 1894 and 1914, three outstanding British golfers dominated the game by winning the Open Championship sixteen times between them. They were Harry Vardon (six), J.H. Taylor (five), and James Braid (five).

Green
In earlier times, the 'green' referred to the entire golf course. Progressively after 1900, it has come to signify the closely mown area at the end of each hole where golfers putt.

Green complex
A collective term that refers to the actual green plus its immediate surrounds.

Haskell ball
The rubber-core ball introduced by American, Coburn Haskell, around 1900.

Hazard
Strictly applied, the word pertains to three types of hazards: sand bunkers; water hazards; and lateral water hazards. Applied liberally, the word may also refer to: wind; structures; rough; and even a hazardous opponent.

Heroic
Heroic shots call upon the golfer to carry an obstacle or hazard to gain a favourable fairway position, with the proviso that there is sufficient room to avoid making such a ploy mandatory.

Klondyke

The name given to the par-5, fifth hole at Lahinch, Ireland. The second shot is famously blind, aiming over a small rock inserted into the large hill that traverses the fairway.

Lay-up

A golfer's measured decision of selecting a club to lay-up short of trouble, invariably, from a hazard or broken ground.

Links

According to eminent geologist, Dr Robert Price, links are 'wind-blown sand landforms'. Typically, linksland is covered by the fine, robust, salt-resistant grass species, fescues and bents, plus dune-binding grasses such as marram and sea-lyme. The noun 'links' applies equally well in the singular or plural form, and is derived from the thirteenth century Old English word, *hlinc*.

Mogul

A steep, rounded, mound. A mogul may appear more like a 'chocolate drop' than most mounds.

Old Course

Pertains to the Old Course, St. Andrews in Scotland. Architect, unknown. The Old Course continues to be the most celebrated and revered golfing ground in golf. The Old Course is home to the Royal and Ancient Golf Club.

One-green system

There are no spare or alternate greens with this system. The eighteen-hole course will have eighteen greens.

Open design

When there is no apparent difficulty in any given golf hole, the design is said to be 'open'. The architect has given the golfer free reign to decide upon the best method of playing the hole. Usually, there will be a complete absence of hazards.

Parallelism

A design where golf holes are routed side-by-side in a parallel fashion.

Penal

When the shot requirement is 'penal' there is an air of finality in the punishment it doles out to golfers who err in judgement or shotmaking. Often, a lost ball, or a stroke(s) lost to par follows. One criticism of the penal school of architecture, is that it doesn't matter to what degree a golfer errs; if they err slightly, the penalty is the same as for those who err greatly.

Pitch and Putt course

These layouts consist of nine-holes, each one usually varying between around forty to ninety metres. This format is a smaller scale version of par-3 courses.

'Playing Four'

'Playing Four' is a strictly Japanese local rule. In case there is a big creek or other waterway in front, and when the first shot failed to carry the hazard, a player may play from a temporary teeing ground set up beyond the hazard. The upcoming shot will be considered the golfer's fourth shot.

Porous

Letting air through; admitting infiltration; permeable.

Routing

The most critical element of a successful golf course design—the course layout. The configuration of holes in relation to the existing terrain and site parameters. The flow and sequence of holes on a site.

Redan

The par-3, fifteenth hole at North Berwick (West Links) in Scotland has become one of the most discussed and copied holes in the golf world. Architecturally, it has distinct features: the green lies along a ridge about thirty-five to forty-five degrees set off from the line of play; there is a guarding front-left hand side bunker with others stationed behind the green; and the slope of the green is front-to-back.

Resort course

The design of a resort course has specific aims: forgiving; bold and brassy; visually appealing; less insistent upon strategic design principles to test the champion; and catering to a market of golfers who strive to enjoy their golf in a luxurious holiday environment.

Restoration

To restore a course back to its original state.

Renovation

To renew or make new again; to make as new; to regenerate.

Road hole

The seventeenth hole at the Old Course, St. Andrews. So named because of the proximity of the right-hand side of the fairway, and its green, to the road running alongside the famous links. Once played as a par-5, it is now a 465-yard par-4. Open championships are frequently decided by the negotiation of this hole. A small pot-bunker located to the front left of the green is known as Road bunker and has ruined many scores, most famously so, Tommy Nakajima in the 1978 Open.

Reverse Old Course, St. Andrews

The Reverse Old Course, St. Andrews (ROC). Golfers play the Old Course in clockwise rotation rather than the customary anti-clockwise manner. The first green on the ROC is the site occupied by the seventeenth green on the Old Course. The second hole heads towards the Old Course sixteenth green, the third hole (ROC) towards the fifteenth green, and so forth.

Shaper
Someone who interprets the architect's plans and shapes the land where needed. Also has earthmoving responsibilities.

Signature course
A style of design that is immediately recognisable as that architect's work, or trademark. The course may present with signature type greens, tees, fairways, or all of these.

Slack
The inter-dunal area, commonly known as a trough is also called a slack.

Sod-revetted
Many bunkers on the older British courses are sod-revetted. Construction sees an almost vertical stacking of strips of turf (sod) up the face, each one slightly laid back from the previous layer. Construction includes filling with sand, brushing, and back filling. Overall, the method ensures intimidation in the mind of the golfer, and helps combat bunker erosion.

Stimpmeter
A metal ramp device that measures the speed of greens by recording how far the ball rolls from a predetermined height. A typically fast green would have a stimp reading of twelve and thirteen.

Strategic
Inherent in most good design principles; allows the architect to lay the strategy required for the golfer to negotiate the hole or course. Also refers to the 'strategic' school of golf course design.

Strath
A broad mountain valley. Also refers to Strath bunker on the eleventh hole at the Old Course, St. Andrews

Tweaking
The altering of the formal design on paper to make the course more functional. Tweaking may occur during the initial staking of the golf hole layout, during construction, or after construction. Tweaking is most visibly noticed regarding the establishment of turf lines and setting maintenance guidelines.

Tiger-proofing
A strategy of design, and/or course set-up that seeks to nullify the brilliance of the power-hitters epitomised by Tiger Woods. In general, the strategy is to toughen up the course and add much length to the layout.

Whins
Another name for gorse, or furze.

Contributors

Bill Amick

Since opening his golf course architectural office in Florida in 1959, Amick has designed more than seventy-five courses in eight countries and served as president of the American Society of Golf Course Architects. He stresses the importance of greater access to golf for greater numbers of people in his design philosophy.

Steve Burns

Before founding Burns Golf Design in 1988, Burns worked for golf course architect, Tom Fazio, for seven years. With a degree in landscape architecture from Ohio State University, Burns has been awarded the *Board Room Magazine* Excellence in Achievement Award in both 1999 and 2000. Steve Burns is a member of the American Society of Golf Course Architects.

Jeff Brauer

Having served his apprenticeship in golf architecture for seven years in the golf design firm, Killian and Nugent, Michigan, he formed his own firm in Arlington, Texas in 1984. Brauer has designed forty-two golf courses and remodeled or consulted with many more. He specialises in public access and resort courses. Brauer is a past president of the American Society of Golf Course Architects.

Michael Clayton

An Australian amateur champion in 1978, Clayton turned professional in 1981 going on to play the European tour for fifteen years. He founded Michael Clayton Golf Design in 1995 with partners John Sloan and Bruce Grant, working at several Melbourne clubs including Portsea, Kingston Heath,

Victoria, Cranbourne, and Spring Valley. Their first solo design, the Ranfurlie Course, opened in 2002.

Dr Thomas Climo

Dr Thomas Climo earned his Ph.D. at the London School of Economics and practiced as a Professor of Economics in England until returning to the United States in 1983. Soon after he entered the golf industry and was the developer with Ernie Vossler of the Paiute Golf Resort in Las Vegas, Nevada featuring three Pete Dye championship golf courses.

Geoffrey S. Cornish

Past president of the American Society of Golf Course Architects and president of golf design firm, Cornish, Silva and Mungeam, Uxbridge and Amherst, Massachusetts, Cornish is also a writer in the field. Co-authoring with Ronald Whitten, *The Golf Course* (1981), this title has since been revised through three editions. With Robert Muir Graves, Cornish co-authored *The Golf Course Design* (1999), a standard college text on golf course architecture. More than 200 of Cornish's designs are in play in the US, Canada, Europe and Central America.

Neil Crafter

With a degree in architecture, Crafter has been designing courses in Australia, Malaysia, Borneo and south China for twenty years. He is a founding member and current president of the Society of Australian Golf Course Architects and co-editor of *Golf Architecture* magazine. He represented Australia in amateur golf 1984-85. Courses include: Fleurieu Golf Club, South Australia; Lakelands Country Club, Western Australia; Borneo Highlands Resort, Malaysia; and Guangzhou South China Golf Club, China.

Paul Daley

An admirer and student of Britain's classic links, the Golden Age of golf design, and Melbourne's sandbelt courses, Daley speaks, writes and publishes on all aspects of golf. He is the principal of Full Swing Golf Publishing, and with David Scaletti, is co-principal of Plus Four Publishing.

Tom Doak

Founder and principal of Renaissance Golf Design, Traverse City, Michigan, Doak has a degree in landscape architecture from Cornell University. He has studied courses in Britain and Ireland and was apprenticed to Pete Dye. Since 1987, he has designed fourteen courses including Pacific Dunes, Oregon. As a golf writer, his titles include, *The Anatomy of a Golf Course* (1992) and *The Confidential Guide to Golf Courses* (1996).

Pete Dye

Dye claims his wife, Alice, as his closest advisor in course design, and both are advocates of environmentally safe courses. Ten of Dye's designs were included in a top ranking US golf magazine's list of the top 100 courses. He was awarded Golf Course Architect of the Year in 1994 by *Golf World*. Among Dye's many notable designs are PGA West, California, and Indiana courses, Crooked Stick and Brickyard Crossing.

Todd Eckenrode

Principal and co-founder of Origins Golf Design, Eckenrode is an associate member of the American Society of Golf Course Architects. His extensive education includes a degree in landscape architecture from California Polytechnic University-SLO. He was senior designer for Gary Roger Baird for several years, including highly acclaimed Barona Creek Golf Club in Southern California. Eckenrode plays the US Amateur and British Amateur circuits, and was the US Public Links medalist in 1998.

Chuck Ermisch

Chuck Ermisch holds a degree in landscape architecture from Kansas State University. He complements this degree with design, construction and field experience gained over a ten-year career. Ermisch has developed his design style and gained valuable industry background under the direction of his mentors, Don Sechrest (Sechrest Golf) and Bob Gibbons (Tom Watson Design).

Dr Ramon Espinosa

With a degree in agricultural engineering, Espinosa has been an independent golf architect since 1965, and a specialty in designing for mountainous and urban areas. As a past president of the European Society of Golf Architects (1994-98) and president of Garden and Golf S.A., Espinosa practices both both design and construction, and has completed more than forty golf projects worldwide.

Ronald W. Fream

Since 1966, Fream has been involved with planning, design, construction and maintenance of golf courses in sixty countries. In 1972, he co-founded the golf company Golfplan with David Dale. Their courses include: Sparrebosch Clifftop Country Club, South Africa; Bonari Kogen Golf Club, Japan; Desert Falls Country Club, USA; Golf de Fregate, France; and Chin Ju Country Club, Korea.

Simon Gidman

Started in golf course architecture with Martin Hawtree in 1983 before forming his own company in 1991. Gidman was vice-president of the former British Institute of Golf Course Architects and later became president of the European Institute of Golf Course Architects in 2001. He has designed many new golf courses including Frilford Heath (Blue Course) and Buckfield Park Golf Clubs, Germany.

Jeremy Glenn

Glenn is a golf course architect based in Montreal, Canada. After obtaining a degree in landscape architecture from the University of Montreal, he has worked with Graham Cooke and Associates as design associate on over twenty golf courses throughout North America and overseas.

Graeme Grant

Introduced to golf as a caddy in the 1950s, Grant gravitated towards greenkeeping, and by 1974 had become a course superintendent. He formed a design firm with John Spencer in 1977, and Jack Newton joined in 1986. Work includes renovation and restoration projects on courses such as Kingston Heath, The Lakes, and Huntingdale. Grant's most prominent original design is Links Lady Bay, in South Australia.

Gil Hanse

Has a masters degree in landscape architecture from Cornell University where he won the Dreer Award, allowing him to study the classics of golf course design in Britain. Hanse is founder and president of Hanse Golf Course Design, Malvern, Pennsylvania. He is committed to handcrafting in the design and construction process.

Dr Martin Hawtree

As a fellow of the European Institute of Golf Course Architects, Hawtree is the third generation in his family's ninety-year association with golf course design practice. He has a degree in arts from the University of East Anglia and a doctorate in civic design from the University of Liverpool. Hawtree has designed sixty new courses, and remodelled many courses worldwide, working mainly in Europe, and occasionally in America, Canada, Africa, Asia, and Australia.

Dr Michael J. Hurdzan

Hurdzan/Fry Golf Course Design can trace its roots back fifty years, three generations, and over 250 golf courses worldwide. It also boasts four ASGCA and GCSAA members. Hurdzan has a doctorate in environmental turfgrass physiology, and is the author of *Golf Course Architecture: Design, Construction and Restoration* (1996) and *The Golf Courses of Hurdzan/Fry* (2002). His body of work includes the two-course

development, Devil's Pulpit, near Toronto, Canada.

Phil Jacobs

With a diploma in surveying and experience in construction and maintenance, Jacobs's major projects include The Links, George, South Africa, which was voted best new South African course, and selected to host the 2003 Presidents Cup. Jacobs has designed thirty-five courses while working with Gary Player Design for fifteen years. Other notable courses include Ria Bintan, Indonesia, and Leopard Creek Golf Estate in South Africa.

Rees Jones

Following a ten-year stint at his father's firm, Robert Trent Jones design company, Jones is president of his own design firm based in Montclair, New Jersey, founded in 1974. With over forty years of design experience, and as past president and long-time member of the American Society of Golf Course Architects, Jones is known as the 'Open Doctor' for his numerous remodelling efforts of US Open courses.

Takeaki Kaneda

Representing Japan, and serving as team captain during the 1960 Eisenhower Cup

(Merion), Kaneda has had a busy life in golf. He has been a writer for *American Sports Illustrated* for twenty years, and has authored thirty books on golf and golf course design. Kaneda worked with Robert Trent Jones Jr. in the early 1980s on Oak Hills Country Club, Japan, thereafter, designing some courses in his homeland. He retired in 1998 as chairman of the Japanese Society of Golf Course Architects, later becoming its honorary advisor.

Mike Keiser

Graduating in 1967 with a degree in English literature from Amherst College, Massachusetts, Keiser co-founded a greeting card company in 1971. He formed Keiser Golf Keiser in 1985, and has since built three courses: The Dunes Club in Michigan (1988); Bandon Dunes (1999); and Pacific Dunes (2001), both in Oregon. He is founder of Sand Hills Golf Club, Nebraska.

Bradley S. Klein

As architecture editor of *Golfweek* since 1988 and editor of *Golfweek's Superintendent News* since 1999, Klein is a former PGA Tour caddie and holds a doctorate in political science. Author of two important golf architecture texts, *Rough Meditations* (1997) and award

winning, *Discovering Donald Ross* (2001), Klein has worked on twenty-four course design restoration projects.

Tim Liddy

A graduate in landscape architecture from Ball State University, Indiana, Liddy practices his golf course architecture in Indiana, splitting his time between projects with Pete Dye and solo design projects. He is a member of the American Society of Golf Course Architects.

Thomas G. McBroom

Has designed more than sixty courses with recently completed projects including Canadian courses, Ussher's Creek, and Rocky Crest. McBroom's design of Timberwolf Golf Club, Sudbury, won *Golf Digest's* award for the top course in 2002, his fourth claim to this accolade. *Score* magazine's top 100 courses in Canada include ten McBroom designs. McBroom is a member of the American Society of Golf Course Architects and has a degree in landscape architecture.

Richard Mandell

Richard Mandell Golf Architecture is located in Pinehurst, North Carolina. His Seaford Golf and Country Club won the 1996 Du Pont North America

Environmental Excellence Award, and Creekside Golf and Country Club was best course candidate in *Golf Digest* and *Georgia Golf News*. Mandell has penned articles for *Golf Illustrated* and *Links Magazine*. With a degree in landscape architecture, he teaches golf architecture at North Carolina State University.

Jeff Mingay

A noted writer and student of the history of golf and course architecture, Mingay is based in Windsor, Ontario. He is an associate of Canadian golf architect, Rod Whitman, and has contributed articles to international publications such as *Golfweek's Superintendent News* (USA), *Score Golf* (Canada), and the Australian Society of Golf Course Architects annual journal, *Golf Architecture*.

Kelly Blake Moran

President of Kelly Blake-Moran Golf Course Architects, based in West Reading, Pennsylvania, Blake-Moran has been designing golf courses since 1984 and had previously worked for many years with Robert von Hagge. Major projects include: Hawk Pointe Golf Club, Washington, New Jersey; Hideout Golf Club, Naples, Florida; and Madison Golf Club, Carmelo, Uruguay, co-designed with Randall Thompson.

Line Mortensen

Danish-born Mortensen works with British golf design firm, Gaunt and Marnoch. After completing a degree in landscape architecture, and the EIGCA diploma in golf course architecture and design, Mortensen became the first Dane and the first woman to join the European Institute of Golf Course Architects. She is a former member of the Danish national golf team.

Chris Monti

Graduated from Cornell University in 1996 and spent a year touring the great courses of the British Isles. He has been employed at Weed Design in Florida since 1997.

Ran Morrissett

Following a family tour of Scotland in 1981, Morrissett became an avid student of golf course architecture. As a former resident of Hong Kong, Australia and New Zealand, he now lives with his wife and daughter in Southern Pines, North Carolina.

Hisamitsu Ohnishi

In 1958 Ohnishi joined Dunlop (Japan) where he developed a golf ball marketing system. Commencing golf architecture in 1976, he has designed and supervised

fifteen golf courses including the Cypress, and has since 1969 organised more than 300 professional tournaments including the Dunlop Phoenix. Ohnishi has been president of the Japanese Society of Golf Course Architects since 2000.

Mark Parsinen

Parsinen's golf course design career began with the development of Granite Bay Golf Club, California in 1994. With a masters degree in business administration from Stanford University, he is one of the few owner-designer-developers in the golf industry. His flagship golf course development is Kingsbarns, Scotland, co-designed by Kyle Phillips. Prior to his golf interests, Parsinen spent many years as a computer entrepreneur in the Silicon Valley.

Jeremy Pern

An agronomist with a masters degree in protected landscape management, Pern has worked as a project manager with architects Robert Trent Jones Snr., John Harris, and Don Harradine. In 1986 he turned to design, and has more than twenty-five golf courses to his credit in Europe and the Middle East. A former vice-president of the British Institute of Golf Course Architects, Pern has a special interest in environmental aspects of course development.

Forrest Richardson

Studied golf architecture across Scotland, and has worked on projects throughout the US and in Russia. He is a member of the American Society of Golf Course Architects citing Arthur Jack Snyder (ASGCA) as mentor. His most notable projects include: Phantom Horse, Arizona; The Hideout (Utah); and Legend Trail, Arizona. Richardson is the author of *Routing the Golf Course* (2002).

Tony Ristola

Ristola's approach to course design is to lead the design and construction process on an all-day, everyday basis. His completed work includes Artland Golf Club, Der Golf Club, Golf Club Emstal, and Golf Club zum Fischland, all in Germany.

Pat Ruddy

Golf writer, golf course designer, and golf course owner, Irishman, Ruddy counts among his designs the twenty-hole The European Club, Ireland, (owner), twenty-four holes at Rosapenna (a new links and a redesign/extension of an Old Tom Morris/Vardon/Braid design) and renovations to the links at Donegal. Inland courses include thirty-six holes at Druids Glen, Ireland, thirty-six holes at Montreal Island (Canada), and St. Margaret's.

Geoff Shackelford

An author of books on golf course design, his body of work includes: *The Captain* (1996); *Masters of the Links* (1997); *The Good Doctor Returns* (1998); *The Golden Age of Golf Design* (1999); *Alister Mackenzie's Cypress Point Club* (2000); and *The Art of Golf Design* (2001). Shackelford co-designed with Gil Hanse, Rustic Canyon Golf Course in Moorpark, California.

Christoph Städler

A former German Amateur champion who competed at the European and World Team Championships from 1968 to 1987, Städler founded his golf course architecture business in 1987. He has designed and redesigned more than sixty courses.

Donald Steel

Steel can point to a lifetime of writing about golf and designing golf courses, and has served as president of the Britain's Association of Golf Writers as well as the British Association of Golf Course Architects. He played golf at a high level, having represented England and qualifying for the 1970 Open championship at St. Andrews.

Robert 'Bobby' Weed Jr.

Beginning his career under the tutelage of Pete Dye as a construction super-intendent at The Long Cove Club, Hilton Head Island, and after twelve years service as chief designer for the PGA tour, Weed formed his own design firm in 1995. His more notable layouts include: The Olde Farm Golf Club, Virginia; and Glen Mills Golf Course, Philadelphia.

Rod Whitman

Beginning his career in the early 1980s as an associate of Pete Dye, Whitman has since designed and constructed six golf courses solo, including Golf du Medoc in France, and Golf Langenstein in Germany. His layout at Wolf Creek Golf Resort, Alberta is perennially ranked among the top golf courses in Canada.

Michael Wolveridge

Wolveridge began his golf course architecture career in 1965, having since designed more than 170 golf courses (at various times five among the top fifty in the world). Australian designs include: Port Douglas Links, Queensland; Hope Island, Queensland; the Ocean Course at The National Golf Club, Victoria; and Moonah Links, Victoria. Wolveridge was president of the Australian Society of Golf Course Architects from 1994 to 1998, and designed the Dukes Course, St. Andrews.

Bibliography

Alison, Charles S. and Colt, Harry S. *Some Essays on Golf Course Architecture.* London: Country Life and George Newnes, 1920.

Darwin, Bernard. *The Golf Courses of the British Isles.* London: Duckworth and Co, 1910.

Cornish, Geoffrey S. & Whitten, Ronald E. *The Golf Course.* New York: Rutledge Press, 1981.

Doak, Tom, Scott, James S. and Haddock, Raymund M. *The Life and Work of Dr Alister MacKenzie.* Chelsea: Sleeping Bear Press, 2001.

Hunter, Robert. *The Links.* New York: Scribners, 1926.

Hutchinson, Horace G. [ed] *Golf Greens and Greenkeeping.* London: Country Life, 1906.

Klein, Bradley S. *Discovering Donald Ross, The Architect and His Courses.* Chelsea: Sleeping Bear Press, 2001.

Koch, Margaret. *The Pasatiempo Story.* Santa Cruz: Privately published by Pasatiempo Golf Club, 1990.

Low, John L. *Concerning Golf.* London: Hodder and Stoughton, 1903.

MacDonald, Charles B. *Scotland's Gift, Golf: Reminiscences 1872-1927.* New York: Charles Scribners Sons, 1928.

Mackenzie, Alister. *The Spirit of St. Andrews.* Chelsea: Sleeping Bear Press, 1995.

—'Round the World on a Golf Tour.' London: *Golf Illustrated* 27 May—24 June, 1927

—*Golf Architecture.* London: Simpkin, Marshall, Hamilton, Kent and Co, 1920.

Osborne, Richard and Lapham, Jr., Roger D. *The History of Cypress Point Club.* Pebble Beach: Privately published by Cypress Point Club, 1996.

Owen, David. *The Making of the Masters.* New York: Simon and Schuster, 1999.

Price, Robert. *Scotland's Golf Courses.* Edinburgh: Aberdeen University Press, 1989.

Ross, Donald J. *Golf Has Never Failed Me.* Chelsea: Sleeping Bear Press, 1996.

Shackelford, Geoff. *Alister Mackenzie's Cypress Point Club.* Chelsea: Sleeping Bear Press, 2000.

Sutton, M. H. F. *The Book of the Links: A symposium on Golf.* London: W.H. Smith, 1912.

Thomas, George C. *Golf Architecture in America: Its Strategy and Construction.* Los Angeles: Times-Mirror Press, 1927.

Ward-Thomas, Pat A., Wind, Herbert W., Price, Charles, Thomson, Peter. *The World Atlas of Golf.* London: Mitchell Beazley Publishers Ltd, 1976.

Wethered, H. N. and Simpson, T. *The Architectural Side of Golf.* London: Longmans Green, 1929.

Wilson, E. O. *Consilience: the Unity of Knowledge.* New York: Alfred A. Knopf, 1998.

Index

Fourteenth green,
Kingston Heath Golf Club,
Melbourne, 1937.

OPPOSITE: **Approaching the
eighth green at Kingston
Heath, 1937. (Photos
courtesy of Kingston Heath
Golf Club.)**